Learning Through Theatre

Mar
Tel:

T   in Education – as both a movement and a theatrical
n   – represents one of the most significant developments
i   mporary theatre. In its short history, it has excited and
i   d, and at times unnerved, actors and teachers alike, and
h   ovided an important and exciting bridge between theatre
a   ducation. In harnessing the techniques and imaginative
p   ial of theatre, TIE can provide an intensely absorbing
a   hallenging experience, and a stimulus for further work on
a   osen subject, be that local history, racism, health or
l   age learning.

I   s fully updated and revised edition of *Learning Through
T*   the contributors chart the development of TIE, identify
its s   gths and provide vivid and illuminating accounts of its
p a   round the world.

Lea   hrough Theatre will be of practical interest to teachers,
edu   lists, theatre practitioners and students of drama
and   tion alike. In particular the chapters that deal with
TIE   actice offer not only an illuminating account of what
has   done in the past, but a helpful guide to methods of
app   for those new to the field.

Tor   ckson is Senior Lecturer in Drama at the University of
N u   ester.

A   g the internationally recognised contributors are: Gavin
Bolton, Wayne Fairhead, Jim Mirrione, John O'Toole, David
Pammenter, Mark Riherd, Ken Robinson, Lowell Swortzell,
Chris Vine and Cora Williams.

Learning Through Theatre

New Perspectives on Theatre in Education

Second edition

Edited by
Tony Jackson

London and New York

Second edition first published 1993
by Routledge
11 New Fetter Lane, London EC4P 4EE

Simultaneously published in the USA and Canada
by Routledge
29 West 35th Street, New York, NY 10001

Reprinted 1996,1997,1999, 2001

Routledge is an imprint of the Taylor & Francis Group

© 1993 Tony Jackson

Typeset in Baskerville by
Ponting–Green Publishing Services, Chesham, Bucks
Printed and bound in Great Britain by
TJ International Ltd, Padstow, Cornwall

British Library Cataloguing in Publication Data
A catalogue record for this book is available from the British Library

Library of Congress Cataloguing in Publication Data
Learning through theatre: new perspectives on Theatre in Education/
[edited by] Tony Jackson. – International ed.
p.   cm.
Includes bibliographical references and index.
1. Drama in education – Great Britain.
2. Drama in education.
I. Jackson, Tony.
PN3171.L38   1993
372.13′32–dc20
93–18375

ISBN 0–415–08609–4 (hbk)   0–415–08610–8 (pbk)

Contents

List of illustrations

Notes on contributors

Tony Jackson is Senior Lecturer in Drama at Manchester University specializing in modern British and American theatre and educational theatre. He has published widely on TIE and was the co-author of *The Repertory Movement: Regional Theatre in Britain* (1984) as well as editor of the first edition of *Learning Through Theatre* (1980). He is currently on the boards of directors of two community and young people's theatre companies in the north-west.

Gavin Bolton is Reader Emeritus, University of Durham, Visiting Professor to the University of Central England, Birmingham and Adjunct Professor, University of Victoria, British Columbia.

David Pammenter was until recently director of the Community Theatre Arts course at Rose Bruford College, Sidcup, Kent. Trained originally as a teacher, he joined the Belgrade TIE team in Coventry as an actor–teacher in 1969, and was its head of department from 1972 to 1977: a fertile period during which many of the Coventry TIE 'classics', such as *Pow Wow, Rare Earth* and *Example: The Case of Craig and Bentley*, were devised.

Jim Mirrione is the playwright-in-residence for the Creative Arts Team, the educational theatre company based at New York University. Since 1974, as co-founder, he has written eighteen TIE plays for the company that have been performed extensively in New York. His 1991 doctorate from NYU was on the subject of TIE playwriting.

Cora Williams is Artistic and Administrative Coordinator of Pit

Prop Theatre, a community and Theatre in Education company based in Wigan. She has been involved with TIE almost since its inception – as an actor–teacher with the Belgrade team from 1966 and as director of the Bolton Octagon TIE Team from 1969.

Chris Vine was a founder member of the Perspectives Theatre Company in Peterborough and a former director of the Greenwich Young People's Theatre. He has worked extensively in educational theatre in Britain and abroad, and is now a freelance director, workshop leader and teacher trainer.

John O'Toole Longtime drama practitioner and teacher, John O'Toole is Associate Professor in Drama at Griffith University, Brisbane, Australia. He wrote the first book on TIE, *Theatre in Education* (1976), and has been involved in numerous TIE programmes in Australia and the UK. Recent books include *The Process of Drama* (1992), *Communicate Live!* (1989) and *Dramawise* (1988).

Penny Bundy Originally a primary school teacher, Penny Bundy was a founding member of KITE Theatre Company. After several years as an actor–teacher with the team, she left to pursue a freelance career as a writer for TIE and young people's theatre. She has had more than a dozen of her plays performed by various companies in Australia. She also lectures at Griffith University in Queensland.

Wayne Fairhead is a teacher, author and workshop leader. He is currently Course Director for the Dramatic Arts Specialist programme at York University, having taught for ten years at the University of Toronto's Faculty of Education, and a curriculum consultant in the city of York (Toronto). Recent publications and articles include *Concrete Daisy and Other Plays* (1991) and 'Drama and cooperative learning' in *Classroom Oral Language* (1992).

Jumai Ewu received her drama training in Nigeria and Britain, and wrote her doctoral dissertation, 'Children's theatre in Nigeria', for the University of Leeds. She has participated in children's theatre workshops in Nigeria, Britain and Canada, has lectured at the Ahmadu Bello University, Zaria, Nigeria, and currently lectures on African Drama at Nene College, Northampton, UK.

Tunde Lakoju was until recently Senior Lecturer in Drama at the Ahmadu Bello University, Zaria. Two of his plays, *The Last Saturday* and *Ava* have been broadcast on the African Theatre Programme of the BBC. He holds a doctoral degree in Theatre in Education from the University of Wales, and is currently the Director of Planning, Research and Statistics at the National Commission for Colleges of Education in Nigeria.

Tove Ilsaas is Senior Lecturer in Educational Drama at the Centre for Teacher Education at the University of Oslo. She has been educational consultant to the National Theatre, the Oslo New Theatre and to Teatret Vårt in Molde. Her current research is in teaching approaches to Ibsen and Shakespeare.

Torunn Kjølner trained at the Royal Scottish Academy of Music and Drama and at the University of Bergen, Norway. For ten years she ran the postgraduate drama course for teachers at the Teacher Training College of Bergen and from 1987 has been Senior Lecturer at the Department of Dramaturgy, University of Aarhus, Denmark. She has been involved with various theatre productions, including three TIE programmes as deviser/ director.

Mark Riherd is the Program Director for the Creative Arts Team at New York University, where he is also an instructor in the programme in Educational Theatre, teaching courses in both drama in education and Theatre in Education. He also conducts staff development workshops in Critical Thinking Through Drama.

Gwendolen Hardwick, a graduate of New York University's Tisch School of the Arts, is currently Workshop Director for the Conflict Resolution Through Drama programme at the Creative Arts Team. Actress, writer, director and producer, she is also the author of three children's plays and her prose and poetry is published in an anthology of new Black women writers entitled *Gaptooth Girlfriends: The Third Act*.

Steve Ball has worked as a primary school teacher in England and Spain and as an actor and actor–teacher in Britain. He is the Director of 'Language Alive!' TIE company and 'Theta', a Theatre in Health Education company, both in Birmingham; he also works as a freelance teacher and director. He has just completed research in TIE and health education at Manchester University.

Lowell Swortzell is Professor of Educational Theatre, New York University, where he teaches courses in musical theatre, American drama and playwriting. He is the author of fourteen published plays, the most recent being *Cinderella: The World's Favorite Fairy Tale* and *Gulliver's Travels*. In 1992 he was inducted into the College of Fellows of the American Theatre at the John F. Kennedy Center, Washington DC.

Ken Robinson is now Professor and Chairman of Arts Education at the University of Warwick. He was the principal author of the report of the National Committee of Enquiry *The Arts in Schools: Principle, Practice and Provision* published by the Calouste Gulbenkian Foundation from 1985–9. He was director of the SCDC/National Curriculum Council's Arts in Schools project.

Geoff Readman is currently Principal Lecturer for Course Development at Bishop Grosseteste College, Lincoln, with specific responsibility for drama. He has been a primary teacher, Head of Department in a comprehensive school and Youth Theatre Director. In 1976 he was appointed Leader of the Wakefield Drama in Education Theatre Team and in 1983 Inspector for Drama in Nottinghamshire. He was the first Chair of the British National Drama Association.

Acknowledgements

The editor is grateful to the following companies and individuals for their kind permission to use photographs as follows:

Pit Prop Theatre, Wigan: *Brand of Freedom*; *Wild Child*
M6 Theatre, Rochdale: *Trappin'*
Young National Trust Theatre (The National Trust, London): *An Endless Maze*
Belgrade TIE Team, Coventry: *Pow Wow*
Creative Arts Team, New York University: *Show of Force*; *It's What You Do ...*
Greenwich Young People's Theatre: *A Land Fit For Heroes*; *Question of Identity*
Tunde Lakoju: *As You Make Your Bed*
Pam Schweitzer, Age Exchange, London: *Keep Warm, Keep Well*

The editor also gratefully acknowledges grants from the British Academy and the University of Manchester which helped to finance visits to the USA, Canada and an international educational drama conference in Portugal during the preparation of this book.

List of acronyms

ASSITEJ	Association Internationale du Théâtre pour l'Enfance et la Jeunesse (International Association of Theatre for Children and Young People)
DIE	Drama in Education
ERA	Education Reform Act (England and Wales, 1988)
GCSE	General Certificate of Secondary Education (England and Wales) (taken at the age of 16)
HMI	Her Majesty's Inspectorate of Schools
LEA	Local Education Authority
LMS	Local Management of Schools
SCYPT	Standing Conference of Young People's Theatre
TIE	Theatre in Education
TYA	Theatre for young audiences
YPT	Young people's theatre

Introduction

Tony Jackson

This book is about a form of theatre that arguably represents one of the most significant developments in British theatre in the second half of the century. In its short history of some twenty-eight years, it has excited and inspired, and at times unnerved, actors and teachers alike, and has marked out for itself a territory that overlaps the domains of theatre and education in ways that are important and unusual. It is moreover part of a much wider development that has taken place across the world in the latter decades of the twentieth century as the theatre looks for new audiences and new ways to speak to those audiences.

Theatre in Education (TIE) as a definable movement began in Britain in the mid-1960s in direct response to the needs of both theatre and schools. It originated as an initiative from within the professional theatre and is now supported by regional arts boards and local education authorities in many parts of the country. It is also now, importantly, an established or emerging force in many countries outside the UK. Essentially TIE seeks to harness the techniques and imaginative potency of theatre in the service of education. The aim is to provide an experience for children that will be intensely absorbing, challenging, even provocative, and an unrivalled stimulus for further work on the chosen subject in and out of school. Subjects dealt with have ranged from the environment, racism and local history to language learning, science and health. But it is the formal innovations that give TIE its special quality and have made its appearance upon the British 'alternative theatre' scene so significant. One of the major and most effective features of TIE is the structured active participation of the children in the drama – frequently placed within a dramatic fiction in which they become caught up in its events, interact with a range of characters and have to make decisions in the midst of 'crisis'; or, at an older age, invited to challenge or advise characters from a play they have just witnessed.

The essays that follow attempt to chart the development of TIE, identify its strengths (and its weaknesses) and give a vivid and stimulating account of its practice, both in Britain and around the world.

This particular edition began simply as an attempt to update the first version of the book published in 1980: TIE had moved on, the achievements were more varied, as were the techniques employed; likewise the problems faced had changed or been accentuated. Time seemed ripe for a reassessment as well as a restatement of principles. However it soon became clear that a very different kind of volume was needed: one that carried through several of the original chapters in modified and updated form certainly, but one that made room for a far wider perspective on TIE. Not only does TIE in the UK look like a quite different animal now compared with the 1970s, requiring a far broader, perhaps looser, definition of what actually constitutes TIE; but TIE is clearly no longer a British phenomenon. Indeed many would argue that it was not that even in 1980. In 1993 however – and I have no doubt that the observation will hold true even more so in 2003 – TIE is alive and kicking in some shape or form, and continuing to evolve, in many countries beyond the British Isles. In most places there has clearly been a linear development from the British model; in others remarkably similar forms have emerged that appear to owe no particular debt to British TIE, and may not be called TIE, having grown out of curricular, social or cultural needs which lent themselves to theatrical treatment. Few would wish to engage in sterile debates about who thought of TIE first; what does bear scrutiny is the common ground and the differences between these various enterprises. This book will make a first stab at that task by highlighting practices in a selection of countries around the world. We make no pretence at comprehensive coverage; rather the attempt has been to represent just some of the developments and achievements in some six countries other than the UK, with enough illustrative detail at least to give a flavour of the projects undertaken, problems encountered and directions pursued. Many of the differences and similarities will become immediately evident to the reader. More probing comparisons must await later studies.

What all the projects share however is a commitment to the exploration of theatre's use as an educational medium, and to ways of actively engaging the audience in the learning process. Whether or not the TIE event consists of a conventional play performance or of active audience-participation there will always be some element that will take that event beyond the self-contained play – through a particularly close rapport with a small group of children, a subsequent workshop, or a programme of follow-up work planned with teachers. Truly these are programmes rather that 'just plays'. Which is not to deny the enormous educational potential of the self-contained play; it is rather to stress how TIE is concerned not just to 'leave it there' but to follow through, to press the issues and the challenge as far and as deeply as possible with the age group in question.

WHAT IS TIE?

In essence, TIE needs to be seen as a new form of theatre. It began, to all intents and purposes, in 1965 at the Belgrade Theatre, Coventry, where a number of pilot projects in schools demonstrated vividly the value of theatre as an educational method and led to the setting up of a full-time TIE unit backed by money from the Belgrade Theatre and the local authority. A pattern was set that soon spread to theatres across the country. The personnel of these companies are usually known as 'actor–teachers' precisely because they seek to combine the qualities, skills and objectives of both actors and teachers (although, as Cora Williams explains later, that term has recently been challenged).

The emergence of the new form was not of course an isolated event. TIE stems from a number of distinct but related developments in theatre and in education evident throughout the twentieth century: the movements to re-establish the theatre's roots in the community and in so doing broaden its social basis – manifested since the war in the revival of regional theatre and the rapid growth of community, 'alternative' and children's theatre;[1] the theatre's search for a useful and effective role within society and an exploration especially of its potential both as an educational medium and as a force for social change – seen most notably in the work of Bertolt Brecht and Augusto Boal and in the wide spectrum of activity ranging from children's theatre to political theatre; and, in education, the recognition during the 1960s and 1970s of the importance of the arts (and drama particularly) in the school curriculum, together with the increasing stress given to the functional role that the arts have to play in helping children to understand, and operate in, the world in which they live.[2] The influences upon TIE have been many and are discussed in more detail later in the book. Within the context of those larger developments, however, the role of TIE is a distinct one.

The most important innovation in this work has undoubtedly been the concept of the TIE 'programme', and it is this element that distinguishes TIE most obviously from other kinds of young people's theatre. The TIE programme is not a performance in schools of a self-contained play, a 'one-off' event that is here today and gone tomorrow, but a co-ordinated and carefully structured pattern of activities, usually devised and researched by the company, around a topic of relevance both to the school curriculum and to the children's own lives, presented in school by the company and involving the children directly in an experience of the situations and problems that the topic throws up. It generally utilizes elements, in a variety of permutations, of traditional theatre (actors in role and the use of scripted dialogue, costume and often scenic and sound effects); educational drama (active participation of the children, in or out of role, in improvised drama activities in which images and ideas are explored at their own level); and simulation (highly structured role-play and decision-making exercises within simulated 'real-life' situations). There is, however, no set formula. The shape, style and length of the programme will vary enormously depending upon the subject tackled and the age range catered for. Thus, to take just three TIE programmes from the past twenty years, not to represent TIE but at least to suggest something of that variety:

It Fits (Perspectives, 1976), a programme about mathematics and problem-solving for 5 to 7 year-olds, involved two clown-like characters and a colourful array of lightweight 'bricks' (cubes, cuboids, cylinders and prisms), and took place almost entirely in the school hall in the space of one hour;

Brand of Freedom (Pit Prop Theatre, 1984) was a three-part programme for 9 to 11 year-olds dealing with the Lancashire cotton famine of the 1860s and relating local history to the American Civil War and the struggle for freedom by black slaves in the South. It consisted, over a three-week span, of a short play, directed project work in collaboration with teachers and a full-scale participation event in which the children 'became' the cotton operatives at a Lancashire mill who had to cope with the pressures of unemployment and the conflicting demands of various characters from mill owner to escaped slave;

Marches, for 16 to 19 year-olds (Cockpit TIE, 1977), was a whole-day programme consisting of a play about unemployment and the rise of fascism in London in the 1930s, followed by a workshop in which pupils were able to interview (or 'hotseat') each of the main characters from the play in turn (including the disarmingly polite Oswald Mosley, leader of the British Union of Fascists) and explore the relevance of the events to their own world, before concluding with a plenary forum in which the issues, attitudes and conflicts were brought fully and often heatedly into the open.

Moreover, the event in the school (or in the theatre–studio to which the pupils have been brought) is not the be-all and end-all of the exercise. The TIE 'programme', as the word suggests, will usually involve a fully conceived programme of work with the theatrical event as the central stimulus for a deeper and richer learning process than the 'one-off' play (or indeed most other teaching methods) could possibly hope to offer. The pattern adopted by most TIE teams is to provide, first, an introductory teachers' workshop for all teachers whose classes will receive the programme, the purpose of which is to explain fully the aim and method of the project and present an opportunity for discussion of the teacher's role; second, a project pack or teachers' notes which will contain relevant research material and suggestions for 'follow-up' to aid the teacher's subsequent work with the class; the programme visits themselves; and finally, some form of 'feed-back' mechanism (often a questionnaire to be filled in by teachers after the programme has

Plate 0.1 Brand of Freedom

A scene from *Brand of Freedom*, a participatory programme for 9–11 year olds (Pit Prop Theatre, Wigan, 1984). Here, in the oakum-picking room (one of several locations), a group of children in role as mill-workers reflect upon the problems faced by their community and, with two of the characters, begin to make decisions.

Photo: Arthur Thompson.

Actors: Ray Meredith, Flo Wilson.

ended, sometimes an open forum for both teachers and performers) through which the teachers can offer constructive criticism and the team can glean some idea of the effectiveness or otherwise of their efforts. Close liaison between company and teachers is thus essential.

TIE AND RELATED AREAS OF WORK

By now it should be clear that TIE as a term implies a kind of theatre markedly different from most other kinds of young people's theatre. The term is all too often confused with those other forms and because it is used here in a very specific sense it may be as well to indicate broadly the other terms that are in general use in this and related areas of work. The distinctions are important, and need to be made if TIE is to be fully understood – although in so doing, it is not my intention in any way to deny the validity or importance of other forms of young people's theatre or to suggest that the forms do not frequently overlap. Without question TIE has much to learn from other forms – and vice versa – and in practice there are very few companies that do not engage in a wider range of theatre activities than TIE alone. The terms most commonly in use, then, are:

Young people's theatre. A broad umbrella term, intended to cover all forms of professional theatre for children and young people, including TIE; it is often used more specifically, too, to cover play performances for the older age range, i.e. usually between 14 and 18 years old (or over).

Children's theatre. Refers to the professional performance (in theatres or in schools) of self-contained plays for younger audiences (i.e. up to about 12 or 13 years of age). This includes the work of national touring companies, productions by local repertory or TIE companies, and those of the building-based children's theatres (of which there are woefully few in the UK).

Youth Theatre. Generally non-professional theatre work involving young people in the preparation and performance of group-devised or scripted plays. Often theatre companies will employ a youth organizer responsible for initiating and fostering this kind of activity.

Education in theatre. There are no satisfactory terms to apply to this area, but it covers two aspects of work very often considered a normal part of a repertory theatre's responsibility, i.e. establishing links with schools, youth clubs, etc. in order (a) to impart a more informed awareness of what theatre is and how it works; and (b) to build new audiences for tomorrow. These aims are generally fulfilled through lectures, backstage tours, open rehearsals, demonstrations and performances of short plays or play extracts both in schools and in the theatre itself.

The set play 'workshops' or 'play days'. These are frequently run by the more enlightened repertory companies, and often by the larger young people's theatre companies, on the plays being studied as a set part of the syllabus in schools in their area. They will often consist of a series of extracts from the play in question linked by a commentary that stresses the play's contemporary relevance and its theatrical dimension, the options available to the director in rehearsal, and how final interpretations are arrived at.

There is then a good deal of professional theatre work taken into schools but much of it is not TIE, although it may appear or even purport to be. This is not to say that such work is of inferior quality in theatrical terms. Far from it. Sometimes it may consist of an excellently researched documentary piece or indeed a fine example of contemporary playwriting on a contemporary issue. Sometimes it may be merely well-intentioned, lacking the rigorous application of educational criteria in its preparation and the skills needed to communicate with the given age group. In both cases the 'programme' concept will be absent and though the 'one-off' performances may well be educational in the broadest sense, the distinction with TIE is an important one to draw.

Finally there are two key areas closely connected with TIE but outside the professional theatre arena:

Curriculum drama or drama in education (DIE). That is, drama as taught in schools, sometimes with a theatrical bias, involving the preparation of a play for public presentation and/or learning about theatre styles and techniques; now more usually concerned with the exploration of themes and problems through role play and improvisation, with emphasis upon developing the child's imagination, self-awareness and expressiveness and upon the social skills involved in group work. DIE differs from TIE primarily in its reliance upon a teacher who meets the children regularly and knows their particular needs, in the relative 'open-endedness' of the experience offered and in the absence of the full theatre resources (characters, costume, set, etc.) available to the TIE company. (Gavin Bolton's chapter explores the differences and the common ground in detail later in the book).

Simulation games. An educational technique that grew enormously in the 1970s, developed for use both in schools and in management training schemes, etc. Such games generally offer a carefully packaged and highly structured programme of activity in which pupils explore 'real-life' situations, solve problems and make decisions in roles that are predetermined but never require acting skill. The simulation technique is one that closely parallels some TIE participation formats and has often been used as an integral part of a TIE programme. Most simulations however, especially those in published form, do not make use of the added stimulus of actors in role.[3]

THE PRESENT STATE OF TIE

How widespread is TIE is Britain now? During the 1970s there was a quite remarkable growth not only in TIE and young people's theatre companies but of 'fringe', 'alternative' and community theatre companies, and the boundary lines between them have often been hard to draw. Many community companies have ventured into TIE and equally many TIE companies have taken up community theatre work as a natural extension of their activities. According to the most recent information,[4] there are at present about thirty companies in Britain who describe themselves as area-based TIE companies or companies with a major commitment to full-fledged TIE work. There are, however, many others (probably well in excess of fifty) whose programme may from time to time include TIE, or whose work, while predominantly for young people and broadly educational, might not strictly be classified as participatory TIE in the sense that is employed here: companies such as the more educationally conscious touring children's theatre companies and the various puppet and dance companies geared to working in schools on a national or regional basis. There are also companies that specialize in work for museums and heritage centres, in health promotion, in theatre for and with the disabled and in rehabilitation programmes for young offenders and prison inmates – all of which employ from time to time participatory theatre techniques that draw upon or closely resemble TIE methodology. The variety is immense, about which more will be said in subsequent chapters. Interest in TIE and debate about its aims and methodology have also widened in a further important respect. Over the past decade, TIE has appeared increasingly as a subject on drama and education syllabuses in higher education, offering as it does a valuable way in, practically and theoretically, to the study of key questions about the role of theatre in society, as well as an alternative approach to educational drama in the classroom.

THE PRESENT VOLUME: ITS AIM, CONTENTS AND METHOD OF APPROACH

Learning Through Theatre: Essays and Casebooks on Theatre in Education was first published in 1980: this version is in most respects a completely new book. Several of the best articles from the old edition have been retained; others wholly revised and updated; most are new. Many of the original chapters (such as Gordon Vallins' on the beginnings of TIE) have been omitted with regret, but different times have required different priorities.

The broad aim in this edition has, then, been to introduce important aspects of Theatre in Education, its development, its theory, its practice and its international dimension. The chapters are designed to appeal both to those who have little or no experience of the subject but who are interested in the educational possibilities of theatre, and to those experienced in some but not all of its various manifestations and who would like to know more. The chapters that deal with TIE practice offer not only an illuminating account of what has been done in the past, but a helpful guide to methods of approach for those new to the field. The intention has been as far as possible to integrate theory and practice, and historical and social contexts, with working examples of TIE practice sufficiently detailed to offer genuine insight.

The essays are grouped in four parts to aid the reader in finding his or her way around the material as easily as possible; each part is preceded by its own short editorial introduction. TIE is still a developing field and the attempt has been made to reflect the most recent developments as far as time and space permit.

The short twenty-eight year period of TIE's existence has been marked by the extraordinary determination, belief, enterprise, imagination and skill of its pioneers in the face of immense difficulties. Its history has been marked too by some confusion of aims and counter-productive struggles for the ideological high ground on the part of some of its practitioners. TIE is still subject to the changing tides in education and theatre, tides that can too easily distort or even submerge its real value and achievement. The achievement, and indeed the potential, are undeniable. But reassessment is needed, now, just as much as in 1980, (a) to help pinpoint and clarify the nature of that achievement and the essentials of its working method; (b) to make TIE and its potential more widely known and understood in educational and theatrical circles and beyond; and (c) to help distinguish good TIE from mediocre.

This book is intended to make a positive contribution to such a reassessment by drawing on practitioners and theorists from seven countries who are not only distinguished in their own field but bring to this subject, between them, a width of experience, a variety of skills and expertise and a wide spectrum of critical standpoints. The book deliberately does not attempt to make any final, unified, definitive statement about TIE, which is of its very nature complex, dynamic and evolving, but rather aims to promote a lively, intelligent debate that will at least clarify the issues and point out some of the most fruitful ways forward. Emphasis has therefore been placed on highlighting the already considerable achievement of TIE, on articulating some of the major governing principles that lie behind the practice and on demonstrating the *how* as well as the *why* of TIE work.

NOTES

1 For a useful general account of these developments see Bradby and McCormick (1978), though their survey oddly includes no

reference to young people's theatre; also Rowell and Jackson (1984) on TIE in relation to regional theatre.

2 For a discussion of recent trends in arts education, see Ross (1978), Witkin (1974), Bolton (1984) and Hornbrook (1989).

3 See Taylor and Walford (1972).

4 Notably the 1992–3 edition of the *British Alternative Theatre Directory*, along with *Theatre-in-Education: What Future? A survey of the threats to TIE provision* (compiled by Trade Unionists at Greenwich YPT, December 1992).

BIBLIOGRAPHY

Arts Council of Great Britain (1991) *Drama in Schools*, London: ACGB.

Boal, A. (1979) *Theatre of the Oppressed*, London: Pluto Press.

Bolton, G. (1984) *Drama as Education: An Argument for Placing Drama at the Centre of the Curriculum*, London: Longman.

Bradby, D. and McCormick, J. (1978) *People's Theatre*, London: Croom Helm.

Hornbrook, D. (1989) *Education and Dramatic Art*, Oxford: Blackwell.

Jackson, T. (ed.) (1980) *Learning through Theatre: Essays and Casebooks on Theatre in Education*, 1st edn, Manchester: Manchester University Press. [Includes case-studies of *It Fits* and *Marches*.]

McGillivray, D. (ed.) (1992) *British Alternative Theatre Directory 1992–93*, Cardiff: Rebecca Books.

Pit Prop Theatre and Neil Duffield (1984) *Brand of Freedom* [video-cassette and accompanying notes], Manchester: Manchester University Television Productions.

Ross, M. (1978) *The Creative Arts*, London: Heinemann.

Rowell, G. and Jackson, A. (1984) *The Repertory Movement: Regional Theatre in Britain*, Cambridge: Cambridge University Press.

Taylor, J. and Walford, R. (1972) *Simulation in the Classroom*, London: Penguin.

Theatre-in-Education: What Future? A survey of the threats to TIE provision (December 1992), compiled by Trade Unionists at Greenwich YPT.

Witkin, R. (1974) *The Intelligence of Feeling*, London: Heinemann Educational.

Part I

Identifying Theatre in Education

Introduction

This section is about developments and definitions. The aim here is, first, to provide an overview of TIE as it has evolved in Britain, identifying some of the key shifts in its development, and, second, to offer a more explorative account of the nature of TIE 'Education or Theatre?' (a revised and expanded version of the 1980 essay) traces in outline the history of the TIE movement in Britain, from its emergence in 1965 to the present, and relates its uneven growth and precarious existence to the perennial problems of how it has been both perceived and funded. Gavin Bolton's chapter is a rewritten version of his excellent essay for the 1980 edition. As an internationally known authority on educational drama and as one who in his own way has had a major impact upon the thinking and practice of many TIE teams, he examines the similarities and differences between TIE and drama in education, between the role of the actor–teacher and that of the drama teacher, and suggests a helpful conceptual framework for understanding the functions of each.

While no simple watertight definition of TIE is possible, or desirable, it is hoped that these chapters will provide the reader with some useful orientation points in the process of understanding the background to TIE, the routes by which it emerged and changed, and some of the theoretical implications. The later chapters will, of course, in various ways put more flesh on the bones. Although the focus here is primarily upon the British experience, the parallels and connections with TIE experience elsewhere will, I believe, quickly emerge.

Chapter 1

Education or theatre?

The development of TIE in Britain

Tony Jackson

The story of the growth of TIE in Britain is one that oscillates between surges of enthusiasm and rapid growth at one extreme and periods of cutbacks, gloom and despondency at the other. The development has of course never been even nor free of anxiety: struggle for survival has rarely been far from its practitioners' minds. TIE is indeed one of theatre's most vital yet most vulnerable forms. At the time of writing, it is facing one of its most devastating threats (from the ramifications of the most radical shake-up of the education system for fifty years), yet survive it will even if in different shapes and more varied and more fluid permutations. Just as several TIE teams fall prey to the economic axe wielded by beleaguered repertory companies or education authorities and as some discuss the imminent demise of TIE in Britain, so new companies form (if with different briefs and even less secure futures) and interest in TIE across the world increases (not always modelled on the British pattern). Why this bumpy ride? Why has TIE not been accepted as an integral, necessary part of our cultural and educational infrastructure? Why does it refuse to go under?

The history and future development of TIE are of course inextricably tied up with how it is and has been funded. This may seem axiomatic but it applies more closely to TIE than to any other form of theatre. TIE is labour-intensive: it usually operates with one or at most two classes of children at a time (i.e. between thirty and sixty) since a close rapport and inter-action with its audience are central to the experience. (Even when circumstances demand performances to larger audiences, the attempt is always made to involve them actively at some point and in some way.) Moreover its audiences are not, and more important should not be, required to pay for the service it provides. Its *raison d'être* lies in its function, first, as a method of education and therefore with a justifiable claim to be seen as an educational resource within the school system, and, second, as an art form in its own right but one that is peculiarly suited to its specific audience and age range (and that, in theatre, is almost unique). However, to say that TIE is an educational resource and therefore belongs in schools is not to say that TIE should be wholly funded and controlled by the local education authority. That may occasionally be the most appropriate arrangement but not always – and historically TIE teams have cherished the strong degree of independence from the school system which is reflected in and reinforced by their funding from more than one source. As David Pammenter argues later in this book, it is significant that TIE was born and nurtured in the theatre. And its characteristic contribution to school-based education does perhaps derive from its roots outside the system.

EARLY DEVELOPMENTS (THE FIRST PHASE)

TIE emerged from the new thinking and atmosphere of experiment that characterized the British theatre of the mid-1960s, and from the developments in educational drama in schools that were taking place at the same time. Beginning first as a project of the Belgrade Theatre in Coventry in 1965, TIE quickly took shape as a unique method of expanding the role of theatre companies who sought to develop relationships with the broader community. At Coventry, the unit of four 'actor–teachers', funded jointly by the theatre and the city and touring schools with programmes of work that embraced both performance and drama 'workshop', set a pattern that was soon followed by theatres in Bolton, Leeds, Glasgow and Nottingham. Before long there were companies offering regular TIE performances in rural and metropolitan communities across the country. They soon proved themselves to be a valuable educational resource, and the participation format, designed for class-size rather than auditorium-size groups, became from the start the key identifying feature of TIE, clearly distinguishing it from the more conventional children's theatre. The format also reflected a philosophical as well as an educational stance. 'Theatre for social change' rather than 'Building audiences for the future' was the way that most practitioners preferred to see their work, allying themselves with – and often in the vanguard of – the progressive movements in both theatre and education.[1]

Since its inception TIE has generally relied upon two main sources for its income: (1) the Arts Council (and more recently the Regional Arts Boards who are now responsible for funding arts work of a specifically local or regional kind); and (2) the local authorities, especially (though not necessarily) local education authorities (LEAs). Thus at Coventry the money for the first project came from a specific allocation of funds from the city authorities supplemented by money from the Arts Council via the theatre's board of management. This was a pattern that seemed to work well and, with some modifications, was applied to companies formed elsewhere during the following few years. The TIE company was based at a theatre and able to make use of its resources (stage management, set and props construction, etc.), and able too to establish for itself a healthy measure of independence, organizationally, from the education authority, while on the other hand, as a separate department of the theatre with funds earmarked for work in local schools, it was afforded the opportunity to build up close liaison with the schools themselves – aided by the appointment of personnel whose background was at least in part in education. When many of the early members of the Coventry company left to set up new companies in Bolton (Roger Chapman and Cora Williams), Edinburgh (Gordon Wiseman) and later, Leeds (Roger Chapman again) and Nottingham (Sue Birtwhistle), not surprisingly it was the Coventry model on which those companies were based. The only main difference was that in some cases revenue came from the LEA rather than direct from the authority itself. The establishment of those first companies, funded on a similar basis in each case, constitutes in effect the first phase of TIE's development. Accompanying those pioneering ventures was a significant shift in the policy of the Arts Council towards theatre for young people.

The Arts Council

The Arts Council of Great Britain operates with funds from central government and exists (a) 'to develop and improve the knowledge, understanding and practice of the arts'; and (b) 'to increase the accessibility of the arts to the public throughout Great Britain'. Given these objectives, it was something of an anomaly that until 1966 theatre for young people had been explicitly excluded from Arts Council support. The anomaly was recognized and corrected in 1965 when, as a result of increasing pressure from many quarters, the Arts Council set up a committee 'to enquire into the present provision of theatre for children and young people in the widest terms, to make recommendations for future development and in particular to advise on the participation of the Arts Council in such work'. The opening paragraph of this report, published in 1966, is worth quoting at some length for the clarity with which it sums up the difficulties faced in the mid-1960s and the inter-relationship between the work done and its sources and level of revenue:

> When the Arts Council originally elected, as a matter of policy, to exclude Children's Theatre Companies from its circle of beneficiaries, it unconsciously set a pattern which has influenced the development of theatre for young people ever since. The amount of subsidy then available for distri-bution to the Arts generally was very small; here, it was felt, was a sphere in which the education authorities, national and local, might give sustenance and guidance. The result, how-ever, has been a failure of responsibility, with help and patronage on a meagre basis and to no particular pattern. It is surprising that so much has been achieved . . . . With some local education authorities, Drama suffers from old puri-tanical overtones. Music, Poetry, Literature, Art: all are 'respectable'. The Drama is not quite yet – even in 1966. And in the ever growing number of enlightened quarters where it is accepted and welcomed, it is still too often regarded as a luxury and an 'extra' in children's education and not, as this Committee believes it to be, a necessity.

During the course of its enquiry the committee travelled to Coventry where 'the unique Theatre in Education team of the Belgrade Theatre was presenting a programme', which ensured that TIE became included in the scope of enquiry. The con-clusions and recommendations of the committee were many and wide-ranging but for the purpose of this brief survey those which had particular significance for TIE were: that financial help should be given to enable the larger provincial theatre companies to establish second companies to play specifically to young people, and also that recommended new young people's theatre companies should be supported. In order to monitor existing work and make new recommendations, the Arts Council was urged to set up an advisory panel composed of people with responsibilities and experience in the professional theatre (including children's theatre) and in education. The report was seminal: it was acted upon by the Arts Council and provided a major boost for those who saw the potential of TIE and for repertory theatres who would now be eligible for additional funds to provide young people's theatre on a regular basis. Hence the developments at Bolton, Leeds, Edinburgh, Greenwich (all between 1968 and 1970), and before long Nottingham and Peterborough (1973) and Lancaster (1975). What the report did above all was assert in no uncertain terms the value of theatre work for young people, including TIE, and the paramount need to subsidize it if there were to be any hope of its flourishing, experimenting, developing and gaining the status it deserved.

What the report also did was to suggest strongly, though it could not insist, that LEAs should finance the work that was done on school premises and in school hours. Not a wholly unreasonable suggestion one might think. But this, the question of who should pay for TIE in schools, has been and still is a bone of contention that has plagued the growth of TIE in many areas of the country.

Local education authorities

Responsibility for education provision in each area of the country is undertaken by the LEAs (at least until the early 1990s, when, increasingly, powers and budgets are being devolved to individual school governing bodies). Policy varies considerably from one part of the country to the next and LEAs have accordingly varied in the extent to which, if at all, they have supported professional theatre in schools. The 1944 Education Act certainly empowered them to do so if they wished. There were still many, however, who expected the individual school to finance an incoming company (whether TIE or children's theatre), either out of its own limited 'capitation' allowance or by requiring the children themselves to pay. Other authorities have taken a more enlightened and imaginative view – a view more sympathetic to the value and use of the arts in education – and either allocated substantial funds to an independent or theatre-based company (as at Greenwich) or, like the Inner London Education Authority (ILEA), set up their own TIE or DIE teams.

THE SECOND PHASE: THE 1970s

It is perhaps from around 1971, with the formation of the Cockpit TIE team by ILEA (along with a companion team, the 'Curtain', to work with younger age groups), that one can see the emergence of a second phase of TIE's development – characterized by closer interest in TIE among a growing number of LEAs and by some considerable strides forward in the work produced in terms of both form and content. TIE had clearly become a definable movement, even in some respects a bandwagon.

By the end of the decade the situation looked decidedly encouraging. By and large some form of TIE even if on an infrequent basis was available in most of the major centres of population, and in many of the rural areas as well. There had been, since the early 1970s, not only expansion but diversification. Although TIE began and initially developed through the establishment of TIE units attached to regional repertory theatres, funded by the Arts Council and local authorities via the theatre board, there soon emerged several alternative patterns. Many companies, especially those which had widened their brief to include community and young people's work generally, chose to go independent, setting themselves up as limited liability companies with non-profit-making and often 'charity' status and receiving grant aid direct from the local authority and the Arts Council (or increasingly from the regional arts association). This gave them, of course, a much greater degree of autonomy and control over their work than would have been the case had they been attached to a main theatre. Other TIE teams, such as the Cockpit, were set up directly by the LEA itself, though London was one of the few authorities to have grasped the opportunity. Elsewhere (such as at Wakefield in Yorkshire), several authorities established drama in education (DIE) teams consisting of peripatetic drama teachers who from time to time worked together as TIE units. Moreover, taking the country as a whole, it was possible to say that TIE companies now covered the complete educational spectrum: from infant schools to further education colleges, from youth clubs to special schools for the 'educationally subnormal', from summer play schemes to work on A Level examination texts. Several companies too explored ways of using the same material both for their school programmes and for their adult shows – part of a widening out from TIE to 'educative theatre' for the community at large.

Indeed some of the most innovative TIE work dates from this period. From 'straightforward' involvement of children in a story, in which they meet and talk with characters and actively become part of the narrative, programmes were developed that put the children right at the heart of the events with responsibility to investigate, interrogate and make decisions that had repercussions for the characters involved – as in *Pow Wow* (about the American Indians: Coventry 1973), *Poverty Knocks* (on the Chartist Movement of the 1840s: Bolton Octagon TIE 1973) and *Marches* (about racism in the 1930s, designed for older students: London Cockpit TIE 1977). Experiments with theatrical form led to 'adventure programmes' such as *Ifans' Valley* (Belgrade TIE, 1973), which involved a school field trip to nearby countryside with children meeting characters en route, and to such complex pieces as *Rare Earth* (Belgrade TIE 1973), a three-part programme about the environment that included an interactive simulation, and a powerful play *Drink the Mercury* which drew on Japanese Noh and Kabuki theatre for its stylized presentation including, most strikingly, the personified depiction of the deadly mercury-emitting factory in Minemata Bay.

A further important step was taken with the formation in 1975 of the Standing Conference of Young People's Theatre (SCYPT) to represent the interests of TIE and young people's theatre to funding bodies and also, perhaps more importantly at that time, to promote debate, the sharing of ideas and experiences and the furthering of the general aims of the movement. This also signalled the movement's growing politicization, a trend already evident in the foregrounding of contemporary social issues in many programmes from the early seventies onwards.

As TIE activity increased on all fronts there was, perhaps

inevitably, some confusion of aims and misdirection of energy. For some repertory theatre directors the newly available funds meant no more than an extra incentive to mount the Shakespeare production they had been planning anyway but link it to the local examination syllabus in order to qualify for the additional cash. Some theatres placed their priority on building new audiences, on promoting an appreciation of what adult theatre had to offer, rather than providing theatre for young people in their own right. And with the expansion of new companies, many actors saw an opportunity to get into the 'real' (i.e. adult) theatre by the back door, to acquire the coveted Equity card by professing immense enthusiasm for performing to 12 year-olds.

None the less, much was achieved during the 1970s, not the least being the acquisition in the latter part of the decade of a greater degree of realism among TIE practitioners about the nature of their medium. TIE companies have always been among the most socially conscious of theatre groups, consistently choosing to examine social issues they believe to be of relevance to the lives of the children with whom they work. Their work is often motivated by a strong sense of the injustices that prevail in society at large, and many companies see it as part of their responsibility to contribute in some way to the making of a better world. Marxist analyses of social processes, and the educational philosophies of such as Ivan Illich, John Holt and Paulo Freire generated not only heated debate about the need for 'alternative' approaches within the state system but also a vital atmosphere of experiment with form, with ways of engaging children actively in their own learning. Inevitably there were mistakes made and blind alleys rushed into: for some groups the idealism slid all too easily into misconceptions about the capacity of TIE to act as a medium for direct social change (and indeed about the desirability of such a role). Theatre may influence attitudes and thus contribute indirectly to social changes, but to expect it to transform on its own and overnight is naive in the extreme. Significantly, though, despite the rhetoric that often emanated from the highly charged political debates at SCYPT conferences, remarkably few TIE programmes of the many hundreds produced actually portrayed society in the simplistic terms common to some of the political agitprop theatre groups of the time. The demands made by the nature of the work to relate one's script constantly to clear educational objectives have undoubtedly enabled TIE companies by and large to avoid the temptation to over-simplify for the sake of quick and easy solutions.

Accompanying the increased confidence in TIE of its practitioners during this expansive phase was also, among a few companies, a tendency towards a somewhat dismissive, even arrogant, attitude to schools, a belief that TIE was somehow vested with a monopoly of wisdom *because* it was outside the school system. Again, fortunately, this has not been widespread, and the major companies have been for the most part notable for the immense efforts they have put into developing close contact and mutual understanding with schools. But where such attitudes have been prevalent and reflected in the work done it undoubtedly set back the cause of TIE by many years, exposing the work to easy hostile criticism.

There was of course bound to be some tension and misunderstanding between TIE companies and those who controlled, or taught within, institutions that tended to be inherently conservative. In 1976, a group of HM Schools Inspectors undertook a survey of the work of theatre companies in schools and published a positive, highly encouraging report called *Actors in Schools.* Two years later, the principal author of the report, Bert Parnaby, assessed the developments and changes since the survey in an article in *Trends in Education* and noted that the biggest shift of emphasis, 'especially in areas where companies have not been fully used or appreciated by schools, by the LEA, or both' (Parnaby 1978: 20), had been a move into the community. While this was to be welcomed (provided that the school 'is realistically regarded as part of that same community'), he was concerned at the lack of any evidence of schools making positive use of TIE as part of the general rethinking of their role and their curriculum, especially in the area of political, social and moral education, that was so acutely needed. And he concluded that, if such were the case, 'the actors' move into community work must be seen as a move out of schools because of indifference and lack of understanding of the work, often by those most closely concerned with curriculum planning'.

By 1980 the picture was not as bright as it might have appeared on the surface. Thus, citing the number of companies in existence (twenty-one fully-fledged TIE teams plus another sixty or so who claimed to undertake TIE work on a less regular basis) disguises the very considerable losses and gains that had taken place in the late 1970s and the fact that many of those gains were due to the use made of government-funded Job Creation schemes which, by their very nature, were only temporary measures and largely dependent upon the will of the particular government in office. Inevitably, many of those schemes (though not all), and hence the TIE personnel involved, soon disappeared.

THE THIRD PHASE (1980–90): CRISIS AND CHANGE IN A HOSTILE CLIMATE

By the early 1980s, with inflation at a high level and a squeeze being applied to the funds available from both central and local government, TIE, generally run on the most minimal of shoestring budgets, was already looking vulnerable. And it was the participation format – so long the key distinguishing feature of TIE – that took the brunt of the new pressures.

Two contrasting trends in the formats of programmes became evident during the subsequent decade:

(1) a shift away from participation programmes to performance-only pieces (*Raj*, about the last days of British rule in India, being a good example of such a 'TIE play'; Leeds TIE 1984) which were only occasionally followed by discussion or workshop; this was accompanied by a reduction in the overall volume of newly devised work;

(2) the redevelopment of participation programmes among a handful of the more firmly established companies, but in different guises and with different emphases.

The reasons for the trend towards performance-only work are many, but have to do with both external and internal pressures. Externally, TIE has not been able to escape the rapid and far-reaching social, economic and cultural changes that came to the fore in the eighties: the decline in the public funding of the arts; the changed, more censorious political atmosphere of Thatcherite Britain; the structural changes being introduced into the education system, involving a new National Curriculum and an emphasis upon skills and training often at the expense of the arts;[2] and the general promotion of an 'enterprise culture' based on the short-term values of the market place. Financial pressures have led to more and more companies looking for increased 'cost-effectiveness': performance-only pieces mean that larger groups of children can be played to per performance. Companies have had to reduce the number of their personnel and spend an increased amount of time in administration, negotiating continually to retain the most minimal of funding. Less time has been available for newly devised, and especially collectively devised, work. It has been easier and quicker to contract a writer to produce a self-contained play, or to use extant scripts. Some excellent work has still been done (*Raj* being just one example), but against greater odds.

Internal pressures have been more complex but just as pressing. There has been some loss of confidence in the participation method. Many TIE actors with a conventional theatre training have felt that participation work was better handled by teachers, others have found it simply exhausting, while others still became frustrated by activating children towards decisions and understandings about the need for change in society only then to walk away, leaving them in the hands of the institution, resulting in little or no change. Surely, it was argued, actors should play to their strengths: could not theatre be powerful through performance alone, through sharper imagery and more controlled, resonant narrative, which too much TIE was ignoring or handling carelessly? If you have to walk away, better to leave children with the memory of a powerful theatre performance that might continue to work, beneath the surface. TIE was, in the view of many, therefore, failing to provide enough of an artistic experience.

But the trend among some companies in the opposite direction was equally salutary. The ideas and methodology of such DIE practitioners as Dorothy Heathcote and Gavin Bolton became more widely known in TIE circles through the 1980s: their approach stressed the pedagogic value of drama and the use of such strategies as teacher-in-role (itself a technique close to the notion of the actor–teacher), and above all insisted upon carefully structured opportunity for reflection by children in classroom drama work. Many in TIE found this methodology highly applicable to their own work. In part this was a response to the sense many had that TIE was too often guilty of pushing children through a programme, gesturing towards participation on the surface but controlling and manipulating their involvement such that outcomes were wholly predictable and participation was of the most superficial kind.

Likewise, debate was greatly stimulated by the work (and visits) of Augusto Boal, especially his 'Forum Theatre' and 'Image Theatre' techniques, which in adapted form offered methods by which young people could exert more control over the problem-solving process. (This approach is discussed in more detail in Chris Vine's chapter.) Both approaches have drawn a number of companies towards a different kind of participation format. In this new variation, performance is often punctuated by halting the action ('freeze-framing') or re-running scenes for closer investigation, so encouraging more detached discussion and reflection, out of situation, out of role, with usually at least one actor as facilitator: this would then inform how pupils viewed, and perhaps influenced, the next stage of the drama. (Notable examples of this approach have been Greenwich Young People's Theatre's *School on the Green*, which looked at ideas about education; Belgrade's *Fire in the Mountain*, a piece about modern Nicaragua; Theatr Powys' *Careless Talk*, about a Welsh community in World War II; and M6 Theatre's *Trappin'*, a play about oppression within a marriage, culminating in a 'Forum Theatre' workshop. Further examples are described in later chapters.)

A closing of the gap between the practices of the DIE teacher and the TIE team was an evident outcome in many parts of the country – and a simultaneous opening of the gap between those companies committed to the participation format and those who increasingly offered plays with just a nod (or not even that) towards participatory follow-up work.

THE FOURTH PHASE: THE 1990s: NEW THREATS, NEW DIRECTIONS, NEW FORMS

As the National Curriculum, LMS and the diminishing role of the LEAs begin to bite, all companies – no matter how strongly they resent the undermining of the long-held principle of state funded arts provision within schools – are now having to look increasingly towards other sources of income to supplement or

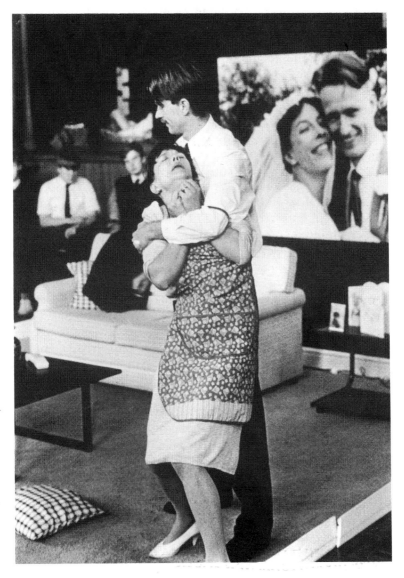

Plate 1.1 Trappin'
A scene from *Trappin'* [local slang for 'getting a boyfriend or girlfriend']
by Frances McNeil (M6 Theatre, 1991). A play followed by a Forum
Theatre workshop.
Photo: Arthur Thompson.
Actors: Maggie Tagney, James Byrne.

even replace grants from the LEAs. Many face extinction if they fail, for the regional arts boards will be unwilling and unable to become sole providers.

Other developments reflect just as clearly the mood of the times – and suggest some of the future directions, both positive and negative, that TIE might take. A number of new teams have managed to obtain funding, sometimes on a project by project basis, sometimes more permanently, to serve the requirements of particular agencies involved with young people – such as the Health Education Council or the National Society for the Prevention of Cruelty to Children (AIDS and all forms of drug dependency along with recent press revelations about the extent of child abuse have clearly promoted intense concern and a willingness to try a wide range of resources and methods in reaching young people). The 'heritage industry' has also started to employ groups of actors, based at a number of major centres of historical interest, whose task is to 'bring history alive' for both tourists and organized parties of schoolchildren – a trend that is viewed with suspicion by many in TIE who place a premium upon artistic autonomy.

At the time of writing a new organization is being formed to represent those companies and personnel involved in Theatre in Museums. In traditional TIE terms these companies may seem a motley assortment – ranging from the impressive Young National Trust Theatre, a sizable company that undertakes full-scale participatory TIE projects for schools which are presented in various National Trust properties around the country, to the much smaller team based at Wigan Pier whose task is to enliven the industrial museum's turn-of-the-century theme ('the way we were'), often for visiting school parties, but just as much for the casual visitor. (The most successful attempt that this writer has seen to recreate and to demythologize history using actors, in as rigorously authentic a way as possible with few concessions to the 'entertain-me' syndrome, is based at the Plimouth Plantation, the reconstructed pilgrim settlement in Massachusetts.)

Diversification has been evident for some years now at all levels – ideological, dramaturgical, financial, organizational – and, in the process, new groupings (such as ASSITEJ–GB, National Drama and Theatre in Museums) have emerged to represent those changing interests, demands and partnerships. It is probably no longer possible to speak of a single TIE movement, just as SCYPT has ceased to be the one voice of that movement. That is not necessarily a bad thing – so long as the dialogue between those new groupings is constantly kept active and broader alliances are made in order to defend the work wherever and whenever it is threatened.

TIE: EDUCATION OR THEATRE?

One of the reasons for TIE's particular vulnerability at times of economic gloom has been its precarious position poised between two main sources of funding. While in some areas and at less financially fraught times the dual system has functioned perfectly well, in a spirit of genuine partnership, there is a very real sense of bewilderment, frustration and, above all, insecurity felt by many companies who feel themselves accountable to two very different bodies and often against very different criteria. Moreover, inherent in this dual system of funding and the continuing argument over who should really pay for TIE, there lies a deeper tension – and that is the debate about whether TIE is really theatre or education. Ideally the terms should not be mutually exclusive but in practice they often tend to be in the eyes of bureaucrats, politicians and even fellow educationalists and theatre professionals. Thus while the Arts Council and latterly the Regional Arts Boards prefer not to fund work undertaken in school hours, many LEAs (and now school governors) will see any activity undertaken by a professional theatre company to be 'entertainment', the 'icing on the cake', i.e. not educational and not therefore to be grant-aided.

The wider dissemination of what TIE means, what it does and how it can be used, is certainly one of the major tasks now facing the TIE movement, just as it was in 1980. But resistance to the notion of theatre as a teaching instrument is not solely due to inadequate public relations: it seems deeply ingrained in institutional attitudes – as Parnaby implied. One does not have to agree totally with the pessimistic analyses of institutionalized education by Illich, Holt and others to recognize that such diagnoses do contain more than a grain of truth – that for example the education offered is all too often dictated by organizational needs, that syllabuses and teaching methods are driven by examinations, rather than the other way round. TIE therefore, because it offers through the art form a vibrant and

Plates 1.2 and 1.3 An Endless Maze
Scenes from *An Endless Maze* (Young National Trust Theatre), a participation programme for 9- to 13-year-olds about life in the reign of Mary Tudor, presented in various historic National Trust properties in 1992. Photo: Kim Williams.

Actors: Plate 1.2: L–R: Antonio Gomez, Nicky Ridley, Sheena Penson, Stephen McEachran, Richard Gay, Hilary Greatorex. Plate 1.3: Nicky Ridley.

'alternative' way of looking at things, has an important and necessary role to play as a 'gingerer' within the system, and also as a vital link between the school and the larger community and its concerns. However, the likelihood of teams being able to persuade institutions, let alone funding bodies, of this function has without doubt become immeasurably more constrained now that delivery of a narrowly conceived and examination-oriented National Curriculum is at the forefront of teachers' minds, not to mention the newly devolved budgets which mean that, separately and with much narrower horizons, schools will place the buying in of an expensive TIE visit as a much lower priority than repairs to the roof or the purchase of textbooks.

It has been argued, in more philosophical vein, that TIE is a hybrid form that represents a disturbing trend in the arts generally towards diluting the quality of artistic experience with dubious and extrinsic social or educational objectives. Is TIE education or theatre or both? Does theatre make the education offered superficial, transitory, untrustworthy? We must surely be wary of seeing theatre and education as totally different commodities whose mingling together is surprising, suspicious and even damaging. The words of Bertolt Brecht, when faced with a not dissimilar resistance to his own experiments with 'teaching plays' in the 1930s, still have relevance for the 1990s:

> Generally there is felt to be a very sharp distinction between learning and amusing oneself. The first may be useful, but only the second is pleasant . . . . Well, all that can be said is that the contrast between learning and amusing oneself is not laid down by divine rule; it is not one that has always been and must continue to be . . . . Theatre remains theatre, even when it is instructive theatre, and in so far as it is good theatre it will amuse.

> (Brecht 1936: 72–3)

TIE at its best has shown, in perhaps the most complete way yet, that theatre and learning need not be incompatible bedfellows. It is possible to learn through theatre.

Part of the problem, for those who worry about such notions, no doubt stems from the fact that we often confuse 'education' with school, with institutionalized State education, and they are not necessarily the same thing. Education can take place in an enormous variety of ways – not least through the medium of the arts. Any good theatre will of itself be educational – that is, when it initiates or extends a questioning process in its audience, when it makes us look afresh at the world, its institutions and conventions and at our own place in that world, when it expands our notion of who we are, of the feelings and thoughts of which we are capable, and of our connection with the lives of others.

One of the main assertions of the Arts Council working party, set up in 1979 to make recommendations on the provision of theatre for children, was that children's theatre, including TIE, is an art, an 'imaginative event using actors', and should be funded as such wherever and whenever it may occur – preferably by the Arts Council so that the independent function of the art might be preserved. The report argued for, among other things, a considerable injection of new funds into children's theatre and a more active part to be taken by the Arts Council in the promotion of this work. But despite the Council's valiant support for children's theatre during the previous decade and a half, its reception of the report, and especially the proposals for a major shift in Council policy, was at best lukewarm. And the ambiguity remains: there is no longer a separate panel to advise on young people's theatre (it being felt that now the work had become more widely established there was no further need to compartmentalize it from other areas of theatre) and the practice of earmarking funds for young people's work was likewise discontinued.

In the 1990s, the Arts Council values 'education in theatre' (see page 8) but still maintains a wary distance from theatre in education; and 'partnerships' between LEAs and Regional Arts Boards have become increasingly fragile. If local government funding for TIE should disappear in all save a few areas of the country, and if schools separately should find themselves unable to pay for, or even contribute to, a full-scale co-ordinated TIE service, then will the work survive? Will TIE increasingly need to go down the road of servicing the requirements of agencies whose major concerns are not educational provision? While TIE must be prepared to respond to the rapidly changing needs of the social world – and there is every reason to applaud the use of TIE methodology in helping to challenge disturbing and anti-social trends and prejudice – it would be a tragic misuse of the skills, imagination and theatrical potential of TIE were it to be wholly appropriated for the purposes of 'crisis management'. Its roots lie in the theatre and its strength in its independence from direct state (or state agencies') control. It must of course be accountable and responsive and it must work through fullest collaboration with schools and other organizations, but ultimately it is an aesthetic enterprise and those who wish to see it contribute energetically and effectively to young people's education in the broadest sense must acknowledge that fact. For this reason, the hope must be that – despite signs of contrary pressures (such as the push to make arts organizations increasingly reliant upon commercial sponsorship) – the majority of TIE work will continue to be funded through enlightened partnerships of local government, schools and Regional Arts Boards: a practice that at its best has so far proved more able than any other to offer the support and long-term security necessary for companies to develop their work and meet the needs of young people.

NOTES

1 For a detailed account of the early days of TIE see Gordon Vallins, 'The Beginnings of TIE' (1980), and Christine Redington (1983); also David Pammenter's account of TIE and 'child-centred' education in chapter 3 below.

2 In 1988 the Education Reform Act ushered in a sweeping series of changes to the structure and content of education in Britain. A National Curriculum was intituted for the first time consisting of three core subjects (English, Maths and Science) and ten 'foundation' subjects (which included Art and Music but not Drama or Dance; Drama as a teaching method was included under English and several other subjects). Equally radical was the introduction of Local Management of Schools (LMS) in which schools were given increasing control over the budget allocated to them by the LEA; the LEA would be allowed to retain only 5–7 per cent of its education budget for central services. Most LEAs that grant-aid TIE companies do so from those central funds. Finally, in an attempt to eliminate LEAs altogether, government has (with financial incentives) encouraged schools to 'opt out' altogether from the LEA and to assume 'grant-maintained' status, which means receiving budget allocations direct from the central government Department for Education. The implications for future funding of TIE companies are considerable, and are discussed further by Geoff Readman (chapter 15 below).

BIBLIOGRAPHY

Arts Council of Great Britain (1966) *The Provision of Theatre for Young People in Great Britain*, London: HMSO.
—— (1991) *Drama in Schools*, London: ACGB.
Brecht, B. (c. 1936) 'Theatre for pleasure or theatre for instruction', in J. Willett (ed.) (1974) *Brecht on Theatre*, London: Methuen.
Jackson, T. (ed.) (1980) *Learning Through Theatre: Essays and Casebooks on Theatre in Education*, 1st edn, Manchester: Manchester University Press.
—— (1986) 'Raj: introduction and critical commentary', in P.S. Petersen and K.-H. Westarp (eds) *British Drama in the Eighties: Texts and Contexts*, Aarhus: Aarhus University Press.
Parnaby, B. (1978) '*Actors in Schools* and after', in *Trends in Education*, London: HMSO.
Redington, C. (1983) *Can Theatre Teach?*, London: Pergamon Press.
Vallins, G. (1980) 'The beginnings of TIE', in T. Jackson (ed.) *Learning Through Theatre*, 1st edn, Manchester: Manchester University Press.

Published TIE programmes referred to

Belgrade TIE Team (1976) *Rare Earth*, London: Methuen.
—— (1980) *Pow Wow* and *Ifan's Valley*, in P. Schweitzer (ed.) *Theatre in Education: Five Infant Programmes*, London: Methuen.
Bolton Octagon TIE Company (1980) *Poverty Knocks* and Cockpit TIE Team (London) *Marches: from Jarrow to Cable Street* (in scenario/case-study form) in T. Jackson (ed.) *Learning through Theatre: Essays and Casebooks on Theatre in Education*, Manchester: Manchester University Press.
Greenwich Young People's Theatre (1987) 'School on the Green' in C. Redington (ed.) *Six TIE Programmes*, London: Methuen.
Leeds TIE Company (1984) *Raj*, London: Amber Lane Press.
McNeil, F. (1991) *Trappin'* (first presented by M6 Theatre Co.) in R. Robinson (ed.) *Ask Me Out*, London: Hodder & Stoughton.
Pit Prop Theatre and Neil Duffield (1984) *Brand of Freedom* (on video-cassette with accompanying notes), Manchester: Manchester University Television Productions.
(Other TIE programmes referred to have not been published.)

Chapter 2

Drama in education and TIE
A comparison

Gavin Bolton

I have never worked professionally in TIE, but since its inception I have found myself caught up in its development. Both DIE and TIE are concerned with dramatic art and pedagogy, but in recent years political and economic expediency have had a reductive effect: some drama teaching has become reduced to a particularly limited form of simulated role-play related to the learning of facts and practising of skills; some TIE has become reduced to performing for large audiences, followed, perhaps, by brief 'hot-seating' procedures as a means of reflection.

Over-reaction to the role-play cul-de-sac has led one or two DIE writers to assert that school drama has nothing to do with pedagogy and that drama teaching is solely about promoting the study of dramatic art. For me this is to exchange one cul-de-sac for another. I believe drama has a great deal to do with pedagogy *because* it is an art. I still hold to the view outlined by me in the 1980 edition of this book, that the richness of classroom drama lies in its potential to achieve change of understanding (a pedagogic objective) along with improvement in drama skills and knowledge of theatre (an artistic objective). The two objectives are interdependent. The current instrumental perspective of education as instruction has upheld a view of drama education as having a purpose either to do with practising life-skills or to do with acquiring prescribed theatre knowledge and skills. Both purposes are reductionist and functional. I believe that classroom drama is to do with creating an art form in a way that is significant for its participants: from the art-making experience something new is understood or something is newly understood.

TIE shares with DIE this emphasis on 'change of understanding'. It is probably true to say that whereas in DIE it is sometimes possible that teacher and children together 'discover' or even 'stumble across' significance in the content of what they are creating, TIE actor–teachers can never leave this to chance. A group of infants with their teacher may use, let us say, a 'secret message' as a starting point or 'pretext' for spontaneously invented drama, not knowing where it is going to lead. For various reasons, not least organizational ones, the TIE team's work has to be planned in almost every respect before the programme is presented.

However, in this chapter I shall confine my discussion to an area of overlap between the two: the kind of drama in education where teacher plays a role has much in common with the input of a TIE team, for both invite the pupils to become engaged, either as participants or as audience, by the teacher's or actors' representation of a character. It is at this particular interface between DIE and TIE that theory and practice coincide, but, of course, interesting differences remain.

I shall discuss DIE under the following headings: mode, structure, purpose and engagement with meaning.

MODE

In DIE today the pupils engage in a wide range of activities, which broadly fall within two bands of 'intentions': the intention to experience and the intention to show. These activities may be grouped into those participated in by the whole class, small group, or pairs; they may be meaning-making or skill-oriented; they may be quick exercises lasting half a minute or sustained for most of the lesson. In this chapter I shall be focussing on 'whole group experiencing' – in other words that kind of classroom activity where it is legitimate for teacher to intervene by playing a role. This is not to imply that other activities are not important – 'tableau' work, for instance, where the class engage technically in showing something to an audience of peers is a valuable strategy – but 'whole group experiencing' is most relevant to this discussion, because of its kinship with TIE.

When children are in make-believe, playing on their own, they are for the most part using an experiential mode. They have 'contracted' to make a fiction; they are agents as well as recipients of the experience. They can say 'We are making it happen, so that it can happen to us.' In 'making it happen' they are also acknowledging and defining the rules related to whatever fictitious context is being created. There are therefore three components to this 'dramatic playing' process: the agent, the recipient and the rules. It is characterized both by spontaneity and by freedom from the burden of putting it in a form that could be repeated and 'performed' at a later date, which features so strongly in many of the other drama practices.

But the burden or challenge of keeping to the rules of the agreed context should not be underestimated. Even a child playing on his/her own, although appearing to have a high degree of autonomy, is in fact setting him/herself a task in restraint, as Vygotski puts it: 'to act on the line of *greatest resistance*' (1976: 548; my italics). Nevertheless, on his/her own s/he may manipulate the rules to suit him/herself. If another child joins in, the rules have to be negotiated and freedom is further constrained. They are both agents but only in so far as they abide by the agreed rules and respond to each other's contriving. The subsequent experiencing is the result of a subtle balancing of these complex factors. Experiencing the fiction spontaneously, from moment to moment, is an existential occurrence to which the participants are both submissive and detached, for they are both participants and percipients, watching themselves even as they are experiencing.

STRUCTURE: TEACHER-IN-ROLE

When a teacher takes on a role as part of class drama s/he is, at a fictitious level, joining in *with* them, but at an educational or aesthetic level s/he is working *ahead* of them. It is, as Geoff Gillham has pointed out, as if there are two plays going on at the same time – the play for the child and the play for the teacher (Gillham 1974). They are different in respect of (a) purpose and (b) structure. Difference in purpose can be illustrated as follows. In their drama about, for example, Robin Hood the children's intentions are, say, to have fun doing a Robin Hood adventure, whereas the teacher's objectives may be to do with torn loyalties, economic pressures, being outlawed or the political history of the times. In other words the teacher is operating at a different level of meaning from the children. (I shall refer to this in more detail in the final section of this chapter.) The drama-making is a partnership between teacher and children as agents, a 'folding-in' of teacher's intentions with the children's intentions.

There is also an interesting interleaving of structures. Left to themselves children will structure for sequence, for the 'what-happens-next' of a story; as Susanne Langer puts it: for a present 'filled with the future' (1953). The teacher, however, will structure for situation. The children will manipulate the contextual rules (i.e. the Robin Hood rules) to suit their wants; the teacher will manipulate the rules to meet what s/he sees as their needs. They are using the fictitious context to submit themselves to experiencing; the teacher is sharpening and deepening that experiential mode by structuring the fiction towards a theatre form.

By theatre form I mean those basic elements of theatre that a playwright employs and a director builds upon: focus, tension, constraint, ritual, contrast and symbolization. (By symbolization I refer to those actions that resonate more than their literal meaning. For instance, lighting a candle may be an unexceptional action in itself, but if we see it in the context of the Waite family lighting a candle in the window of their home for Terry to return to, then the symbolism of hope and faith become part of that simple action.) A teacher-in-role, therefore, in a very special way, is working in theatre. Just as a playwright and director will consciously create tension etc. so that an audience might experience, so a teacher-in-role uses elements of theatre so that the participants might experience.

But experiencing, in itself, is of little value. It is reflection on the experience that leads to change in understanding. Obviously it is beneficial for a class or an audience to reflect after the experience, but the greater potential may lie in reflection during the dramatic experience. I referred above to both participants and percipients – that the children watch themselves as they create. The drama teacher has an advantage over the TIE team, in that s/he can, by slipping out of role at regular intervals, keep this 'spectator in the head' functioning effectively. In role as, say, a messenger from the Sheriff of Nottingham, to the class in their role as a village of craftsmen making weapons for Robin Hood s/he may have spoken the line: 'The Sheriff's attention has been drawn to this village' – and almost immediately the teacher can slip out of role and invite the class to ponder on the implications of that remark ... and then, but a few moments later, the 'Messenger' resumes his role again, and the 'spectator in the children's head' is now working on 'red alert'!

When a TIE team works with pupils its function can usefully be seen as an extension of teacher-in-role. Although TIE normally lacks the degree of flexibility for slipping in and out of role as described in the last paragraph, there is nevertheless an intention to adapt to the needs of an audience. The team is not just offering the children a play, as in traditional children's theatre: it is anticipating a 'play for the children' where the audience/participants, at their own level of meaning, can discover and retain their own dynamic within the action.

Where the type of subject-matter embodies a great deal of factual information, as in *Labour for the Lord* by Phil Woods (Tyne and Wear TIE 1992), there is a danger that the children remain submissive 'passengers' within the complex experience. In this particular TIE experience, which creates the context of a child-employing chemical factory in the 19th century, the audience of 9 to 10 year-olds, although actively engaged throughout the drama, never have the chance to take the initiative. And yet they seem to find the activities absorbing and to relate to the characters to an extent which seems to justify the structure.

It does not however match those TIE programmes (such as *Poverty Knocks*, Bolton 1973, or *Brand of Freedom*, Pit Prop 1984) where the young participants are genuinely involved in decision making. This question of 'ownership' by the pupils applies to both TIE and DIE drama. It is fairly common in DIE drama for the teacher and children together to go through a series of dramatic exercises before a sense of ownership by the pupils can be achieved. We may be talking here in terms of minutes, hours or even, in some circumstances, days! So we must not expect too much from a TIE programme in this respect. I would prefer to see the kind of over-tight structure in *Labour for the Lord* where the actors keep the initiative in their own hands than the programme I saw a few years ago, *Fight for the Forest* (Tyne and Wear TIE 1989), an environmental project by Rob Marsdon, in which the young participants appeared to be making decisions based on their likes and dislikes of particular characters rather than on a grasp of the issues.

PURPOSE

As I mentioned at the beginning of this chapter, I believe that DIE is concerned with change in understanding, but it is a mistake to isolate this objective by treating it as a commodity separate from form. I suggested that such a tunnel vision leads to extreme views of drama as either functional role-play or theatre 'studies', both skills- and information-based and both in the long run doing a disservice to drama as an art. If content is important then so is form. The relationship between the two is complex (I have written about it in detail elsewhere (Bolton 1992)). The very term 'content/form' may remind teachers that in setting up a dramatic experience for change in understanding, they are at the same time working towards improving the pupils' understanding of and skills in *theatre*. Some teachers fail to acknowledge this and opportunity for reflection on and articulation about theatre form is missed.

But there are other objectives that might from time to time in DIE have priority over 'change in understanding'. Drama can have a strong influence on personal and social development. Problems related to 'group interaction', 'discipline', 'language usage', 'self-esteem', or 'movement skills' etc. may become a 'hard' objective during a drama lesson. The flexible teacher will adapt to the current requirements.

Now TIE cannot have this breadth of purpose. Indeed it would usually be impossible to switch objectives to suit the particular needs of the group. Impossible and inappropriate, for the TIE team's priority must always be 'change in understanding'. Nor is it teaching about theatre. It may be afterwards that the school's drama teacher will want his/her class to discuss the theatre forms employed in the TIE presentation, but that is not the responsibility of the actor–teachers.

Thus the overlap between DIE and TIE lies in the shared objective of 'change of understanding'. Does that imply that the teacher-in-role and the TIE actor–teachers are virtually doing the same thing? This is a more complex question than it may first appear.

ENGAGEMENT WITH MEANING

One obvious difference is that whereas a drama teacher can attempt to tailor the stimulus for the drama to meet the specific needs of the class (s/he can set up a drama dealing with 'going off with strangers', 'bereavement' or 'bullying', for example, because something has recently happened to class members to make such a topic a matter for urgent attention), a TIE team cannot select their programme with such finesse. I recently observed a brilliantly devised programme on AIDS presented to students aged 16 to 18 by Tyne and Wear TIE company. The play, especially written for the company in 1991, was *Sex, Lies and Tricky Bits* by Stuart Blackburn. Although there were firm indications at every performance that members of the audience found the experience compelling, the audience's 'readiness' for the material of the play and for the workshop that followed varied considerably; some audiences seemed more mature or better informed on the subject-matter than others. Also it was noticeable that the ethos of the school or college affected the students' responses. (One school audience asked for the teachers present during the workshop to leave!) The TIE company, unlike the DIE teacher, cannot abandon or even re-shape the material for the sake of a particular class. There were a number of occasions when the workshop needed to be pitched at a slightly different level or to be moved along at a slower pace – school lunches or buses put a stop to such refinement. Of course it was envisaged that the final stage of the programme (probably taking place next day or later) included follow-up work by the health education teacher or tutor, who would be in a strong position to readjust the material to the needs of his/her students and to reflect on the dramatization and workshop experience in a way appropriate to the group – providing the tutor actually *saw* the play and workshop: some school timetables did not allow for that! But of course the TIE team had achieved what no class teacher could do: they offered a powerful, moving theatrical statement about sexual relation-ships; the audiences were both engaged and yet sufficiently distanced to cope with the reflective workshop.

Drama teachers (most of the time) and the actor–teachers (all the time), in thinking about the material they propose to handle, think retrospectively. That is, in their minds they perceive an end-product – and they then work backwards to make it available for the pupils. They know what it is they want to teach; they have given careful thought to the 'meanings' to be drawn from the dramatic experience; they have expectations of what the drama will look like when it is over. These retro-spective meanings are universals or generalizations, necessary components of reflection.

Thus in the AIDS programme the particular dramatic events concerned a young woman who after a one-night affair became HIV positive. But the company are not teaching about a par-ticular character becoming infected; the company defined their purpose as 'wanting young people to understand that sex is a matter for *negotiation*, that respectful communication between two people, in providing the basis for all sexual interaction, will also be the best protection against HIV infection'. The devisers' starting point (in this case the 'negotiation in sexual communi-cation' objective) is to be the audience's discovery. The audi-ence's starting point, however, is the particular context of a girl who has a holiday fling with a waiter. For some form of change in understanding to occur, members of the audience make their personal journey through the play and workshop to arrive at the 'negotiation' destination. They need to experience the power of the process's particularity, in order to reflect on the product's universality.

To summarize then, there are two broad levels of meaning to be engaged with. There is what might be called the particular or contextual meaning – the holiday fling, for example. In *Labour for the Lord* the contextual meanings are about child employees in a Victorian chemical factory. In the drama about Robin Hood the contextual meanings are about mediaeval craftsmen making arrows for Robin Hood's men. If the learning outcome of these experiences were to remain solely at this level, the participants might feel they had become better informed about the actions and objects and other facts to do with those times – rather like reading *War and Peace* for information about Russian history.

The converse level of meaning relates, as we have already seen, to significant generalizations that can be drawn from the particular contexts. So 'Robin Hood' becomes about, for instance, 'hero worship versus expediency'; *Labour for the Lord* becomes about 'victims of industrial progress'. These might be described as universal or thematic meanings.

There is a symbiotic dependency between the particularity of 'contextual meanings' and the generality of 'universal meanings'. If the drama is working as art, the participants' or audience's response will be a holistic one: attention will not be given to one or other level of meaning, but to each in the other.

There is a third level that is personal and idiosyncratic. I have mentioned that the TIE team cannot anticipate the 'readiness' of a particular audience. Neither they nor a teacher can cater for the individual background and feelings of a particular child. For each member of the class or audience there will be personal meanings that remain unarticulated – someone present at the HIV programme who has AIDS, for example.

The TIE company has a huge advantage over the teacher in respect of the contextual meaning. The actors can create, three-dimensionally and with immediacy, a believable context that arrests attention and interest and, above all, creates the potential for a multi-level experience of theatre. This is well-named *theatre* in education. The context itself can be rich in meaning and significant for the children, not simply as a vivid simulation but because it also taps universals and personal connotations of meaning that all good theatre provides. The teacher rarely has these resources. The equivalent in the drama classroom is a slow, often painful process of 'building belief'; much well-intentioned drama-making founders in this early uncomfortable stage. The converse of this is that because in the drama classroom 'ownership' of the material is so often hard come by, the pupils' personal investment in successful material can be profound.

BIBLIOGRAPHY

Bolton, G. (1992) *New Perspectives on Classroom Drama*, London: Simon & Shuster.

Gillham, G. (1974) 'Condercum School report' for Newcastle-upon-Tyne LEA (unpublished).

Langer, S. (1953) *Feeling and Form: A Theory of Art*, London: Routledge & Kegan Paul.

Vygotski, L. (1976) 'Play and its role in the mental development of children', in J. Bruner, A. Jolly and K. Sylva *Play: Its Role in Development and Evolution*, London: Penguin.

Part II

Ways of working

Introduction

The chapters that follow examine different working practices in TIE and the principles that, in the view of the authors, underpin that practice. David Pammenter's essay has become a classic statement of what has been at the centre of the TIE process since its inception: devising. For that reason it is reprinted here with only a few minor amendments. Indeed the fundamental questions he raises about the function of education in relation to devising seem just as pertinent now as they did in 1980.

Jim Mirrione offers a complementary and, in many ways, a counter-view of the devising of TIE programmes: while he shares many of Pammenter's philosophical assumptions about the purpose of TIE, he argues forcefully for a far more prominent role for the writer as artist in his or her own right. In part, as he explains, this derives from the particular experiences and pressures of operating a TIE team in and for New York City; but his view is also reflective of the trend away from collective devising in many companies in Britain and elsewhere.

A yet further angle on the creative processes involved in TIE work is offered by Cora Williams (like Pammenter, someone who has immense experience of TIE in a variety of conditions yet still at the 'cutting edge' of the work). In discussing the 'TIE actor' (note: no longer the 'actor–teacher'), she describes yet another distinguishing feature of much TIE practice: the engagement of the performers in all stages of the evolution of a programme. There are not only specific craft skills required but a philosophic commitment to a working process that begins often with the very germ of the idea, a process that is essential in her view to the genuinely educative and enriching experience that TIE can provide.

One of the theatre practitioners to have had most influence upon TIE over the past decade has undoubtedly been Augusto Boal. It is fitting that it should be Chris Vine, one of Britain's leading TIE directors and someone who has done more than most to promote and adapt Boal's theory and practice, who contributes this chapter on Boal's influence and, just as importantly, on those areas of difference between Boal's practice and that of many TIE companies.

Chapter 3

Devising for TIE

David Pammenter

INTRODUCTION

The TIE movement, during its short history, has had to rely almost entirely on its practitioners for its material. Its whole history has been one of self-devised work either with or without writers, so the central activity of most teams has been devising. The devising process has differed much from company to company and cannot be discussed as if there were one definitive method or as if the process were not always in a state of change. What follows then will inevitably not satisfy all schools of thought on the matter and within the space of one article it certainly cannot be comprehensive, but I shall attempt to deal briefly with the major factors, restrictions, responsibilities and skills in relation to devising.

Self-generated work has never been a soft option for TIE teams. It is very demanding. The TIE programme or play is not a watered-down version of adult theatre, nor is it seen by most of its practitioners as a method of introducing young people to the 'real' theatre which will follow later: it is an experience provided for children or young people in their own right. It demands therefore an understanding of its potential audience/participants; objectivity, clarity and analysis in the researching process; creativity, vision and vitality in the structuring and writing process; and, at every stage, a sense of theatre and dramatic order. Always the deviser is calling on both the skills and resources of the theatre and the skills and resources of the educationalist.

Before TIE had established itself there was clearly no extant body of work for the teams to draw on, so TIE as a movement, though drawing much from current theatre and education practice, has been obliged to create its own work from the start. There is now a growing body of material generated by TIE teams in the form of programmes, plays, research material and project packs for use in school which teams may draw on, but still devising remains central. There are many reasons for this, the most obvious being that much self-generated work has been devised with a specific regional or local relevance in mind. It is often the case with such programmes that whilst the structure or the methods employed may be useful to another team, the specific content may not (as, for example, with the Bolton TIE 'classic', *Poverty Knocks*, set in Bolton in the 1830s).[1] Another reason is that as long as it attempts to make the issues that face our society, of which our children are part, accessible to children; as long as it seeks to liberate understanding and not impose order; as long as it seeks to make sense of the chaos of the real world and by doing so allow children to perceive and understand the changes and contradictions going on around them, and of which they are a part, then TIE must go on changing too and, as a consequence, go on generating its own material. The danger for teams who do not attempt this is that they will become enshrined in their own institutions and be of little value to the children they serve.

INFLUENCES ON TIE AND ITS DEVELOPMENT

TIE grew from a climate of social change and the accompanying developments in educational theory in the late 1950s and early 1960s. It was during that time, following the period of post-war austerity and during something of an economic boom, that the more liberal attitudes of society at large found their expression in educational theory. This liberalism, heralded in the Education Acts of 1944 and 1948, with the ensuing development of comprehensive education, began the stirring consciousness of another development, that of 'child-centred' education. Whether or not it was, is, or ever will be 'child-centred' is a large question which I will touch on later. However, change was definitely on the cards.

Initially, TIE – this new form of theatre which Gordon Vallins and subsequently Rosemary Birbeck and others piloted in Coventry from 1965 onwards – was deeply rooted in the newly adopted educational theory and was to do with 'learning by doing'. It did not base itself in its content – that which was to be communicated or explained – but rather it focused itself on the methods by which communication could take place. Programme aims at that time were largely to do with creating a forum for the stimulation and development of the imagination of the child, the development of social behaviour and the extension of creative play. Much time was spent with teachers on in-service training courses making them aware of the relatively new concept of educational drama, its aims and methods. Great emphasis was laid on myth, legend and folk stories. But also, in this early experiment with form and method, which has been of enormous help and influence ever since, were the seeds of how TIE was to develop. There were programmes about real people in real, readily identifiable situations. In these programmes the involvement of the children led to problem-solving and decision-making based on an exploration of a problem or situation. An early example of this development is to be found in Coventry's *Who was to Blame?* (1970) – a programme for 10 to 13 year-olds which explored, through performance and subsequent discussion, the forces operating on a young milkman who ended up on a charge of grievous bodily harm. This kind of exploration and decision-making, developed in the context of audience participation, has become a backbone of many programmes since. Examples of the success of this now highly-developed technique are Coventry's *The Car Makers*, a programme which explored the chequered history of the Coventry engineers and car makers (1971); Bolton Octagon's *Poverty Knocks*, a programme about the history of the cotton operatives (1973); Coventry's two-part mining programme *The Price of Coal* (1977); and Pit Prop's more recent three-part programme about the Lancashire cotton famine of the 1860s, *Brand of Freedom* (1984).

Perhaps the cornerstone of TIE's development, which was to allow its devisers freedom to experiment with form and method, was the insistence of the early practitioners that their work required an in-depth relationship with the participants and thus should be restricted to small groups of children – one or two classes – at a time. Having avoided a restriction which, usually for reasons of finance, the children's theatre companies were obliged to work under, the TIE teams were able to adopt more specific educational aims and explore new approaches with the licence of the theatre to create new forms.

This theatrical licence has been of great importance to the deviser in the development of TIE. Although, in the early days, many theatre directors and workers did not fully understand what TIE was about, and although many thought (and some misguidedly still do think) that TIE was the responsibility of the local education authorities (LEAs) rather than the theatres, only the theatre could have allowed the development to take place. Educationalists inside the schools system, hands tied by the controllers of that system, could not have ensured the freedom for experiment and growth which has been the hallmark of TIE. It was, however, the active support and advice from progressive educationalists within the schools system which enabled the new forms to connect and succeed with teachers and children in the schools. This remains the case, and if this line of contact were broken, or if the mutual trust and respect, where it exists between the TIE company and the recipients of the work in the schools, were lost or discriminated against by those with political interests and power over either discipline, then the prospect for future development would be bleak.

The devising team must have a clear perspective of the purpose and function of their work before they start devising at all – in the same way that a conscientious teacher or writer has. They must have a clear understanding of the forces at work both on themselves and on the children they wish to work with, and a real awareness of the parameters or confines set on their work by the morals, values and ethics of the society we live in – whether or not these are subsequently to be challenged. It is this understanding which lies behind the selection of subject material and definition of aims, and it is this understanding – or lack of it – which ultimately determines the nature of the programme.

The deviser and practitioner, who are usually the same person, must have a genuine commitment to the subject area they choose and the questions they raise if the mechanics of the programme, the structure, the words, actions and characters are to be of any value to the children. Without this, the result will be poorly thought-out, poorly put-together work which will succeed only in communicating the lack of this commitment.

The most obvious and immediate forces at work on the TIE

devising team which set the parameters on its freedom to choose what or how to explore, are the institutions of the education system and the theatre of which it is a part. Both of these institutions of course reflect the economic, social and political forces at work in society at large.

What follows may best be seen as some preliminary observations and reflections on the education system and the theatre industry which help to place in perspective my own personal approach to TIE as a movement within both that seeks, in some small way, to counterbalance the pressures and demands of an institutionalized system of education.

THE EDUCATION SYSTEM AND TIE

Broadly speaking, during the nineteenth century there were two types of 'schooling' in Britain. Neither had much to do with real education, neither saw their function as helping the child to fulfil his or her maximum potential, but each had its own curricula to suit the purposes defined for it by the then rulers of society. There were the public or grammar schools for the sons of 'gentlemen' destined for leadership who studied accordingly – and there was the elementary school tradition, especially intended to train the 'lower orders' in sufficient skills to equip them to work as needed by their 'masters' whose law and property, place and position they were taught to respect. In short they were taught how to be of use and to know their place and, in that, religion and religious instruction had their role to play.

The questions to be confronted are as stark now as they were 150 years ago, despite the tremendous steps forward during the intervening years. What is education? Who is it for, and what does it say and do? Is the schools system the means by which we instil the inadequacies and contradictions of one social class or generation into the next? Or is it really concerned with freedom for children to develop their potential to the full; with equipping them to take an active part in shaping their world? Is it 'system-centred' or 'child-centred'?

The Newsom Report of 1963 stated: 'In short, drama [as part of the syllabus] along with poetry and other arts is not a frill . . . . It is through creative arts, including the arts of language, that young people can be helped to come to terms with themselves, more surely than by any other route' (Newsom 1963: 157).

Few today would disagree with this as a statement, but is our practice in schools really concerned with helping our young 'come to terms with themselves'? The arts cannot on their own achieve this laudable aim, and much else within the schools and certainly in the society outside, is concerned not with the young 'coming to terms with themselves' but rather with making sure that any development services the prerequisites of the system as it exists. Our education system, with some welcome exceptions, has little to do with freedom for development of the child, it has much to do with the demands of an industrial and technological society to perpetuate itself at the expense of its young. Our society is making sure, both generally and through the agency of the schools, that our children come to terms with it on its terms.

These observations are confirmed by the writings of a number of prominent educationalists. Michael Duane for example (1971) suggests that our education system reflects and reinforces the class structure that created it, a view endorsed by Dennis Lawson (1975). I do not make this point dogmatically; simply it is necessary for the devising team in TIE to be part of this educational debate and for its theory and practice to be clear in relation to it, as it will inevitably have a direct influence on content selection, aims, relationship to schools, teachers and children. If TIE is really to do with freedom for development of the child; if it is to attempt to base its approach in child-centred education, then its practitioners must be aware that they are swimming against the tide; they must consciously ally themselves with the many inside the education system who share the same perspectives, honestly and openly, so that full and proper focus can be brought to bear on aims, objectives, methods and achievements and, in so doing, they must create an atmosphere where real evaluation is possible.

For our young people to be free to develop their potential, for them to have the tools with which to effect change, the central freedom they must have is unrestricted access to knowledge. Here TIE has a responsibility: the deviser has an important role to play but has to know how to play it.

It was not until the 1970s that serious enlightened focus was put on the curriculum itself in our secondary schools. Previous changes had been largely structural and organizational but had not, in the main (despite the Newsom and other reports), concentrated on *what* was being taught (or, alternatively, what was not!). More recently the discussion has been about the new National Curriculum and the transmission of a common culture. Clearly these are crucial debates which are vital to the future of TIE and to the way the devising team perceives its role and function. They have obvious repercussions on the team's freedom to devise and are central to its deliberations over content selection and treatment.

TIE's role in the opening up of children's minds to ways of looking at the world, in the explanation of ideas new to them and of concepts of history and the present, as opposed to preaching some or other accepted truth to them, is certainly important, but its impact should not be overestimated and the deviser must always view it in the changing context of the schools system and society at large.

THE THEATRE AND TIE

The theatre and its current precarious state is also an important force at work on the TIE teams which requires examination.

In the theatre chapter in *Leisure for Living*, the policy statement on the Arts and Leisure adopted by the Labour Party in 1959, the state of the theatre was described as 'simultaneously hopeful and precarious'. Now, over thirty years on, the picture is no better but could hardly be described as 'hopeful'. There exists in particular no real policy for the provision of theatre for young people and, given the priority of recent governments and the climate of cut-backs in the arts through the late 1980s and early 1990s, the future of TIE is bleaker than it has ever been. The concept of the provision of TIE as a service to young people is rapidly receding over the horizon as is any hope that the government or Arts Council will undertake further or even guarantee existing funding, already woefully inadequate for this area of work.

What is theatre, who is it for, and what does it say? Theatre, at its best, is the communication and exploration of human experience; it is a forum for our values, political, moral and ethical. It is concerned with the interaction of these values at a philosophical, emotional and intellectual level. I say at its best, because much of what passes for theatre these days has little to do with any of the above. Much of our theatre has to do with sexual titillation of the worst order, is nostalgic, backward-looking and safe. It plays to a small percentage of the population which is, in the main, middle-class. The values it reflects, often reinforces and usually fails to explore, are mostly middle-class values and assumptions. There are of course welcome exceptions to the above in the form of fringe or community companies and some regional and repertory theatres, but it is true to say that, in general, the theatre does not provide a quality service to its audiences, to working people in general or to young people in particular. It is not that the skill, ability or intention are not there: they often are; rather, with the state of funding as it is, few people will take risks at the box office, and children in groups of thirty do not allow of a commercial return. Where attempts to make provision for working people and the young are made, the product frequently panders to undeveloped taste, fails to challenge easy assumptions on the part of its audience and rarely concerns itself with the question of whose or what values it is communicating.

THE CHOICE OF CONTENT

If what I have said is true, the question of content for the TIE devising team is not an arbitrary one, not if we are aware of its implications and consequences. We cannot pretend that the socio-political factors that govern the lives of adults are different for children, so – if access to knowledge is an important freedom – then we must make those factors accessible to the young so that they may explore and challenge them if they choose. In some areas of the country, given the persuasion of some LEAs and some theatres, it would doubtless be easier and more acceptable for TIE teams simply to dust off a few safe morality tales or Edwardian nursery stories, present them, challenge no assumptions, open access to no knowledge, liberate no understanding and go home content that the children had at least been entertained. However, we know that entertainment is not devoid of content and content relates to values and ideas, so again, whose ideas and values do we communicate? Clearly, the thinking TIE deviser could not follow the course outlined above any more than the thinking teacher would want that in his or her school.

Entertainment is a much broader and richer concept than

the usual context in which it is placed implies. Once the programme aim has been decided and the content chosen then it requires a rich imagination on the part of the deviser or writer to find a structure and form, a style of presentation and performance that will engage and involve the audience or participants. Entertainment does not necessarily imply a light-weight relationship between content and audience, or actor and audience. It does not mean 'make 'em laugh'. It is the engagement achieved, the involvement and trust established, the rapport between content, actor and audience that provide for entertainment, be it light or heavy, comic or tragic. The selection of content must then take account of what its theatrical or dramatic potential is, otherwise we could have worthily chosen and performed pieces which bore our audiences and fail to involve.

Adults and children alike are capable of understanding intellectually, physically and emotionally the world of which they are a part. There are all sorts of factors that govern the extent of their understanding, some of which I have touched on. Perhaps the most important is the extent to which they have been able to secure access to knowledge and the extent to which social conditioning has succeeded in mystifying them. Children, of course, learn and develop different concepts and areas of understanding at different speeds at different times, and the deviser must be ever conscious of this. But the deviser must also be aware of the barriers that our society has thrown up around young people, consciously or unconsciously, which ensure that our young are rendered incapable of challenging this state of affairs in any informed way.

If we draw the conclusion that much of what passes for education and certainly much of our theatre has the effect of clouding over real and important issues, social, political and personal, of distancing our children from them, then the priority for the deviser in choosing the content for the programme is to take up those issues. It becomes the responsibility of the devising team to raise those issues in the forum of the programme in a clear, accessible and meaningful way that avoids mystification and so does not fail our children.

THE QUESTION OF BIAS

If we wish to raise political questions such as racism, conservation, questions of law, philosophy, the role of women in society, unemployment, old age, violence etc. (the list is endless) then the work will be criticized by the short-sighted or bigoted as being politically motivated. Of course it will be political, in that the word 'political' embraces every emotional and material condition of our lives. Whilst the devising team must be aware of this kind of charge, levelled usually by those who see child-centred education as a threat and who are themselves definitely system-centred, it would be wrong to get so worried by it that a kind of self-censorship becomes imposed. If we are serious in our attempt to understand the movement and change that we and the children are caught up in, and if we seek to order and transform this into programmes so that it is made accessible to children, then we should not be surprised by it. Neither do I believe that devisers should be afraid of the related charge of presenting a bias in their work. Because the work is being devised and the devisers have a *de facto* bias, it is bound to be there. The question is, is it a useful bias? If the team has something important to raise, uncover and explore in the forum of a programme, then they must have some kind of perspective on it. Learning is a dialectical process and the true dialectic can only exist if real positions are taken. Bias in this sense is not a bad thing provided that it is part of a dialectical learning process as opposed to the dogmatic presentation of a perspective which admits no opposites and permits no learning. Most thinking educationalists understand and welcome this approach. If a programme sought at each point to present all points of view or all possible perspectives without taking any line at all, then the chances are that the child is unlikely to have his or her assumptions challenged or have a wish to challenge in return. No play ever written was able to do it and no school lesson ever did either. Bias, responsibly handled in a programme, can be educationally beneficial in that it will provoke a response or exploration as part of an opening-up process. Dogma on the other hand is clearly part of a closing-down process and has nothing to do with real education. Dogma in this sense, whatever the intention of the deviser or teacher who perpetrates it, can do little except provide for the maintenance of the 'status quo' in that it reinforces the status relationship of teacher and taught. It makes no room for discovery so, even if it intends to inculcate a different perspective from the accepted norm, the net effect of doctrinaire theatre is to alienate the child.

The unthought-out charge of bias often comes from the same quarters as the charge of the work being 'politically motivated', namely the extreme right wing who have little hesitation about foisting their own morals and values on to our young and who would reject the idea that learning is a dialectical process. Many teachers would agree that educationally it is useful to challenge accepted truths and norms as part of the process of enabling the child to discover his or her own responses – it is to do with liberating one's understanding, rather than imposing order. A crucial part of the devising process should therefore concern itself consciously with critical analysis, both of the material to be performed and the effect of the performance, of the ideas that it may stimulate and is intended to stimulate, and of the relationship between what is intended and what actually takes place. Unconscious bias is not useful and dogma is unacceptable.

The presentation of alternative perspectives on periods of history has often given rise to questions about bias. Many teams, seeing that there has been and still is much mystification in relation to history, have taken up the documentary or quasi-documentary approach. This is largely because young people, cut off from history, often have no historical perspective, no way of seeing the present in terms of the past. Obviously there are those who do not see it as important, and some teachers who are happy to see history as a dead or purely academic subject, but many teams have not accepted history that way and wish to use history to raise questions about today. This trend has given rise to some highly imaginative work. Examples are M6 Theatre Company's *No Pasaran*, and Cockpit's *Marches*, both about the rise of fascism during the 1930s. Several programmes mentioned earlier in the context of role-play participation again deal with a historical perspective at junior-school level. In many of these programmes, whilst it was necessary to explore real conflicts, not too much time was spent 'putting the other point of view' (though *Marches* was an interesting exception to this),[2] and yet there were few complaints about bias.

I once read a headteacher's report on *Drink the Mercury*, a Coventry TIE programme performed as part of a trilogy about conservation. The programme deals with a chemical company in Japan which poisoned the waters of Minemata Bay, killing and maiming many of the local fishermen and their families whose principal diet was fish from the bay. Of course the programme raised political questions about the actions and responsibilities of private enterprise in relation to the victims of the pollution it had caused. He thought it 'dangerous' because of its 'political overtones'. He felt it less than diplomatic to present such work whilst the debate on 'political education' was in train. The programme has become something of a TIE classic, endorsed by nearly all the educationalists who have seen it (Belgrade TIE Team 1976: 59–63). This particular head-teacher was simply voicing his own fear that knowledge is dangerous. This static view of the process and practice of education is perhaps more biased and damaging than anything a TIE team could perpetrate. We must keep TIE in perspective: its actual impact on the education system is still minimal.

I begin to be afraid when certain areas or subjects are proscribed or barred as being 'unsuitable' for children or young people. TIE teams have a responsibility to the education system but a greater responsibility to children. There are areas which demand much careful thought and analysis before they are raised with young people, but what should guide the deviser is whether or not he or she can do justice to the children by making accessible the ideas involved and by creating the correct forum in which learning can take place. This task should, as far as possible, be carried out in liaison with the teachers.

THE RELATIONSHIP OF CONTENT TO FORM

Usually during devising the aim and content will suggest a form, a structure, a way of communicating. An early question for the devising team is about the level and kind of involvement required. Involvement can mean full-scale active participation with the pupils themselves in role, or at the opposite end of the spectrum it can mean passive but attentive watching and listening. Either way, involvement is to do with how the children relate to plot, characters, situations, the things that happen and the people that make them happen, or that they happen to. It is only through this involvement that the children will engage fully and productively with the content.

Where the involvement is to be of the physical participatory kind with the children in or out of roles, the deviser has to create a situation which contains the necessity for the child to deal with the problems and contradictions raised by the plot – to cope themselves with the conflict at the centre of the piece. When devising such a programme, it is essential to understand that there is a real problem to be faced: the involved child's understanding changes and develops only to the extent that he or she is committed to the situation, and that child needs to be involved in its resolve in some concrete and meaningful way, not in a tokenistic way. The deviser must create a structure that will satisfy that need.

How an event happens, how a situation develops, is always dependent on conflict, on opposites, and the deviser must be careful to ensure that the involved child's participation also relates directly to the clash of those opposites and interests. Otherwise, it is not a discovering situation for the children, they will not be agents in their own learning; you are merely organizing them, telling them something and expecting them automatically to agree because you have said it. The deviser must focus not just on what he or she would like to happen but on what actually happens. A useful example of this kind of involvement is the role the children play in *Pow Wow*, (Coventry 1973), a programme in which they first identify and develop a relationship with a racist, acquisitive cowboy who runs his own Wild West show and later with an Indian who tells a different story about the demise of the Indian tribes in the face of the advancing white man and his technology. At one point the children have to decide whether or not to free the Indian from his cage and later, at the end, they have to decide on questions of ownership, trust and allegiance. They are deeply involved with both characters and have to make real, binding decisions which they know will incur the wrath of one or other adult. It is a difficult task when you are seven or eight. They discover a situation and their involvement in it demands action on their part. The programme could not proceed if they chose to opt out. It is significant that in my experience they never do opt out, as their own involvement through the structure and form of the programme does not permit it.

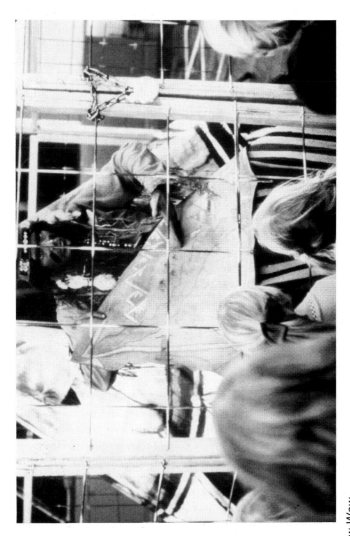

Plate 3.1 *Pow Wow*

Pow Wow (Belgrade Tie Team, Coventry, 1973). The caged Black Elk describes his village to an apprehensive but fascinated class of 7 year-olds.

Often a problem in devising is to find a form or structure that enables the deviser to raise all that needs raising in order fully to explore an idea or subject without the programme becoming lengthy and rambling and hence boring. It is often difficult to find an actual incident which encompasses everything – which is why the quasi-documentary is a useful form. This technique allows the deviser to make the general truth of a problem or historical period clear to the children in a situation where the actual historical events get in the way, or are too long-winded. For this reason *The Price of Coal* programme on the history of the mines near Coventry uses some fictional and some actual characters and events. The programme also takes the liberty of compressing events out of their time-scale for it covers the whole history of mining from the start of the first pits right up to 1845. The actual chronological order was found to get in the way of what the programme sought to do. The odd historical fact is bent a little as well, but this is not important if it is done in service of the child's understanding of the larger truth or issue. An example in this programme is that the coal owner whom we drew from historical fact was actually a reasonably fair employer by the standards of the time. To present him simply as such would have allowed the children to imagine that he was typical of the coal owners of the period, which would have been a gross distortion of the truth, so we created a character who had worked as a 'Butty' in Durham and would perpetrate the malpractices, on behalf of the owner, more in keeping with the industry at the time. We wished to generate an understanding of the general conditions of mines whilst focusing on local pits. The local history did not adequately reflect the general truth of the period so we adapted it to suit our needs rather than slavishly follow local history at the expense of the larger understanding.

The *Rare Earth* trilogy, part of which I have mentioned in a different context, is a good example of the more passive kind of involvement which is another approach open to the deviser. Here the more traditional structure of a theatre piece is used to create the forum. The problems the programme raises are the issues of pollution and man's relationship to his environment and the natural order. Though the style of the programme is very different from *The Price of Coal* it does a similar job in opening up an area of knowledge, making concepts, ideas and events, both historical and contemporary, accessible to children.

There is no blueprint or formula for the devising company to follow, no 'right' way to create a good programme, but clearly the experienced deviser is more aware of some of the pitfalls; if not, then there is not much learning or analysis going on. Aim and content together frequently suggest or even dictate a form or structure, but there are many other factors to take into account. It may well be that the aim and content cry out for role-play participation, but if the programme is intended for fifth-year secondary pupils then there are a number of factors such as sexual embarrassment to deal with which may lead the programme too far away from its main aim to make the role-play participation worth while; consequently it may be necessary to explore a different style of presentation. Clearly the kind of participation that a team can use with infant children may not necessarily work with sixth-formers; account must be taken of conceptual development, maturation, the extent to which 'schooling' has stifled the imagination, the effects of social conditioning on behaviour patterns, etc. Form should be chosen on the simple basis of whether or not it best enables the children or young people to make sense of, or respond to, the content of the programme. It is possible to devise a programme in such a way that the form says one thing while the content is desperately trying to say another. For example, if a company wishes to raise the issue of sexism in society and then uses sexist images drawn from, say, the world of advertising to illustrate its point, then it must ensure that that is what is *actually* taking place and that the sexist images are not reinforcing the very attitudes that it seeks to challenge. The same problem occurs when the deviser wishes to work through symbols. Often symbolism can make a more immediate impact and be more economic than naturalism (as with the stylized portrayal of the Chisso factory in *Rare Earth*), but devisers must be sure what they wish their symbols to communicate, as vagueness in this area could lead to the same problem outlined above.

In this article I have separated form and content for reasons of analytical clarity, but the deviser must remember that in practice the form *is* the content as experienced by the child. The event, not the intention, is the arbiter of success or failure. The event is the focus for the actor–teacher and the child. This means that the exploitation of the material's theatrical potential requires the same thorough analysis as the rest of the process. Theatricality does not imply irresponsibility or tinsel. Often the kind of educational stimulus that is required to motivate the child's involvement comes from a carefully planned and artistic-ally well-conceived theatrical presentation which depends totally on the actor's skill to communicate. There has been in some companies a tendency to undervalue the craft skills of the actor, the argument being that the motivation for doing what you do is more important than how you do it; whilst in other companies the tendency is to undervalue the need for educational analysis in the belief that if you can get up and hold your audience, that is enough. Both tendencies are shortsighted and will be re-strictive in relation to the work. It is important to restate: no matter what you think your content is about, or how you think your form serves it, the final arbiter is the child's experience and for him or her there is no analytical separation of the two, only the quality of the experience received or participated in. The child's involvement or lack of it is determined by the validity of the experience.

CONCLUSIONS

This focus on content or on reality-based content is not intended to denigrate or preclude the telling of a traditional story, nor does it exclude any particular subjects, topics or ideas from investigation. Rather, I am saying that theatre is a social art and therefore the practitioner has a social responsibility for the conception of the material. TIE, because it appears before the child uninvited, must take its social responsibility very seriously. Ultimately its responsibility is only to the child. If the material presented is slight, lacking emotional or intellectual depth, then the intellectual and aesthetic capabilities of the children are being underestimated and the resulting work will be patron-izing and hold little meaning for them. If learning is to take place through the forum of the programme, if the programme is child-centred, if learning is to do with experience, then the responsibility of the deviser is to create a rich and meaningful experience: an experience that has been well planned, has depth, truth, usually has its own internal logic and has an artistic integrity that reaches and involves the child, and is challenging to both child and performer.

The deviser, actor, director and designer faced with challenging material must respond to the higher than usual demands being made on their craft skills. This will, in performance, place demands on the children who, by respecting the experience and involving themselves in it, will wish to learn and themselves help to deepen the experience. If all this happens, then the programme becomes a genuine forum for learning and exploration of concepts and ideas and perspectives. If all this is prevented from taking place because of lack of understanding, analysis or commitment on the part of the deviser or actor, then the experience will not hold much for the child, and the TIE team may become agents of mystification or dogma, neither of which can liberate any understanding in the child.

NOTES

1 Eileen Murphy's case study of *Poverty Knocks* (1973) is included in the first edition of Jackson (ed.) (1980) *Learning through Theatre*. Bibliographic details of other published programmes referred to in this chapter are given in the Bibliography on pp 285–8.
2 In this programme, Oswald Mosley, the leader of the British Union of Fascists in the thirties, was a central player in the drama and his views were explored, and challenged, extensively by the pupils (16 to 18 year-olds). This was felt to be a necessary part of the educational process by which students should be confronted with, and have to find effective ways of dealing with, racist attitudes.

BIBLIOGRAPHY

Belgrade TIE Team (1976) 'Follow-up', in *Rare Earth: A Programme about Pollution*, London: Methuen.
Duane, M. (1971) 'Freedom and the state system of education', in J. Hall (ed.) *Children's Rights: Towards the Liberation of the Child*, London: Elek Books.
Holt, J. (1969) *How Children Fail*, London: Penguin.
Jackson, T. (ed.) (1980) *Learning through Theatre: Essays and Casebooks on TIE*, Manchester: Manchester University Press.
Lawson, D. (1975) *Class, Culture and the Curriculum*, London: Routledge & Kegan Paul.
Leisure for Living: policy statement on the arts and leisure (1959) The Labour Party.
The Newsom Report (1963) *Half our Future*, London: HMSO.

Chapter 4

Playwriting for TIE

Jim Mirrione

INTRODUCTION

As I begin this chapter, I am also engaged in writing my
eighteenth TIE play for the Creative Arts Team (CAT), the
professional Theatre in Education company in residence at
New York University. Thus, my thoughts and statements regarding the process of TIE playwriting will be reflective of the many
styles and techniques that have influenced my work since 1974.
I shall attempt here to outline what are, in my estimation, the
general principles as well as the specifics that I have found
helpful in the crafting of the TIE play. Several of the plays in
CAT's repertoire will be used as paradigms of these principles.
Finally, it is both an honour and an irony to be contributing to
this new edition of *Learning Through Theatre*, because the authors
of that first edition were all influential in my development as a
TIE writer.

BACKGROUND

When I first encountered Tony Jackson's text, CAT was evolving
out of the group devising experience that marked its first six
years as an American version of a British TIE team. Many of the
principles espoused by such writers as David Pammenter were
incorporated into the company's work. Yet, as CAT continued
to adapt the methods its members had studied and observed in
England – especially the work of TIE teams such as the Belgrade,
Cockpit and Greenwich – there began an analysis of how to
move beyond the traditional parameters of British TIE. This was
initially necessitated by the needs and composition of an

American inner-city audience of predominantly minority students, many of whom had been hobbled by substandard education and a variety of social and economic ills. During this period, CAT had worked exclusively with smaller classes in both its TIE and drama in education (DIE) programmes. By 1980, due to the success of the programmes the company had been offering to the New York City Board of Education, it was asked to broaden and expand audience size. That year the traditional TIE format, consisting of a show and workshop in a few classes, was overhauled to include long-term residencies in various school districts in the city. This new format also included a series of pre- and post-performance DIE workshops that incorporated the theme of the current production into the overall structure of the programme. Because the performance had to move beyond the intimacy of a classroom environment, new production values had to be implemented for a show that would now take place in a school auditorium, for an audience of up to – but no more than – 250 students. This limitation was essential to the preservation of the educational content of our productions. Teachers and principals had to be informed that, simply because we were no longer performing to one or two classes, we were not going to allow the massive audiences customary to the traditional school play.

Other educational imperatives, such as evaluation of our programmes and their impact upon larger audiences, were soon mandated by our funding agencies. This led to the creation of activities that were designed to increase critical reasoning amongst our audience members. One of the most salient techniques was the post-performance discussion. Immediately after each show, the actor–teachers would remain in character to answer challenges and questions from the audience as to the choices their characters made in the play. In addition, the TIE play had to provide enough DIE material for the workshop component of the residency, while still being a complete drama in itself. These conditions forced the company to re-evaluate whether the group devising process could still deliver a coherent and appropriate TIE product. Similarly, I, as a senior member and co-founder, grew weary of the endless debates, discussions and negotiations that ensued in the attempt to craft a single script. Inevitably, there was also the realization that the effectiveness of our overall programme could be compromised by the various and competing agendas of writers and non-writers alike. All of these factors led to my contention that: the writing process of a TIE play is most effective when a single dramatist works with a director and an executive administrator (producer) of a TIE company to create a unified product that enables educational content to be illustrated and communicated by the particular dynamics of theatre.

Thus, by 1978, there was a certain convergence of factors in the growth of CAT as a TIE company, as well as my own development as a playwright. The TIE plays that would be written from henceforth, while recognizing the valuable input of the other actor–teachers in the company, would be the creation of only one playwright who could both incorporate traditional tenets of dramatic construction, and develop new methods appropriate to TIE. Actors' ideas about the script were now limited to the dynamics of motivation and acting, not creation. Yet, as it applies to our subject here, the four early plays of CAT (1974–8) did provide an insight into some of the more fundamental elements important to the construction of TIE plays. Group narratives, dramatic tableaux, improvised scenes, archetypal characters, a central narrator and the use of a musician or some other musical element to bridge scenes, were all part of the staple of group-devised plays; and these components were all refined as the focus shifted to a single playwright for the company. These early building blocks influenced the later dramaturgical steps that I took in my playwriting; and it is these underlying principles and methods that I will discuss in this chapter as an attempt to provide a possible useful model for other TIE playwrights.

FIRST PRINCIPLES

The question of how one writes TIE scripts can be answered from both an empirical and an analytical framework. Thus, if you have never written a TIE play, then the best way to start is to see one in action, or to assess what have been the recurring dramatic elements in TIE scripts. My own study of the TIE movement, and the many plays it has produced, has led me to formulate the following observations, some more obvious and less contentious than others but still important to state:

1 TIE has always sought to be a combination, in some manner, of theatre and education.
2 While the disciplines of theatre and education are usually thought of as separate, they are in key respects very similar especially in their primary aims of promoting cognition and imparting comprehension.
3 TIE utilizes the resources of the educational system it serves, and is cognizant of the needs of educators when exploring a particular topic for a play.
4 A TIE play will usually be preceded by some form of preparation such as the workshop component and followed by the post-performance discussion (or other forms of follow-up).
5 The content of TIE, i.e. the social, political, topical and curricular issues of society, are the staples of TIE plays. Pure entertainment alone is not TIE; however, pure pedagogy or political orthodoxy also fails to constitute a valid TIE play.
6 All theatre genres, forms and styles are possible in TIE plays. Although realism is the most utilized style, TIE can also incorporate allegory, historical incidents, science fiction, music hall, comedy, melodrama and any other element to convey its message.
7 A TIE play has enough content to support the various workshops that will accompany it, as well as such ancillary materials as the teacher and student follow-up packets.

While by no means all-inclusive, the above features are important for a TIE writer when considering the task at hand. Inherent as well in this formulation, is the necessity to see the writing of the TIE play as taking place in two steps: the pre-scripting phase (purpose and methodology), and the scripting phase.

PRE-SCRIPTING PHASE

It is in this stage that the TIE playwright must formulate what are the basic questions that will impact upon the creation of the script. These considerations are, I believe, constant and essential to any proposed TIE play, and should be addressed before it is written:

1   What is it that the playwright wants to impart to this student audience?

2 What do the school or the educators want imparted about the particular subject-matter of the proposed play?

3 Is the subject-matter of the play strong enough to hold the students' attention, impart important information and meet with the educational goals of the school or teachers?

4 What new information or experience will the students receive from this material?

5 Will this information or experience be compelling enough to induce critical thinking among the students, or will it merely reinforce preconceived ideas?

6 Does the information in the TIE play contain enough material to produce a post-performance discussion and/or workshop?

7 Does the play complement the pre- and post-classroom workshops in order to create the total TIE programme?

8 What is the point of view of the writer regarding the information inherent in the TIE play?

9 Does the information seek to set up an intelligent dialectic between two opposing ideas, characters or forces, or does it espouse only one opinion throughout the play?

10 Does the dramatic material challenge the audience to rethink the political, social and cultural issues it presents, and then allow a balanced discussion to emerge after the play?

Combined with the overview of the traditional elements constant in TIE plays, the above queries can serve as the creative brakes, as it were, before the act of playwriting takes place. This is essential because the TIE playwright does not exist in isolation from the company he or she writes for, or from the audience and educators he or she must work with in the fulfilment of the project. Furthermore, the demands of TIE are different from those of children's theatre, where the writer can usually create a script for a wide range of audiences within broad age limitations, but with less regard for educational content. Because all TIE plays are age-specific and are usually performed by a team of actor–teachers who both act and conduct workshops, the playwright must take into consideration, when writing, the personnel who will perform the roles. Furthermore, because the TIE team is not assembled merely for one show, as in the commercial theatre, but rather are skilled individuals who have made a commitment to the work of theatre and education, the

TIE playwright can draw upon their expertise when formulating these investigatory questions. Concomitantly, the TIE playwright should also be a skilled actor–teacher in his or her own right: one who is able to devise workshop plans, theatre exercises, improvisations, movement techniques, simulation games and other DIE experiences in a classroom setting. This will provide the playwright with a first-hand knowledge of the type of student he or she is writing for, and the conditions, problems and aspirations of various students in different school and societal environments. Again, because the writer is always working in close association with the actor–teachers and the director, he or she should also be able to consult with teachers, evaluators and other individuals who are instrumental in suggesting and monitoring the educational content of the script. Thus, the writer must know before the script is written that it can provide the basis for the ancillary TIE materials, i.e. the follow-up student and teacher packets.

I have so far been speaking primarily of the practical considerations that must be dealt with before the onset of the writing process. But I now wish to turn to what I have termed 'purpose', that is the philosophical predisposition to the work of TIE. Too often, there has been a self-conscious shrinking away from admitting that the task of writing for TIE is not within the domain of all who propose to do so. No one would contend that an accomplished but tone-deaf sculptor could automatically become a concert pianist, simply because he is already engaged in an artistic field. Similarly, the most erudite public speaker or educator does not axiomatically qualify as a dramatist merely because both disciplines require the use of words. Even those who claim their profession to be playwriting, still cannot assume that the usual dramaturgy that has served them before will easily translate into a valid TIE script. Thus, there are several concepts and considerations that a TIE playwright should address before tackling this type of dramatic writing.

Purpose

A primary motivation of the TIE playwright should be the desire to engage and educate students, by presenting dramatic material that directly relates to their concerns and needs. This type of dramatist should share the same drive and ambition of an educator and an artist: the urge to impart information that stimulates critical thinking and transmits a creative and cathartic experience through the dynamics of drama and theatre. This will necessitate, on the part of the TIE playwright, that he or she be open and receptive to the concerns of students and youth in the world of today. My experience has taught me that a TIE play written in a vacuum, without any close observation or knowledge of the argot, conflicts, codes and concerns of young people living in contemporary society will undoubtedly fail. Writing should not take place with preconceived ideas without first testing those notions in the laboratory of the classroom. This can be accomplished by means of workshops, interviews and observations of the different age-group audiences particular to the intended script. I have often used the schools and classrooms CAT has worked in as my primary source of inspiration for the themes of our plays. There is a rich and abundant world of dramatic situations, characters, language and conflicts in these environments.

Very often, just an overheard conversation can trigger the genesis for a TIE play. A case in point was the scenario for CAT's 1992–3 TIE play entitled *The King of Twelve Blocks*. In this particular instance, a group of actor–teachers were working in a classroom of highly disruptive students. Attendance was generally sporadic but one student was particularly fickle in showing up for the sessions. When the other students were questioned about this, they replied that the student failed to show up to school that often because of his overriding concern: the maintenance and control of the drug traffic on twelve square blocks outside the school, thus earning him the moniker 'the king of twelve blocks'. The following year, when the same actor–teachers returned to this class, they inquired as to the whereabouts of this student. The students replied: 'Didn't you hear? The dude got shot dead. He crossed the thirteenth block.' Immediately upon hearing this I felt that there were more than sufficient dramatic possibilities for a TIE play; one that dealt with peer pressure, the lure of drugs, the loss of long-term goals and the seduction of instant gratification status symbols.

But mere reportage is not the central characteristic of TIE playwriting. The writer must also be willing to question the social, political and curricular issues that affect youth and society in general. The script should contain content that seeks to broaden the range of information a student may receive in school. However, while working within the school system and incorporating information provided by educators about a particular subject, the TIE playwright should still retain a healthy scepticism about the assumptions, assertions and conclusions schools and society tend to make about any issue. This may require the writer to challenge previously held ideas and, through the dramatic medium, ask students to examine more critically the political, societal, curricular and cultural information they have been provided with by schools, parents, society and the media. Finally, although no litmus test is proposed here, the TIE playwright benefits from being a keen observer of the educational trends, societal developments and political issues affecting the community, city, state and country. Although TIE writers should avoid doctrinaire political ideology in their writing, they will find the task of writing a TIE script more difficult if they are not attuned to the critical political issues of the day.

Finally, as the last category in the pre-scripting phase, a rigorous methodology is required to prepare the ground step by step for the task of scripting the TIE play.

Methodology: Research

The process of scripting TIE plays involves more than the traditional putting of words onto a page and being cognizant of the essentials of plot, character, dialogue and action. The process also includes an understanding that certain passages, material, characters and conflicts must be educationally sound as well as dramatically charged. This balance is often a complex and difficult task because, unlike a purely commercial writer whose main aim is to see how the art of the play is communicated, the TIE writer must also be aware of what educational information is conveyed and how that information is transmitted. Students may experience a TIE play initially as theatre, and thereby aesthetically, but they also are being educated simultaneously in different ways through a wide variety of techniques. All of these concerns lead to the research phase.

It is essential that all TIE plays be fully researched before they are written. Research, both historical and contemporary, enables a playwright to decide which materials are appropriate, and what quantity of information is necessary for the play to succeed. Yet, the major criterion for selecting material (both historical and contemporary) is whether or not that material has dramatic possibilities. In the area of historical material, dramatic possibilities will emerge if major characters are evident, conflicts between characters or points of view are clearly established and a clear dilemma is uncovered that propels individuals to make choices and face consequences. Likewise, the TIE playwright can determine dramatic possibilities from contemporary material if the material has relevance for the intended school audience; if it presents characters and situations that are easily identifiable and similar to the concerns of a student's world; if the language and idiomatic expressions have resonance for that audience; and if the emotional pull of the subject-matter is within the range of the audience for whom the play is intended.

Within the two areas of research, historical and contemporary, there are several additional concerns that have to be addressed. If the proposed TIE topic is of an historical nature, the playwright must undertake extensive investigation of files, documents, news accounts, slides, photographs, abstracts, editorials, videos, films and articles, and where applicable conduct interviews with individuals knowledgeable about the subject and the times in which the characters lived. After all historical material has been culled, the playwright must scrutinize it for the various biases and interpretations it contains, as well as seek out alternative sources and interpretations of the research material. With regard to contemporary material, there should be a familiarity on the part of the writer with the current literature and opinions expressed about the proposed topic. This will include newspapers, periodicals, journals, books, films, radio, TV programmes and interviews. In both categories, the reading of other plays available from the dramatic repertoire or other TIE plays that have dealt with similar proposed topics is also useful.

In my own work with CAT, all the plays written have benefited in particular ways from this kind of research. In 1978, when CAT left the group devising approach behind, I completed the first 'single-handed' scripted play, *The Trial of Mary Wade*. This was an historical TIE play in its truest form, because it resurrected the events of an American 16th-century witchcraft trial and presented them to a contemporary audience. The parallels regarding historical and contemporary issues such as racism, peer pressure, hypocrisy and political chicanery became even more resonant when the audience was placed in the role of witnesses and jury. The primacy of historical research was also evident in the trilogy of plays: *Rosa Parks: Back of the Bus* (1980), *Joe Louis: The Brown Bomber* (1982) and *Hannibal* (1983). All of these plays reflected the advantages that verbatim dialogue, historical anecdotes and the historical and social conditions of a particular period can have on the process of dramatic construction. Furthermore, as a consequence of steeping myself in the texture and times inherent in the period in which these characters lived, I found that the use of music heightened the telling of the story. This was especially true in the case of Rosa Parks and Joe Louis who both lived when blues, jazz and gospel were the dominant musical idioms.

From 1984 to 1990, a series of what I would term the topical/social issue TIE plays were written for CAT. These plays dealt with such topics as child abuse (*I Never Told Anybody*); drugs (*Home Court*); racial prejudice (*The Divider*); and handgun violence (*Show of Force*). All of these plays were written to focus a particular topic, or incident, within a continuing social problem. Often they were marked by reference to a current event, such as the drug death of Len Bias in *Home Court*, or the racist attack at Howard Beach in *The Divider*. In terms of dramatic construction, I found that the TIE story line for these four plays was enhanced by researching, first, all the references to the subject that had appeared in print or on television, radio or film, and then supplementing this background by observations of, and interviews with, students and school personnel who were encountering similar problems.

The elements of the pre-scripting phase, while never completely possible in every situation, are none the less important prerequisites for the TIE playwright to aim at as he or she embarks on the task of dramatic construction in the scripting phase.

SCRIPTING PHASE

TIE has been influenced by many different authors and writing/devising methodologies. Yet, there is little universal consensus on how to go about scripting the TIE play. In my own work I can easily side with Aristotle on the need first to construct a scenario (plot) and to be cognizant of the necessity of theme, character, dialogue, song and spectacle; however, I am also drawn to the dictums of Brecht, especially in his scepticsm about 'catharsis' in a play and his belief in direct (rather than vicarious) confrontation of a dramatic problem by an audience. But because TIE is the product of many modern theatre developments, there are some other important antecedents that must be acknowledged (even though space does not permit due consideration of them). The most significant one in the United States would be the Federal Theatre Project in the 1930s (together with its highly innovative Living Newspaper plays); and the parallel Workers Theatre Movement in Britain whose 'agitprop' dramas flourished from the mid-twenties, elements of which were still present in Joan Littlewood's Theatre Workshop in London in the 1950s. Both movements saw as their mandate the creation of issue-based plays that were performed in a variety of non-commercial venues, designed to dramatize current events in educational and entertaining terms understandable to a mass audience.

Antecedents such as these all underline one of the key starting points for a TIE writer – that he or she must first have a fundamental desire to *write about a pressing problem that will bring about a change of consciousness in an audience.*

This is perhaps the 'ur-scripting' phase aspect that must be established before the more exact elements such as scenario, content, language and characterization can be discussed. As with any play, the TIE script should be well constructed with a cogent and clear beginning, middle and end. Action, plot and characterization are all essentials, as are exposition, foreshadowing, conflict, major crises, rising action, climax, reversals, irony, mood, repetition of theme and resolution. While these are the usual and traditional elements of dramatic construction, they are utilized within a TIE framework that takes into consideration educational content.

The issue of 'educational content' has always been a contentious one. Is a TIE play simply an ordinary drama that has been diluted or altered from its true dramatic intent by pedagogical concerns? The best way I can answer this is to point to a specific example from the CAT repertoire. In the play *Last Year,* the issue of adolescent suicide and the pressures that lead to such an act were paramount. Thus, would Tyrone the main character actually be seen jumping off the roof of the building that, for most of the play, had been the symbolic battleground of emotions as the plot progressed? The educators that I met with, who were either experts in adolescent psychology or administrators who had dealt with cases of attempted or successful suicide, all had reservations about my original ending. In that draft, Tyrone was clearly seen taking his own life: a dramatic moment that I thought would drive home the point of the futility of such an action based on all that had previously transpired in the play. Although I pressed for the original ending, the eductional arguments were most persuasive. All the literature and studies had indicated that the actual depiction of a suicide attempt only glamorized the act in the minds of those who were most at risk, whether or not that was the intention of the dramatic ending. Quickly reminding myself that Sophocles had put Jocasta out of sight when she took her own life, and realizing that the educators' comments were sound, I was able to create an even more dramatic moment by having the set turn at just the moment that Tyrone stood poised on the roof. This 'cliffhanger' turned out to be the better choice, because it allowed the post-performance student discussion to focus on issues of choice and responsibility as they related to Tyrone and his friends. Tyrone himself was challenged as to why he felt so despondent as to attempt to take his own life; which in turn forced the students to examine how they could unwittingly push an at-risk friend to the edge in real life. All of these same elements impacted upon the workshops that were held after the performance. Thus, instead of being a hindrance to the plot, the educational content actually advanced the story line and contributed to the students' overall interest in the play.

Scenario

Because of the integral nature of TIE within an educational system, it is essential that a working scenario be constructed before writing takes place. This scenario will provide the blueprint for the eventual script and is best decided upon by the playwright, director and the TIE administrator responsible for educational content. Often the input of a school's educational liaison teacher or other professional consultants will be made at this stage, although it is rare that they will exercise veto over a scenario or script. All the TIE plays I have written for CAT were first developed as a scenario, and then analysed by the assigned director and programme manager. Once approval of the basic direction and content was given, I was free to construct drafts of the play, meeting at different intervals with the director and programme manager to discuss the progress of the play. In several instances, as in the case of *The Divider, Show of Force* and *Last Year*, different draft versions were given staged readings so that I could get, respectively, the opinions and suggestions from professionals in the fields of race relations, handgun violence and suicide prevention. The advantage of this document is that it can be used during planning stages as a means of judging whether or not the dramatic flow is consistent, and if educational elements have been incorporated into the script.

Content

Content is perhaps the most important aspect of a TIE play. Not only must the play be artistically sound, capable of conveying an effective dramatic story, but it must also contain educational material that is woven seamlessly throughout the entire fabric of the play. Educational content may range from the use of certain vocabulary words an educational liaison teacher deems important for an age group, to the presentation of certain historical characters that relate to what has already been studied in the curriculum (which are then explored more critically in the play). But mere inclusion of educational content is not enough; there must also be a critical viewpoint presented in the script. TIE sets out to challenge previously held positions or to examine more critically ideas and information that are perceived to be the 'norm'. It is simply not enough to parrot back information that students receive in school. An example of this need for more critical content was demonstrated during the writing of *Rosa Parks* and *Joe Louis*. In both these plays, that dealt with racial attitudes in the United States before and after World War II, it was essential that students be exposed to subject-matter that went beyond the facts that were in their textbooks. This was made apparent to me when, in my own research with students, I found that an overwhelming majority knew little about the above individuals, the roots of racial prejudice in the

United States, the origins of Nazism in Germany and the legacy of 'Jim Crow' laws and their effect on their own lives.

Language

The most common mistake made by writers of children's theatre and subsequently anyone attempting to write for youth audiences, is that the material has to be oversimplified in plot, action and dialogue. However, language in a TIE play should mirror the phrases, colloquialisms, codes and styles of a contemporary audience, while at the same time introduce to that audience new words and ways of speaking that enable it to understand the manners, poetry, diction and syntax of diverse characters who have lived in different times. This will mean that language will have to be authentic, especially if the subject-matter is of an historical or documentary nature. An example of this point is again provided from the CAT repertoire, in the 1978 play *The Trial of Mary Wade*. Because the play centered on the events of a sixteenth-century witchcraft trial, the language of the period, although at times archaic, was essential to the style of the drama. Therefore, no attempt was made to update any of the characters' speech. Several dramatis personae such as the judge and Reverend Mather all spoke in the phrases and style of the period, which combined legal, spiritual and medical terminology into the text. This was contrasted with the protagonist Mary Wade and her chief accuser Elizabeth, who spoke in short declarative sentences.

With regard to the use of contemporary language in a text, the TIE playwright should be able to utilize the idiomatic expressions, slang, connotations, phrases and other contemporary jargon culled from media, culture and students themselves. All of the above can serve to ground the play in realistic terms, and there is an immediate identification on the part of the student when this type of language is used during the course of the dramatic action.

An example of the use of this type of argot culled from observation occurred in *Saloogie* (1981). The play is set in a fantastical world where a group of 'Kids' are pitted against a duo of scientists (Labs), who have been assigned the task of coming up with the ultimate theory as to why young people turn to violence and vandalism. Throughout the play the Labs attempt to present their theory to the audience whom they refer to as scientific colleagues assembled to hear a lecture-demonstration. Similarly, the Kids attempt through song, scenes and monologues to present their position to the audience. There is a continuous conflict of personalities and points of view, as both sides compete for the attention and sympathy of the audience. The final conflict occurs when the Kids are pitted against the full forces of 'Behaviour Modification' exerted by the Labs. Because of the subject-matter of the play, the 'Kid' characters had to mirror the same students that would see the play, and who had also been part of the activities in one of CAT's DIE workshops ('Conflict Resolution Through Drama'). Thus, a new type of speech would have to be created, one that was accurate and which reflected the language of many of these students. In researching these words, I discovered that their language was a vastly confusing, jargon-ridden, strangely poetic stream of consciousness. Meanings for words were always reversed. Connotation became the rule, denotation the exception. The result was this opening monologue by Kid 1:

> Now these weird ass jive motherfuckers have got to be the most gone turkeys I have ever seen. Serious! They got no other tools than those bang-a-gong tinker toys they make us play with. Sometimes it's a snap but usually I chill out and let them play the fool. I'm down but I ain't gonna snap to this action, 'cause any minute I get the feeling they is gonna drop the dime on me. I mean they don't even speak the same language. They is foreign like. So I keep telling them to get out of my face, 'cause they ain't no homestyle and later for the chili dog. I'm serious. These dudes are bugged and them females are definitely busted out. I mean they are always trying to act bad, but they ain't really bad because they is too busy trying to be cool. Me? I just take a chill pill, get a blotter of some C & C and blow this joint, while I blow on one .... But some of these people they got it bad for you.... But I show 'em, I just give them the old hotel treatment. And I'm checking out. See, like I say: slow you blow, fast you pass.

It was my experience during production that students, after they had seen and heard a play with these expressions, reacted as if someone had broken a code and spoken to them about the things they knew. This reaction can immediately ease the tension student audiences have, especially those who have never seen a play before. However, the TIE writer should avoid gratuitous use of slang because it is only part of a character's total verbal quality. Furthermore, the mere repetition of these phrases merely for shock value or comedic effect only cheapens the text when there is no justification for them in the context of the entire play. Language should also not be one-dimensional; that is, in an attempt to present a youth-oriented play the playwright erroneously makes all the characters speak the current slang of the day. The elements of simile, metaphor, irony and figurative language are all necessary in a TIE play. When, because of the language requirements of grade levels, the educational liaison teacher or the programme evaluators sometimes request incorporation of certain vocabulary words into the script, this presents a challenge for the writer: he or she must avoid artificially placing a required word or phrase into the speech of an inappropriate character.

As has been cited in the example from *Saloogie*, monologues are useful ways to anchor TIE material for a student audience and a means of providing important information about the story line. Monologues can also bridge the various scene changes that occur in the drama especially when different characters connect the action, motivations and conflicts of the previous scenes or foreshadow further dramatic developments. I have concluded, through my own 'back of the house' observations, that there is no mathematical rule that determines the length and effectiveness of a monologue for a student audience. However, although the restlessness factor is important, a well-written, detailed monologue that conveys its information with strength, humour and with a colourful sense of language can be most effective. Similarly, dialogue between characters is most efficacious when it keeps the central story line of the play moving. Complicated sub-plots, numerous reversals of action and too many flashbacks and flashforwards – while all legitimate dramatic techniques – can tend to detract from the primary plot. Their use should serve only to further the main story, not because students are incapable of following more than one story line; rather, because a TIE play has to transmit its information within the confines of the time restrictions and production limitations of the school setting. (It is my experience that the TIE play should be no more than ninety minutes:

sixty minutes of performance and thirty minutes of follow-up workshop.)

Characterization

Closely associated with language in a TIE play is the use of characters to convey the artistic and educational content of the script. One of the most useful is the narrator, because of the ability of that character to impart information at significant moments in the play. This is especially true in documentary TIE plays, where the setting, characters and major problems of the drama can be stated clearly from the onset of the story. The narrator can also function as a facilitator and guide to the dramatic process when the drama shifts to simulation or participatory workshop. Characters in a TIE play can be realistic, historical or symbolic. What they cannot be, however, is opaque to the point that the action becomes incomprehensible to a student audience. There must also be a certain economy in the choice of characters to tell the story. Because most TIE teams employ no more than six actors for the production, there is not the luxury of writing parts for ten to fifteen subordinate actors. Every play that I have written for CAT has had no more than six to eight actors, and many times as few as four. This situation necessitated much doubling and tripling of roles by the actors; a common occurrence the TIE playwright should take into consideration when faced with cast limitations. It is essential, though, that the main character(s) always remain constant: student audiences identify strongly with a central character, and may become confused when they see that character double in a secondary role.

Several illustrations from CAT's repertoire reflect the above considerations. Damien, the deceased son in *Home Court*, is capable of being the narrator in his own story as it unfolds in flashbacks, which reveals him to be a ghost witnessing his own undoing. Alva Simpson, the reporter in *The Divider*, takes control of the investigation of the death of Lin Pang and serves as both commentator and protagonist in the action. Randall, the student in *Show of Force*, becomes involved in taking a handgun to school and relives his own tragic nightmare as the weapon causes the death of one of his classmates. In *Joe Louis*, the narrator and central character were shared by two versions of Joe played by two different actors: the old and feeble man who reminisces from a wheelchair, and the young victorious heavyweight champion of the world. Rosa, the civil rights heroine in *Rosa Parks*, conveys her centrality to the story by song and her involvement in almost every scene of the play.

It is important to note, when speaking of central characters, that they immediately make known their conflict and how it relates to the play. Overly stylistic foreshadowing, indirect references to the main character and other delays in getting the central protagonist on stage to tell his or her story, only serve to slow the action and obfuscate the content of the TIE play. This does not mean that there should be an oversimplification of plot development, or a too hurried exposition of the problem. Rather, the directness of the protagonist's journey and intentions should create an immediacy for the student audience. Likewise, the antagonist and subordinate characters should not be cardboard or one-dimensional presentations. Even a character who represents an immediately negative position can also evoke sympathy. I believe that the strength of a TIE play may be ascertained when the heroes have clay feet, and villains are not always dressed in black. Thus, there should be a complexity in characters that does not allow students easily to cheer or dismiss them. Reversals in the lives of different characters (as when the antagonist and protagonist exchange roles), can also serve to keep the student audience analysing the various choices these characters make, and the consequences they suffer in the play.

Finally, all the characters in a TIE play must undergo a basic change in their lives or in their previously held positions. This is essential because student audiences must be allowed to think along with the characters on stage, and should come away with a new outlook on a problem that encourages critical thinking. Damien in *Home Court* attempts to say that his drug problem is manageable; Randall in *Show of Force* refuses to accept his responsibility in the shooting dead of another by his gun; Priscilla in *The Divider* negates the impact of her racial slurs and the possibility that they may have contributed to the death of Lin Pang. All of these characters constantly provoked the audience and emotionally affected them because they were seen in highly charged situations similar to their own lives. This identification with characters also allowed them to scrutinize

Plate 4.1 Show of Force
Show of Force by Jim Mirrione (Creative Arts Team, 1990) addressed the consequences of using weapons as a means of resolving conflict, centring on the experience and dilemmas of one high school student.

their motivations and to see how all actions resulted in choices and consequences. All these elements can immediately affect the quality of a post-performance workshop and any subsequent workshops in the classroom.

CONCLUSION

Cervantes is quoted as saying: 'No fathers or mothers think their own children ugly; and this self-deceit is yet stranger with respect to the offspring of the mind.' As I look back at some of my earlier plays, it is clear that they could have benefited from more discipline, although they have retained at least some of the respectability their siblings gained from a maturing in the writing process. It was this continuous experimentation with the form and style of TIE that I believe enabled me to grow as a writer. I was also fortunate to have as a laboratory the thousands of students who came to hundreds of inappropriate school auditoriums to attend the repertoire of CAT plays. The considerations that I have submitted are a product of trial and error, were not always adhered to in my own plays and are not meant to be applied in any orthodox fashion. The creative impulse is first and foremost the desire to communicate something through the power of words and action. This is the essence of drama. But I believe there can emerge from these processes a recognizable methodology that may serve as a flexible model for future writers of TIE plays.

Chapter 5

The Theatre in Education actor

Cora Williams

In 1965 when Coventry Education Authority and the Belgrade Theatre started Theatre in Education, unknowingly they invented a new breed of actor. Some were employed from theatre, some from teaching; they were called actor–teachers. The term encapsulates the very nature of the then new theatre form, a hybrid, one species emanating from educational drama and the other from a traditional British theatre background. The new breed was viewed with suspicion from the start and little has changed over twenty-eight years. Those who are concerned about status are distressed to acknowledge that each of its two root professions undervalues the TIE actor. This suspicion is largely a product of ignorance. TIE is a hidden theatre form. It plays in private behind closed school doors. Yet when directors and actors from mainstream theatre are persuaded to attend as visitors they note with surprise the talent of the actors; teachers, also with surprise, remark on the effective teaching techniques the actors deploy.

Over the years the term 'actor–teacher' tended to be replaced first by 'performer' and then by 'actor'. All three job descriptions remain valid and their use illustrates the rich history of the theatre form. 'Actor–teacher' is useful as a reminder of the important common ground between the theatre practitioners and the teaching practitioners, exemplified for example in the increasing number of teachers who attend TIE conferences, and likewise actors who attend education conferences. For a period, roughly from the mid-1970s to the mid-1980s, the term 'performer' was used by some companies in preference to 'actor–teacher'. It seemed to be a desire to emphasize their professional craft alongside all performers in the entertainment industry, perhaps a humble attitude to a job of work. However, as the reader will discover in subsequent pages, the 'performer' in TIE does not only 'perform' a character in an extant play, arduous and skilful though that single task is, but has to be a specialized creative being. Therefore the more artistic term 'actor' has now replaced the modest term 'performer'.

The reclaiming of the term 'actor' is a reminder too that TIE, however close its ties are with education, primarily emanates from art. This declaration has been important in recent years, as restructuring of national and regional arts funding bodies and the rewriting of cultural policy have hinted that the main responsibility for funding TIE might be off-loaded to local education authorities or to the schools themselves.

From the mid-1960s to the mid-1970s, probably due to the buoyancy of the British economy and the civic pride that led to the development of the repertory movement, the vulnerable new hybrid survived. Nottingham Playhouse, Watford Palace, Sheffield Crucible, Bolton Octagon all flourished and boasted their TIE companies. But the movement has been dogged by the low status of its actors and indeed all its workers. Consequently it has been painful to observe the drain of highly skilled and talented actors away from TIE and into more lucrative jobs in arts administration, into higher education and into mainstream theatre that is publicly more conspicuous. They have drained away sometimes due to the need for greater financial security (and who can blame them?), sometimes because they could not cope with being undervalued by the theatre profession. Still, however, TIE survives, and counts among its practitioners a remarkable number of well-educated, highly skilled actors, many with decades of experience behind them, that have resisted the lure of other more prestigious kinds of theatre. And still large numbers of young actors emerging from drama schools and universities want to make a career in TIE. For all that it is hidden from public view, escapes media interest and is largely undermined by the Arts Council, TIE remains a most productive form of theatre, and for the actor offers constantly new challenges and rewards – in devising and in performance.

In the early days there were no specialist TIE courses in higher education. In addition to those trained for either teaching or traditional acting, a company might be comprised of people who had previously worked in broadcasting or social work or the book trade. They were an eclectic group of people and it was inevitable from the start that the outcome of their research – the crafting of a new theatre – should have been to push back the boundaries of theatre form.

Its practitioners, conscious both of the unique qualities and of the vulnerability of this new movement, created before long an organization to represent its interests, the Standing Conference of Young People's Theatre (SCYPT) – a move that came out of a sense of 'mission' and perhaps a premonition that from the start there would be a struggle for a future. From the mid-1980s, as the concept of 'enterprise culture' replaced to a large extent society's pride in the notion of state subsidized art, and with the daily intrusion of 'market forces' into arts provision, TIE companies have increasingly come under threat of closure. During this period, companies (inside and outside SCYPT) have raised 'emergency funds' by voluntary donations from members' wage packets in order to save companies on the brink of crisis. The early sense of mission to create new theatre forms has been transformed into a fight for survival. It is as well that we are not strangers to adversity; today's practitioners have inherited from the early pioneers the inspiration that is a product of the deep gratification of working with children and young people. Children who have benefited from a rich arts education are the wonderfully responsive audiences of today; they will also be very ambitious audiences in their adulthood, if TIE is permitted to have an influence on the development of British theatre outside the stifling clutches of the predominently white, male, middle-class culture.

THE ART AND THE CRAFT OF THE THEATRE-IN-EDUCATION ACTOR

When appointing an actor a company will be alert to three broad criteria:

The craft skills

An ability to act is of course essential; the quality of this skill is no different from acting in any other theatre form. Music, dance and mime skills are also looked for, as is a facility with accents, and indeed languages other than English. The actor in

TIE must be able to work in unconducive circumstances, in a classroom cluttered with furniture, or in a school hall with intruding sounds from adjacent rooms. Hence the paramount need for actors who can combine a deep concentration on character with the ability to create a theatre arena for, with and amongst children. The ability to adjust to scale is highly desirable; the large scale often comes easier to a trained actor than do the intimate circumstances of a classroom or corner of a hall and maintaining character whilst speaking to one individual child or a small group of children.

Improvisational skill is essential, for devising (as in the 'gestation' stage below), for exploring ideas with a writer, and in performance when an actor will have to improvise away from the script, engage in character/audience dialogue and wind back onto the prescribed script.

The company member factor

An actor and all employees, whether in a collectively or hierarchically managed company, will need to be prepared to engage with colleagues outside rehearsal and performance in the general company organization and in the advocacy of the work to outside agencies, for example at teachers' meetings. The employing company can only judge suitability for this function by ensuring that the applicant has a clear understanding of and commitment to the nature of the work. An applicant using TIE in order to enter the profession and obtain a union card is to be avoided.

Special qualities of artistry

A TIE company seeks to employ an actor but not an aesthete. The actor who is appointed will be one who perceives the pedagogical function of theatre and the opportunity it offers to explore, express and test social opinion through the art form.

IN PROTECTION OF THE ART AND THE CRAFT OF THE ACTOR

A standard curriculum vitae for an actor in conventional theatre will include her age, hair colour, height, eye colour and skills such as swimming, car driving, horse riding. It is as if an employer is casting to a photo-kit, for example a portly matron with a large handicap. Perhaps this is too cynical a view but many female actors in particular, from their application to drama school and throughout their employment, are ruthlessly categorized. They find employment if their face fits one stereotype and the dole queues when they are to be replaced by someone who looks good in a swimsuit.

The feminist movement together with the principles of equal opportunity and employment rights have all been a strong influence on TIE. On rare occasions, for example if an actor is employed to cover for illness or study breaks, she will be employed on a short and limited contract. Far more commonplace (at least up to 1992) is a contract with a starting date and no termination date. It is not uncommon for actors to stay with a company for seven or eight years, or even longer.

In employing an actor, the company must, then, take account not only of her ability to fulfil the immediate employment needs, but also the creative potential of that actor over a prolonged period of time. TIE has fought through its union Equity for job protection without which the opportunity to work as an ensemble would have little or no future. Creating work in close harmony, which suggests a peaceful process, is not the usual experience of most companies. The reality is that, painful though it might be at the time, creativity is wrought out of conflict. Conflicting arguments, divergent thinking, risk taking and often abrasive processes are frequently the ingredients of a progressive production. Actors may be cautious of taking intellectual and artistic risks if their job is in jeopardy. The concept of ensemble-creating and ensemble-playing therefore takes on a new meaning; it is collective working that allows and invites disharmony in the interests of the longer-term goal. Within a single production, and especially over a span of productions, creative leadership will pass like a baton from actor to actor in a collective working process, and sometimes there are injuries! In such a process, true ensemble is often achieved in a moment of enlightenment: in the collective discovery of the idea which will become germane to all the actors. It is a moment which might only be identified retrospectively. Ensemble therefore is a concept without which one cannot conceive a successful production, it is also a concept which is unachievable without decent and secure working conditions.

THE JOB OF THE ACTOR

Each new production is developed over four stages: inspiration, gestation, transcription and rehearsal.

Inspiration

The idea for new work is found from many diverse sources, and the responsibility for finding new ideas does not lie with one company member – anyone is entitled to put an idea to the company and everyone has the responsibility for searching for ideas for future work. At Pit Prop Theatre many ideas emanate from social and political change: for example, the break up of the Soviet block; the world crises of refugees caused by natural disaster, such as cyclone and flooding in Bangladesh; the Gulf War; economic collapse of a country; Nicaraguan revolution. Many productions are prompted by acute awareness of oppression, racism and sexism. A book or short article may be the starting point. One production was given impetus by a remark made by a teacher of a reception class when actors were researching a production for 4-year-olds. She said, 'Of course they know nothing when they first come here,' presumably intending to impress upon us the challenges faced by the first teacher a child meets in her/his school life. Whatever was intended it prompted the actors to dwell on the learning achievements of a child in the first three years of life –a language, considerable motor control, the social behaviour of family and peer group. The production *Wild Child* (1990) became a celebration of early achievement, largely self-motivated, and its consolidation through giving the children the responsibility of teaching a feral 'child' (an actor) the skills and concepts of human behaviour.

Over a period of years an area-based company needs to provide TIE to all school age groups. The 'good idea' becomes an appropriate idea if it is going to be suitable for the age of children the company needs to be working with. If a company has artistic autonomy, priority is given to fashioning the inspiring idea to the age that will most benefit from it. The company member, or group of members, who puts forward the idea for the new production, takes a leadership role at this stage in the process.

Plate 5.1 Wild Child
Wild Child (Pit Prop Theatre 1990), a programme designed for 'reception' classes of 4-year-olds. Here a character is being taught by the children about their world.
Photo: Donald Tonge
Actor: Adrian Stokes

Sometimes the kernel of a production is subliminal for months or even years, waiting for more appropriate circumstances, the presence of new skills in the company or a sharpening of political concern in society.

Gestation

This period usually commences months before the designated rehearsal stage. It might first feature on the year planner as a day or longer set aside for discussion around the idea, involving the whole permanent company, or it might be extra work taken on by individuals in their spare time. This is also the point when the company appoints additional specialists with skills in writing, design, directing or music directing, though their contracts will not commence until the rehearsal period. From this time to the opening of the production the company will seek advice from other professionals, teachers, advisers, social workers and grass-root political workers; and books, newspaper articles, videos and pictures will be accumulated.

As soon as the last performance of the previous production is over the company embarks on the intensive rehearsal period. If the company is to self-devise the new production, actors in TIE relate to the director and designer in a uniquely creative way. In traditional theatre the public perceives actors as having a high status in the industry during performance, but the uninitiated public is not aware of the low status occupied by the actor in rehearsals. At the same time writers often protest about their new work's vulnerability in the hands of both actors and directors. In TIE, actors deserve and are usually accorded a high status in the rehearsal period of self-devised programmes.

In the gestation period there are two distinct requirements of actors: (a) research; and (b) creative exploration of the idea. In the early weeks, in broad terms, there is more research than exploration, and in the middle weeks there is more exploration than research. An actor who is hostile to research will not be content in TIE. However there is sometimes a gender divide in the application of research to the exploration of ideas. Male actors are often more comfortable when intellectually arguing the product of their research. Female actors tend to prefer to express their findings through character and situation in improvisation. Only the more sensitive and astute male directors can cope with this problem, while female directors tend to be more intuitively in tune with female actors.

The director needs to set up opportunities to diffuse research into drama by an osmotic process. Towards the middle of the gestation period is the most exciting phase; it feels almost dangerous. Actors and director are under pressure to describe the new play and give it a title so that it can be advertised, but if this pressure is allowed to dominate it may well close down the play into a documentation of the research. Actors are now having to produce characters that provide a vehicle to express their passion for the original idea, clothed with the findings of their research, and actors are having to service other actors' character needs too. And the director is jockeying all the creative opportunities that emanate from the rehearsal room floor.

The end of the gestation period is enshrined with a search for the *Gestalt*, the gathering of, as it were, single notes of music into musical phrases, and musical phrases into melody. When the production meets with its audience, it will need to have clarity but not simplicity; it will need to be rich enough to have meaning for its young audience with its diversity of experience and understanding, whilst also being sufficiently vivid to provide the audience with ripples of recollection long after the event. During this period there can be times of despair, the fear that all the efforts of devoted company members will fail to produce the theatre they believed was contained in the inspirational idea. Now the right conditions need to be present in order for the actor and director to be able to draw on their craft skills. Here they must rely on their instinct for finding the crucible of the drama – the theatrical vessel which will be able to contain the intensity of the dramatic action – and when you find the crucible you recognize it with great relief. In *Dancer* (1991), a production for young people of 15 to 16 years old with special educational needs, it seemed to me the crucible was manifested by sand marking the periphery of the set (the town) and by a wind machine. These technical devices signalled for the audience the isolation of the townsfolk forced to examine their differences. The sand was their desertedness and the wind their chill at the break-up of the Soviet block. The crucible can become the physicalization of ideas that helps actors refine their characters, both to sharpen the fundamental conflicts and to address their divergent self-interests. It is a stage in the creative process when we move out of gestation and into transcription.

Transcription

One of the features that characterizes the rehearsal room during devising is the amount of paper around. Strips of paper marking passages in books, notebooks that are personal logs of the process, metres of rolls of paper crossing the rehearsal room floor, single sheets describing scenes pegged like washing on a string. Finally there will be a script filed away when the company embarks on the next new production.

Very few TIE companies can afford a resident writer. The contribution that the writer can make in devised TIE is highly desirable, but there are few who are prepared to concede to the actor creative pre-eminence in the devised theatre process. The writer who is prepared to share with actors the craft of play-writing is much valued by the company. The role is not one of collecting up all those pieces of paper and making sense of their desperate nature; it is one of creative companionship. If the writer, who has researched the product along with actors, can witness improvisations and transcribe the actors' work, adorning and developing it with her craft, she can move the process through to rehearsal smoothly.

In the absence of a writer actors will be left to write up scenes in their unpaid hours. Some actors are also good natural writers; some need the process of writing to help them draw on their research to support their improvisation of a speech. However, the craft of the writer is to be valued and it should ideally be an essential and ever-present post in a company.

Rehearsal

Rehearsal, in comparison with the other stages of the process, is the easy part. The rehearsal period is much inspired by the work of the designer, who has worked through all of the other stages with actors and director, but who will have departed from the rehearsal room for lengthy periods after the middle of the gestation period. She will have taken the essence of the ideas stage and the research into the improvisation stage and pursued her own particular research. In traditional theatre, design serves the needs of the play; in TIE design has the creative weight equivalent to at least one actor in the finished product. The designer's visual communication has often made sense when verbal communication was breaking down.

All the investment of time and commitment in the ideas, the gestation and the transcription stages of the production, coupled with a TIE company's collective way of managing its affairs, leads to ensemble rehearsal and performance. The TIE actor has an extra quality: her character is dedicated to the inspirational idea and sustained by the wealth of research and creative experiment. There is a power in this actor which will become evident in performance.

TIE is a radical wing of the arts industry. In the rehearsal stage actors and director are preparing to entice the audience into engagement with the theatre event and finding the means to challenge the audience into thinking for itself. This is manifest in the way the ensemble of actors plays the scenes. The art form rejects the notion of complete, well-rounded characters; instead it sets out to puzzle and disorientate its audience, for their emotional journey with the characters is the essence of the educative experience.

Meaningful theatre and certainly all TIE examines the human condition at times of crises. At such times the ordered part of the brain is subordinated to the brain stem, or the chaotic influence. Human behaviour is less predictable and the audience's commitment to the play's characters is at risk. The characters' vulnerability in the context of their circumstances is exposed in the drama, and *if artistically marshalled* as the story unfolds, draws the audience empathetically closer. As the character behaviour is buffeted by the turbulence of fast-changing circumstances, so the emotions of the audience are disturbed. The chaotic is further reflected in events which change rapidly just when the audience is seeing a logical pattern emerge.

This rough theatre is a characteristic of TIE. In his book, *The Empty Space* Peter Brook had courage enough to spare when he wrote so passionately about 'rough' theatre. In the context of TIE, which actively and verbally invites the participants' dialogue along with the actors' prepared lines, which in turn often have to be modified in order to make cogent responses, 'rough theatre' is incomplete theatre; it is not perfectly rounded. If well-rounded theatre is the perfect impenetrable theatre, TIE is the irregular sphere which invites and needs the audience to perfect it. Each performance will complete the sphere differently; performances will conclude unsatisfactorily if one is seeking a perfect geometric conclusion. Involvement TIE, then, needs to be 'rough' so that the audience, in small numbers, can actively engage with the event. Most of Pit Prop Theatre's productions have no cosy seats in which the audience can settle impassively to watch; the audience is actively, physically and verbally engaged, as well as being engaged emotionally and intellectually. The company must therefore give prime regard to the place and identity of the audience – the other participants – throughout the gestation and rehearsal phases. In improvisation and rehearsal an actor has to see with her mind's eye the audience at all times.

But the event of theatre, if it is to be an organic experience, does not rest when the actors and the audience depart. Each member of the event, audience and actors alike, will have brought to the occasion a past; during the event of fiction (the play) they know real events are changing minute by minute; all members of the theatre event have a future and if the play has been useful it will be carried forward. Six months or six years hence, a participant may need to match up real-life experience with the fictional experience of the play – for that person the theatre event is still not complete, it remains an imperfect experience. At that moment there is insufficient time to re-collect the second by second, chronological theatre event. In order to best serve the means of recall the theatre practitioners need to have built into their performance mechanisms for that purpose: sensory, intellectual, political or linguistic. They might be described in symbol or metaphor or ritual, and they need to be consciously written into the play. In this process lies the art.

There have been phases in the historic development of TIE when stress was laid on the linear development of plot and character. This panders to the institution of education which strives to create intellectual order out of disparate experience. Recently TIE practitioners have been experimenting by putting to one side logical progression and allowing the art to flourish by focusing on the chaotic influences most of us experience in our lives, the disparate and fragmented experiences, and positively encouraging the juxtapositioning of apparently conflicting influences. Therein lies a fruitful partnership between teachers and actors. The former are needed to guide us in marshalling our experiences towards a sense of order; the latter make legitimate a process of investigation into the disorder of our experiences.

The production *Fighting for our Lives* (Pit Prop Theatre, 1992) was given its physical and locational form by the designer who after collaborating in the rehearsal room, turned up one day with a model for the set. There were two distinct areas, both in a museum.

a) The first area entered by the audience was the public space, clinical, perfectly presented, with a restricted use of colour, and history described in chronological order;

b) the second area entered by the audience was the private space, the archive of history, fragments of people's lives in other cultures and other times, and a turbulence of history.

The design became an inspiration to the actors, director and writer from whom it is important to note it had emanated but unconsciously.

The audience of 13 to 14 year-olds behaved differently in each of the two spaces and their instinctive behaviour was encouraged by the signals given out by the actors. In the public, or ordered, space, using questionnaires, the students researched the presentation of orthodox history, and they did not like being distracted from their task. In the private, or chaotic, interior, they allowed the theatre event to take them over, picking up and committing to memory the bits of it that were usefully significant to them as individuals, and sometimes with a group or collective response.

This production could not resist the inherent third element, that of invading the two separate theatre spaces, and this the audience baulked at. Order in the public space they could cope with: it reflected the institutional aspects of education; chaos in the archive space they revelled in. Trawling through time, culture and place is what most of us do as we grapple with the past and with other places in our search to make sense of today. But when the theatre event invaded the other space, that was difficult for the audience. The company was reminded that official education applauds a one-way process, that of making order out of chaos; that chaos might impinge on order for a

pose, goes against our training as pupils and students
ıg.

THE ..ТOR IN PERFORMANCE

During the preparation period, the TIE actor has been preparing, not for a performance (she can give a performance of
her artistry in the rehearsal room) but for an event of theatre.
When it starts the dynamics will be on three planes:

1 The audience, one class of the same age will need to be
   addressed collectively, in friendship groups, and as individuals.
2 The actors, now at the start of their performance, will be
   focusing on their skills, their props and all the other necessary practical arrangements.
3 The third and the most important dynamic is the inspirational
   idea: that which gives energy and purpose to the whole
   performance.

The event of theatre begins, the actors listen intently to assess
the mood of the audience, the audience does a sensory search
to assess whether the experience is threatening or conducive.
The four stages – inspiration, gestation, transcription and
rehearsal – are now reversed by the company so that the
confidence and skill they have gained in rehearsal is their first
display, leading to a confidence on the part of the audience. As
narrative (that is, the script or 'transcription') takes over so the
audience is embraced by story. If all is working so far via
character and emotion and sensory perception, the audience is
engaging with the actor, who in performance is now the
manifestation of the inspiration, the gestation, the transcription
and the rehearsal phases of the production. The casual observer
will see only the actor's character, but the audience will be privy
to the skills of the 'actor–teacher', the craft of the 'performer'
and the creativity of the 'actor'.

Inspiration for a TIE production is the company's most
precious commodity and by now is its binding force. It is what
has given energy and guidance to the company in the weeks
leading up to the performance; it is the reason for going on
working on the production over the months of its active life; it
is what inspires actors to perfect their acting performance in

order to make more 'rough' and therefore more effective the dynamic of the theatre event, both as a learning forum in the here and now and as an inspirational force hopefully long after the event itself.

It is regrettable that so few scripts of audience-involved TIE exist in a readily transferable form. It is not that rough theatre is equatable with inferior theatre, but that the script alone represents only one part (though an important part) of the whole interactive experience. Thus the TIE actor must constantly be making and re-making sense of the play right through the rehearsal period and beyond, even up to the last performance. I recall that actors in a two-hander during a very long run of a TIE play for 3 and 4 year-olds (*Wild Child*) chose to learn each of the two parts. After the set had been put up and the props arranged, they would come to the final stage of preparation which was to put on their costumes. It was at this moment that they would decide which character to play. If it was the eightieth performance, the simple explanation for their chosen ploy was to keep the performance fresh; but there was also a deeper purpose: to be frightened into continually learning from the play. In this way the interplay with the audience was continually renewed and enriched and developed.

Take two adjacent boroughs, fictionalized but out of factual experience. Call one the Depressed Borough and the other the Enlightened Borough. The same production by the same company is played in each of the two boroughs. In the Depressed Borough the performance is received by pupils and teachers displaced from formal teaching; they are anxious. Their anxiety is displayed by the teacher underscoring the theatre event with strict rules, serious glances and firm whispers. The anxiety is displayed by the pupils in the form of hyperactivity, a lot of physical and usually aggressive contact, and a constant banter of chat. In the Enlightened Borough both teacher and pupils are excited but calmly in control of positive expectations. The teacher metaphorically sits back and the pupils lean forward.

In each of the boroughs the actors are alert and super-sensitive to respond to the needs of the audience. In the Depressed Borough the actors' energy is mostly spent circum-navigating the class to embrace its people with a sense of ease and confidence in the event and to capture the interest of each individual in the substance of the production. The actors will have analysed the programme for its potential in performance and identified specific moments or 'markers' when a heightened response can be expected from the audience. If the response is disappointing, the actors will approach the next marker with intensified alertness and skill, reaching out to the periphery of the class to draw their attention into the minutiae of the action. If the response exceeds expectation, the actors then work to reveal the play's greater complexities.

In the Enlightened Borough, the modifying and controlling of responses will be less needed, but the energy of the actor is just as great as in the former borough. The actor's investment of internal energy here is being led by the pupil's capacity for reading beyond the superficial display of theatre. These pupils and this teacher will not be dependent on a simple linear development of the drama. If an aspect of the production is not comprehensible at the given moment they do not panic, the section is registered and they will move on knowing that revelation will happen either inside the theatre event or later working with the teacher. In both boroughs, Depressed and Enlightened, actors can feel equally gratified by their achievements in transforming perceptions through educative art. The progress has however been unequal.

We do not need art, except that it helps us to examine the chaotic experiences of our lives, except that it reminds us of the potential of our humanity, except that it advances our political literacy. Depressed Borough might be made up of children in a privileged socio-economic community and Enlightened Borough made up of underprivileged children, or the other way round. I would differentiate the two groups not because one is passive and the other active, but because one, the Enlightened Borough, has an arts education curriculum and the other has not. The former is enlightened not necessarily because stage crafts and the greats of British stage writing are examined, but rather because these children have learnt how to read the symbolism of the art, have learnt to search for the purpose of the ideas; these children's expectation of theatre art is not three acts, two intervals, and a comforting self-congratulatory story. The arts curriculum in the Enlightened Borough has been as exacting as scientific pursuit. It is a searching to find the true meaning of the hostile and oppressing experiences encroaching on the lives of working-class people; the poverty, homelessness, unemployment, erosion of public services; war and all its consequences. Finding the truth is the embarkation point towards change, and articulating that knowledge with a political literacy – the impassioned language of the oppressed – is the skill every young person has the right to learn. The teaching of facts, the selection of which is dictated by the dominant culture, is oppressive and in itself an arid pursuit. TIE can contribute to an education which transforms information, via analysis, into knowledge, a powerful tool enabling the next generation of adults to challenge present injustices. Art is therefore not for art's sake, nor for behaviour modification; it is rather the conscience of a nation by means of which we can examine society's values.

Artists working with children are united by one commonality: through our young audiences we are inspired towards the real needs and the aspirations of humanity.

Chapter 6

TIE and the Theatre of the Oppressed

Chris Vine

In 1982 the Greenwich Young People's Theatre (GYPT) began integrating the methodology of the Brazilian director Augusto Boal into its existing TIE practice. It was the first British TIE company to do so, and those early tentative steps marked the beginning of an experiment which was not only to enrich its own work for the next decade but to spread the influence of Boal throughout the TIE movement and to presage the introduction of the Theatre of the Oppressed to a wider constituency of practitioners and teachers in many reaches of the British theatre world. This chapter will examine the reasons for Boal's work proving so peculiarly appropriate for translation to a TIE context and providing such an enduring source of inspiration; it will also highlight the significant changes and developments made by the GYPT company in the process of adapting his methodology to its own usage.

In order to appreciate the potential relevance of Boal's work within a British TIE context, it is important to remind ourselves of some key features of Theatre in Education itself: that its prime motivation lies in its explicit educational purpose and that its distinctive formal feature is its use of active audience participation. Central to the work, in all its variety of theatre forms and educational strategies, are the twin convictions that human behaviour and institutions are formed through social activity and can therefore be changed, and that audiences, as potential agents of change, should be active participants in their own learning.

It was within this TIE mainstream that GYPT was working when it first encountered the ideas of Augusto Boal: their relevance to its own practice was immediately apparent. The

GYPT company had a long tradition of innovatory participation work: from the mid-1970s it had given particular prominence to the development of complex forms involving the audience working alongside the actors in a theatrical context, often framed within elaborate theatrical environments. This practice was part of a conscious attempt to enhance the cognitive and affective experience of the audience by combining the power of the theatrical experience with techniques developed in the field of drama in education (DIE). GYPT, like many companies, was subject to a wide range of influences; inspiration was to be found in diverse quarters including the theatre of Brecht, the DIE work of Gavin Bolton and Dorothy Heathcote and the pedagogy of the Brazilian educationalist, Paulo Freire. But this apparent eclecticism (common to most companies in the early years of TIE's evolution) was tempered by a determination to build a progressive practice within a coherent theoretical framework. At this time GYPT was working to develop a dialectical and materialist practice through which its audiences could be actively engaged as the *subjects* in the learning process (as opposed to passive objects who are filled with knowledge by and from others) but simultaneously be challenged to take a critically *objective* view of their experience, recognizing themselves as part of the same social reality from which the contents of the TIE programmes were drawn.

The central educational concern of the company was to find ways of reuniting feelings, thoughts and actions in its audiences, and thus create a *praxis* in direct opposition to those practices in both theatre and education which tend to keep them separated.

The company's first encounter with Boal's ideas was through his book *Theatre of the Oppressed*. The connections with its own concerns were immediately apparent:

> In order to understand the poetics of the oppressed one must keep in mind its main objective: to change the people – 'spectators' – passive beings in the theatrical phenomenon – into subjects, into actors, transformers of the dramatic action. I hope that the differences remain clear. Aristotle proposes a poetics in which the spectator delegates power to the dramatic character so that the latter may act and think for him. Brecht proposes a poetics in which the spectator delegates

power to the character who thus acts in his place but the spectator reserves the right to think for himself, often in opposition to the character. In the first case a 'catharsis' occurs; in the second an awakening of critical consciousness. But the poetics of the oppressed focuses on the action itself: the spectator delegates no power to the character (or actor) either to act or to think in his place; on the contrary, he himself assumes the protagonic role, changes the dramatic action, tries out solutions, discusses plans for change – in short, trains himself for real action. In this case, perhaps the theatre is not revolutionary in itself, but is surely a rehearsal for the revolution. The liberated spectator, as a whole person, launches into action.

(Boal 1979: 122)

Here was the first coherent theory of the relationship between the actor and the audience (including a view of the social responsibility of the artist) to be propounded since Brecht. In his struggle to make his work increasingly relevant and effective as a tool for liberation, Boal had come to the conclusion that traditional forms needed reworking and, specifically, that the relationship between the actor and the audience must be changed. He believed that feelings as well as the intellect were crucial to the development of people's perceptions and understandings and saw in the language of theatre the means to help them think with their whole being – not passively but 'in action'. For him theatre was a dialectical process concerned with the movement of people and matter: 'Theatre is change and not simple presentation of what exists: it is becoming and not being' (Boal 1979: 28).

It was no coincidence that a crucial stage in the development of Boal's work occurred while he was working in Peru on a literacy project inspired by the methods of Paulo Freire. Freire believed education should be an active process in the service of social change:

Teachers and students (leadership and people) co-intent on reality, are both subjects, not only in the task of unveiling that reality, and thereby coming to know it critically, but in the task of re-creating that knowledge. As they attain this knowledge of reality through common reflection and action (praxis) they discover themselves as its permanent re-creators. In this way, the presence of the oppressed in the struggle for their liberation will be what it should be: *not pseudo-participation but committed involvement.*

(Freire 1972: 44; my italics)

Both Freire and Boal espoused the cause of human liberation, and Boal, like Freire, came to realize that the process of liberation begins with a critically active response to your own experience: this will not be developed by those – be they teachers or actors (or political leaders) – who *tell* others what their problems are – or how to solve them!

It was not surprising, given the particular concerns of the GYPT company, that the Theatre of the Oppressed created so much interest. A real sense of excitement was generated both by its theory and by the descriptions of Boal's methods, particularly his use of Image Theatre and Forum Theatre, forms which encourage the spectators to intervene directly, in the first to 'speak' through images made with the actors' bodies and in the second to 'act' in the place of the main protagonists. The company sensed that these ideas could add an important new dimension to its work but they remained insufficiently clear to be translated into practice.

Then, by fortunate coincidence, an opportunity arose in 1982 for three company members to attend an international workshop run by Boal in Austria under the auspices of the International Amateur Theatre Association (IATA).

At that time the company was re-mounting a programme for the fourteen-plus age range. The programme, *A Land Fit For Heroes*, was designed, by an extraordinary coincidence, to explore, at the conceptual level, the relationships between experience, thought and action. At the heart of the programme was an extended role-play which took as its starting point the historical events of the 1926 British General Strike. The school pupils were carefully inducted to a variety of roles chosen to reflect a cross-section of society in a provincial industrial town of the period. The roles included coal miners, railway workers, shop-keepers, farmers and landed gentry. One group of pupils were journalists and produced a small newspaper. The different socio-economic interests of different groups (e.g. the railway workers) were cross-threaded with individual family and class loyalties. Once in role the pupils worked alongside the actor–

teachers, also in role, within a carefully designed theatrical environment. Although the experience was carefully structured to produce a number of different initial conflicts between groups, there were no predetermined outcomes. Once the action began, the actor–teacher's choices and actions proceeded in response to those of the pupils. No two 'performances' were ever the same, and the finishing point was determined solely by the strictures of time.

The whole undertaking was extremely complex, but we knew from experience that it was very effective for revealing the discrepancies that arise between what people say they will do (in theory) and what they actually do when confronted with the immediacy of a situation. The pupils always became emotionally involved and felt very keenly the dilemmas that arose. They were often able to reflect upon their own actions during the event itself, stepping in and out of role of their own volition (the company never stopped the action), and were certainly able to do so once the role-play had finished, often expressing surprise at their own contradictory behaviour during its progress. However, the drama operated at a very high level of emotional intensity as a 'lived through' experience in real time: the educational challenge lay in trying to find a method to help them examine, objectively, after the experience, the forces which had been at work on them and which had preconditioned many of their responses. What was needed was a new activity which would maintain their emotional engagement, and at the same time allow them to reflect upon and analyse their recent experience.

The techniques demonstrated by Boal in Austria seemed as though they might offer a way forward. On our return we decided to experiment with the use of Forum Theatre.

Working from improvisations the actors created a short piece of theatre containing conflicts which mirrored many of the dilemmas the pupils had faced individually and in groups during the earlier role-play. The piece ended with the central character, a railway employee, facing a difficult choice: should she comply with the wishes of her employer and derive considerable benefit for herself and children, but at the expense of her brother, friends and workmates; or should she refuse to co-operate and risk the promised security for herself and family?

The pupils watched this scenario unfold knowing in advance

that it contained a series of problems similar to those they had already experienced. When it was over they were asked what they thought she *could* do. They discussed the possible options open to her and speculated on their ramifications. The many different suggestions were noted. They were then asked what they thought *they would do* if they were in that situation. Again many suggestions were offered and there were some strong disagreements. Some said they would avoid making a choice and have the best of both worlds, some that they would put their children first, some that loyalty to friends and workmates was more important. Others thought that they could talk their way out of the dilemmas by explaining the problems to the employer (the main oppressor) and others maintained they would go to their workmates for support and not try to tackle the situation alone. After the different opinions had been clarified, the next stage began.

Individual pupils were invited to step into the shoes of the central character to test out their ideas. The results were impressive. Hardly ever did the pupils consciously 'perform'. They wrestled with the problems as they arose, sometimes were devious, sometimes became very angry, often ended up doing the opposite of what they had intended – or something very different – but seldom gave up. Sometimes they worked alone and sometimes they drew other pupils into the drama to represent their friends or workmates. The audience was spellbound. Not only were the pupils 'watching a performance' but they were weighing the chances of their own proposals against the results of the other, different proposals being tested in front of them. Interestingly, there was seldom a sense of competition engendered: the focus was on helping the protagonist – and defeating the oppressor.

Between interventions the pupils were asked to give their analysis of what had happened. As a group they became the sounding board for objective reflections on the continuing action. Often a pupil who had just intervened would say, 'I did such and such . . . the problem is solved', and the others would say, 'No it isn't . . . now this will happen'. If the disagreements persisted, the opinions could be tested by going back into the drama. In this way they worked as a whole group, tackling the problems *collectively*.

This method of working placed particular demands on the

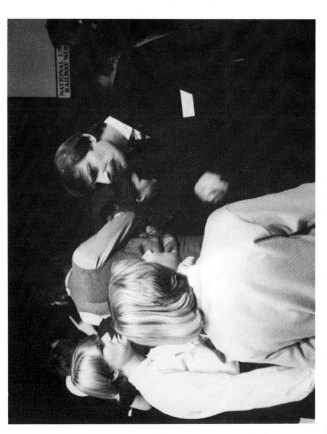

Plate 6.1 Land Fit for Heroes
Two pupils confront Sir Robert, the railway magnate, during the role-play from *Land Fit for Heroes* (GYPT 1982). Later in the session pupils were able to apply the lessons of this 'lived-through' experience when they again encountered Sir Robert within a Forum Theatre drama.
Director: Chris Vine. Photo: John Daniell.

actors, requiring an interesting new orientation of the synthesis between their acting and teaching skills in a way not normally needed in role-play situations where there is not the same element of performance to an audience. The actors needed to be very clear about the motivation of their characters and pursue their objectives as truthfully as possible; at the same time they needed to reveal those motivations as subtly as possible and make clear the means, both social and personal, that were available to help the characters achieve their objectives. Only by doing this could they begin to show both their strengths and weaknesses and demonstrate, in the Brechtian sense, the truth of their characters as social beings, rather than individual psyches. But this was happening in improvisations with non-actors which also needed orchestrating physically and vocally to make them as accessible and engaging as possible for the rest of the audience.

In addition the actors were also working as teachers: they needed to give the participants the maximum support and allow them time to explore their ideas and actions. They had to provide them with options to pursue, offer questions that would challenge them, help them to clarify their ideas and spur them on to struggle with the problems they were confronting. It was crucial that the pressures on them were truthfully maintained and no easy or 'magic' solutions allowed, but, at the same time, it was counter-productive, both theatrically and educationally, to overwhelm them with the full force of the character's (or actor's) powers. The aim was to enable the audience to think and act, not to defeat and paralyse them. The pupils could only do this in an informed manner if they were able to recognize the truth of the situation. The task of the actors was paradoxical: they had to reveal the reality through distortion, not obscure it by reproducing its outward appearance.

A key figure in the Forum process is the 'Joker'. The Joker is the facilitator, the direct link between the audience and the dramatic action; she or he has the responsibility for orchestrating the whole event. The Joker must encourage and enable the spectators (or 'spect-actors' as Boal calls them) to intervene. We discovered that this entailed taking time to clarify the possible courses of action, and making sure that pupils who wished to intervene were clear about the situation, and their intentions within it, before the intervention began. It was also important to ensure the actors understood what a participant wanted, where the intervention was to begin, which characters were present, and so on.

After each intervention, the Joker was responsible for developing the analysis of what had happened. Contributions were elicited by a questioning process, beginning with the individual who had intervened and opening it to those who had been watching: How did you get on? Did you achieve what you intended? What helped you? What stopped you? How did you feel? What have you discovered about the employer? Do you (the audience) agree? What else have you (all) discovered? What will he do next? What power does he have? What power does our central character have? What else could be done? ... and so on, helping the group to develop a wider understanding of the situation and to formulate more informed courses of action for testing by means of further dramatic interventions.

The role of the Joker proved particularly exacting. No two performances of the Forum ever followed the same course and it was impossible to predict all the suggestions the audience was likely to make. In rehearsal the actor–teachers had prepared for as many different kinds of intervention as they could anticipate; they were used to responding 'in the moment', through drama, to the demands of young people, and were confident they would be equal to the task as each intervention arose. In the event this proved a great deal more difficult than anyone had foreseen, demanding intense concentration and continuous reassessment of educational and theatrical strategies. For the Joker the challenges were even greater. She or he (in our early experiments two actor–teachers alternated in the role, supporting and learning from each other) was responsible for the ultimate success or failure of the whole Forum. We discovered the functions were numerous.

In the first place the Joker must make the aims and procedures of the Forum clear, and then set the process in motion. At all times she must be responsive to the desires of the spectators, listening extremely carefully and enabling them, individually and collectively, to pursue their journeys of exploration, without imposing the wishes of the company upon them.

At the same time, choices have to be made: not all interventions are equally productive and not all suggestions can be pursued. The Joker has to judge when to move from one line of enquiry to another, when to stop pursuing one action and its consequences and allow someone else to open up a new possibility: she must keep the audience focused on the central problems, select the appropriate questions to further the dramatic debate, support the spectators and the actors, challenge the spectators, know when to listen, when to speak and when to insist on action ('Don't tell me, show me!'). At all times the Joker must transmit energy, excitement and an enthusiasm for tackling the problems, combined with a genuine interest in all the contributions from the audience. But above all else, the Joker must carry the overall responsibility for structuring and deepening the learning experience as it is unfolding.

For the experienced actor–teacher many of these skills were not in themselves new: what was new was their convergence and concentration upon one individual in a single event. Although the Joker was still part of a team, the focusing of demands on that individual reminded us most sharply of the responsibility and skills required of the drama teacher who, working alone, strives from moment to moment to structure and deepen the learning of the group and each individual pupil within it.

It was an important realization that inspired us to re-examine and refurbish the range and depth of our educational and theatrical skills. It also raised a number of questions about the teaching function of the Joker as originally conceived by Boal. The answers began to emerge as we discovered more details of Boal's actual practice.

The first experiment with Theatre of the Oppressed techniques was an extremely exciting and powerful experience. The GYPT company was in no doubt that it wished to explore their application further, experimenting with the use of both Image and Forum theatre, and extending their use into its work with younger age-groups and to students with special educational needs. Over the next few years the process of experimentation and adaptation was rapid and thorough. As it progressed other companies and individuals also began to see the potential of the Theatre of the Oppressed techniques in the TIE context, recognizing the similarities, both in intention and in the skills required, between the two genres. This spread of interest had a number of effects which further encouraged the development of the work.

More practitioners wanted first-hand exposure to Boal and

his ideas and a small group, including GYPT members, attended his workshops in France and Holland; in 1984 GYPT led a Theatre of the Oppressed workshop for the Standing Conference of Young People's Theatre (SCYPT); and in 1985 the Rose Bruford College of Speech and Drama, supported by GYPT personnel, organized the first workshops to be led by Boal and his French company, Le Cetitade, in the UK.

As Boal's ideas spread different companies and individuals adopted his methods in tune with their own needs; others in the TIE movement rejected them altogether. In the GYPT company, experimentation continued, but it was now more thoroughly informed by Boal's own intentions and processes and one thing became rapidly apparent: in the first instance the structure of Forum Theatre had been misunderstood and the techniques misapplied in a number of particulars.

In its early use of the Theatre of the Oppressed techniques, the GYPT company would always invite the audience to intervene at a predetermined moment of decision and choice (as described above); the play, as performed by the actors, was never completed. Boal's theatre does not work in this way. He presents a complete piece in which the main protagonist fails to overcome his or her problems: the movement, as in a classical tragedy, is from fortune to misfortune, happiness to despair, success (or anticipated success) to defeat and failure. The audience sees the whole story and is invited to consider whether or not the outcome could have been different; the play is then re-run and the audience invited to stop it at any moment it feels a crucial mistake is being made. At this point individuals or groups can intervene to do things differently and try to alter the course of events.

One of the merits of this approach is that it objectifies a complete experience (as portrayed through the play) and asks how we might generalize from the particular, learning from the experiences of others and re-applying those lessons to produce different outcomes in our own lives. It therefore also conveys the implicit belief that outcomes and futures are not predetermined; we are simultaneously the products and creators of our own history.

GYPT decided to experiment with the method in its original form; it found the perfect vehicle in a one-woman show entitled *No Going Back,* a short play originally devised by the Coventry

Belgrade TIE Team. It is set in a women's refuge. The central character, a woman physically abused by her husband, tells her story. She describes her relationship from her early courtship, through her marriage and the birth of her children. She tells how her husband first assaulted her, how the attacks increased in regularity and severity, how others, like her parents, refused to take it seriously, how she kept forgiving him, and even after leaving him would always go back, convincing herself he would eventually change. Now, she says, she will never make those mistakes again, she will never return to him. As she draws her story to an end, the telephone rings; it is her husband begging her to go home. She agrees and leaves.

Under the direction of Lynne Suffolk, the play was produced with the characters from the woman's life peopling the stage as she spoke of them: it was no longer a one-person play although none of the other characters ever spoke. As the woman left the refuge at the end of the play the teenage audience was already calling out to her in exasperation.

Two of Boal's techniques were applied to this programme. Before the pupils saw the play they made still-images, using themselves as the characters, to examine the discrepancy between romantic dreams (the 'Ideal') and the everyday reality of relationships. In this way the area of exploration was delineated in a very concrete manner. The pupils were asked to consider what prevents people from changing their circumstances even when they are extremely unhappy. The pupils then watched the play.

After the play there was a short discussion about the behaviour of the woman. The play was then re-presented as Forum Theatre. The pupils were able to stop it and intervene whenever they thought the central figure, the woman, should have taken a different course of action. During the interventions, the other characters (the husband, parents, police and others) did speak, responding directly to the participants.

By contrast to the approach used in *A Land Fit For Heroes*, this method did not focus on one moment of choice and decision, but allowed the pupils to examine a number of key incidents, over a long period of time, in the lives of the protagonists. Some pupils focused on the early attitudes of the woman to the man, before they were married, and began questioning social attitudes to gender roles. Others were more interested in the responses of the police or the parents to intimations of violence, and began to examine how society often encourages its victims to believe they are the ones at fault. By experiencing this directly, through the drama, they were able to analyse the complexities and contradictions of people's responses in such situations and – frequently – by re-applying this awareness, display the new strength and persistence they realized was necessary to change them. On several occasions pupils told their teachers that these things happened in their families: for them speaking out for the first time was perhaps the first step towards changing their reality.

The success of this new model, closer to what Boal had intended, did not invalidate the model first employed in *A Land Fit For Heroes*. That approach had helped the company to focus very precisely on a single moment of choice which contained in embryo a world of personal and political perspectives, under-standings, misunderstandings and illusions. By investigating a single moment in a particular relationship between an employee and an employer, it had been possible to survey a wide terrain of class relationships, vested interests and power. In one sense the two figures were emblematic, but this did not diminish the social reality of their conflict nor simplify the underlying complexity of their options and the probable consequences.

In *No Going Back* the perspective on the central relationship was different. The emphasis was on examining how people become victims, unravelling how they allow their emotions to be distorted and unwittingly collude in their own oppression. In this instance it was essential to examine the early choices and influences on the characters. To have focused solely on the moment at the end of the play when the woman decided to return to her husband would not have illuminated the causes of the problem. Everyone could agree that she should not have gone back, but only by exploring the earlier subtle and more insidious pressures did the pupils begin to understand why she did so, and begin to reflect on the importance of those appar-ently insignificant responses and choices which, in their cumul-ative effect, predispose us to collude in our own oppression.

By now the increasing familiarity with Boal's own working processes was leading to a reappraisal of a number of the practices which GYPT had originally, and mistakenly, attributed to him. This new awareness was also producing a different, more critical perspective on his theory and practice as it was now more clearly emerging. In some instances the newly under-stood authentic techniques were applied with impressive results, but in other cases the company's earlier 'errors' were deliberately compounded and embedded in its approach to Forum work or further adapted to suit the needs of specific groups. An example of this is provided by the way the company inserted Forum techniques into storybuilding workshops developed for students with moderate and severe learning difficulties.

In these workshops the students were encouraged to create characters and develop their adventures. The stimuli from which the work began was provided by personal artefacts and articles of clothing. Thus an old alarm clock, a wide-brimmed hat, a black handbag, a used railway ticket and a framed photograph gave rise to the creation of Emily, an elderly woman who lived alone, had trouble waking up in the mornings, and once a year visited her daughter who lived by the sea. Once established, Emily could enjoy numerous adventures, and in these adventures any member of the group could take her part simply by donning her hat; she had been created by everyone and was, as it were, common property. Similarly, group members could become the many other characters she encountered and could work alongside the actor–teachers to recreate her adventures.

The creative act was in itself extremely important to these students, but within their stories the company recognized a further opportunity. With very little adjustment it was possible to create situations to which Forum theatre techniques could be applied in order to develop decision making, self-assertion and advocacy skills. The key to this was Freire's concept of 'problematizing' reality.

The groups' stories were often a seamless stream of events, sometimes bizarre and fantastical, but usually progressing to a happy ending; as in fairy tales all difficulties were, in the end, magically surmounted. Instead of letting the difficult moments pass, the company began to isolate them, to look for moments of conflict which could be re-presented to reveal a difficult 'real' problem which needed confronting. For example, on one occasion Emily found herself on the beach next to someone playing very loud music on a cassette player. Emily was unhappy about the noise, but in the original story she avoided the problem by leaving the beach. By applying Forum techniques this moment was re-examined and Emily's passivity was challenged; an actor–teacher took the role of the person playing the music and successive students took the role of Emily and tried to change the situation. Emily's right to a peaceful afternoon was suddenly an issue demanding attention! In another episode Emily fell out with her daughter; again the students assumed the role of Emily, this time exploring different ways of negotiating a difficult emotional situation whilst insisting on a recognition of her rights and feelings. Although the situations which were explored had been drawn from fiction, the fiction itself had its roots in the lives of the students and the challenges presented were very real indeed. The drama generated by the interventions was often correspondingly intense.

During this period the company essayed many experiments with different variations on the techniques for many different age-groups, but whatever the nature of the audience or the fictional context, one revision to Boal's methods remained constant: this was the insistence on analysing the results and implications of the various interventions *as they occurred*. This meant there was a great deal of discussion as the Forum progressed. By contrast, Boal insists that the Theatre of the Oppressed is about acting not talking and maintains that over-analysis disrupts the dynamic of the theatre and the nature of the 'theatrical' debate. He prefers to let the audience's experience, individual and collective, speak for itself, and warns of the dangers of the actors imposing their own solutions upon the spectators. There is much to commend this cautionary impulse: all teachers, actors or not, should be aware of the fine line to be drawn between challenging the views of the students and imposing their own upon them. But there is an important philosophical and pedagogical distinction to be made between the imposition of a dogma, which closes debate and inhibits thought, and a dialectical process which recognizes bias, admits of real contrary positions and acknowledges the conflict of opposites.

It had long been an accepted wisdom within TIE that an absence of educational bias is neither possible nor desirable. Indeed, the overt challenging of received truths and accepted norms is seen as an essential step towards encouraging pupils to deepen their own thinking. The view of the GYPT company was therefore very clear. If the Forum was allowed to develop its own momentum moving from one intervention to the next without comment, it would rapidly become a theatre of alternatives which failed to offer any criteria for choosing between them. Each individual would be left to draw her or his own conclusions and would be likely to attribute the success or failure of the various interventions to the individual qualities of the participants rather than to the intrinsic effectiveness of those actions which were based on an understanding of the real world: all actions would simply be applauded as equally good ideas, all of them originating merely in the minds of the participants. In this case our existing judgements of ourselves as more or less intelligent individuals would be perpetuated.

If on the other hand the Joker was prepared to intervene in order to challenge the perceptions of the audience and help them towards an analysis of the inherent contradictions of the real world, then a less comfortable but more profound learning process would become a possibility. This approach did not merely raise a question of technique: it isolated important philosophical differences between the company's view of education (and the concomitant responsibility of the educator/artist) and Boal's own view of the role and function of his theatre and the artists within it.

The GYPT view was that the audience should be encouraged to reflect upon their actions as a group, articulating thoughts and feelings, challenging and being challenged by each other and by the Joker. The Joker should not impose his or her views but should most certainly accept the responsibility of the teacher to challenge assumptions, highlight contradictions and pursue disagreements. What is at stake is not only the possibility of taking different courses of action, but an understanding of the merits of those actions in relation to what people are trying to achieve, and the material circumstances in which they are trying to achieve it. (Do *I* want to keep *my* job or do *we* want to control *our* place of work? Who will oppose us? Why and how?) Even more important is the question of the *real* nature of the problem. (Is it my inadequacy or the employer's unreasonableness or our respective relationships to the means of production?) If the different perspectives are articulated and made openly available for debate then a shared learning can begin: if they are not, the danger is that the whole experience is at best therapeutic and at worst depressingly negative, circumscribed by the strengths and weaknesses of each individual's *isolated* attempt to solve a misapprehended problem. The intended strength of starting from the experiences and perceptions of each individual becomes a fatal weakness if these are not drawn into the social framework provided by the Forum and re-appraised collectively under the guidance derived from a progressive pedagogy – a pedagogy which recognizes that many of our received beliefs and perceptions are in fact false. The collective task is to distinguish truth from falsehood in our present reality in order that we may better construct our future reality.

These views do not imply that the educators should know the answers in advance or ignore the need for others to find their own solutions. But they do mean that we must abandon a position which says that all points of view are equally valid and that the teacher should only present the alternatives. It is the great fallacy of democracy that choice itself is beneficial: unless people are equipped to understand the true nature of the choices given, and can create their own agendas, the existence of alternatives is meaningless.

Boal's recent work seems, wittingly or unwittingly, to have ignored this problem. In the concluding paragraph of the new English version of *Games for Actors and Non-Actors* he proclaims, 'Let us be democratic and ask our audiences to tell us their desires, and let us show them alternatives' (1992: 247). This is a long way from the 'rehearsal for the revolution' and the language of dialectics to be found in the original *Theatre of the Oppressed*. He appears to be increasingly at pains to avoid being labelled or identified with any recognized ideology, perhaps in an attempt to avoid being pre-judged or constrained by expectation, or perhaps as a result of the political uncertainties besetting so many people in a rapidly changing world. In his practice his insistence upon the importance of personal experience appears to have turned much of his interventionist theatre towards a theatre of alternatives at the cognitive level and a theatre of therapy at the affective level. Indeed his newest original work is entitled *Méthode Boal de théâtre et de thérapie: l'arc-en-ciel du désir* (1990). This bears testimony to his increasing commitment to therapy and the development of the individual. Meanwhile, elsewhere in Europe, the spread of the Theatre of the Oppressed has spawned many groups using his techniques

Plate 6.2 A Question of Identity
A pupil intervenes to tackle a racist character in the Forum following
the performance of GYPT's *A Question of Identity*, a TIE play by John
Wood (1991).
Director: Lynne Suffolk. Photo: Martin Thomas.

to create their own theatre about their own oppressions to play back to their own groups. The groups can thus become locked into a circle of self-perpetuating perceptions and under these circumstances the work easily becomes diverted into an exercise in self-expression and mutual commiseration, a far cry from Boal's original intentions. TIE has never operated on this basis. It has always taken responsibility for selecting and shaping the material for its audiences in such a way as to help them make connections and deepen their understanding of their own experiences and other experiences which may *appear* to be very remote from them. Whilst elements of the Theatre of the Oppressed can be used to this end they will continue to be employed and developed, though perhaps diverging more and more markedly from Boal's own practice. Some companies have already rejected the work in its entirety. For them it is the product of idealistic thinking, and as such inherently reactionary. But for the GYPT company much of quality remains. As recently as the autumn of 1991 it used its own TIE version of Forum theatre to address the issues of contemporary racism. Whatever the present divergence, the debt to Augusto Boal for inspiring a decade of experimentation, development and debate remains incalculable.

BIBLIOGRAPHY

Boal, A. (1979) *Theatre of the Oppressed*, London: Pluto Press.
—— (1990) *Méthode Boal de théâtre et de therapie: l'arc-en-ciel du désir*, Paris: Editions Ramsay.
—— (1992) *Games for Actors and Non-Actors*, trans. Adrian Jackson, London: Routledge.
Freire, P. (1972) *The Pedagogy of the Oppressed*, London: Penguin.

Part III

International perspectives

Introduction

The chapters in this section represent just some of the developments and current practices in TIE or TIE-related work across the world. This is not a comprehensive coverage – among the many other countries that could have been represented are Eire, Finland, Poland, Tanzania, Kenya and the Philippines, to name only a few; nor does it represent all the main types of work to be seen. Rather it is an attempt to illustrate the range of that work and some of the ways it has emerged from and been influenced by the particular circumstances in which it takes place. Some countries (such as Australia) have clearly taken the British TIE model as their main starting point, with several British personnel having played pioneering roles; others have evolved similar models influenced at least as much by other developments in education and theatre. In all these countries however the work is evolving in its own way, and I have allowed contributors a fairly wide brief in how they describe it. While some have endeavoured to offer a broad overview of TIE work in their country, others have been more selective and have attempted to illustrate approaches through case-studies of recently presented programmes. Others again have chosen to highlight some of the particular problems or challenges, practical and/or theoretical, that are currently being faced. Thus the style, approach and emphases vary from chapter to chapter and country to country.

Despite the difficulties that may be faced in terms of funding, educational demands and social and cultural biases, what is clear from these essays is the strength and vitality of those experiments and the sense of collaborative exploration that characterizes them. Even where conditions do not allow for participative programmes with small groups of children, all the companies described here share a broad understanding of the need to reach young audiences in ways that go beyond the straight performance of a play, and have between them explored a variety of strategies to encourage the active engagement of children in their own learning.

Given the size of the USA and its long and impressive history of children's theatre, it is important to stress that the focus here upon the Creative Arts Team is not intended to represent all educational theatre across the country. CAT is indeed one of the most progressive TIE companies, and certainly the largest, in the USA, but there is a variety of other American companies too, some of whom are doing what we in Britain would recognize immediately as TIE or something closely related to it, but which has developed from quite different starting points. Thus, to take two contrasting companies: History Theatre of Ideas in Rhode Island developed from a concern with promoting an interest in local history in schools across the state. Professional actors are used to enact some of the major debates from American history in the classroom, structured so as to provide pupils with an opportunity to question the characters about their views and actions, thus bringing to life not just the historical figures but the felt experience of moral and political choices and the pressures to act in certain ways: history was not to be seen as a series of facts but as problematic tussles that for the participants at the time seemed far from matter-of-fact. In Minneapolis-St Paul, on the other side of the river from the prestigious, superbly resourced Children's Theatre, is the small schools-touring CLIMB Theatre company, founded originally to work exclusively with the disabled, but now also performing plays which touch children's most immediate concerns, such as peer-group pressure and bullying, and running drama workshops for children with and without disability throughout Minnesota schools. Their programmes, presented by 'actor–educators', are always accompanied by substantial teachers' packs and helpful information on further ways of dealing with seemingly intractable problems.

Chapter 7

Kites and magpies

TIE in Australia

John O'Toole and Penny Bundy

'TIE is dead' – or so assert a progressively larger number of major providers of all sorts of theatre in places called schools, during the last decade.

> I am now at a point where I believe only in the word 'Theatre'. All other terms serve only to keep the funding and power base status quo in place.
>
> > (Dickins 1992)[1]

> The desire to distance oneself from the term TIE over the last few years has been marked . . . . Dance in education may be OK but TIE is a no-no. Why? Is there a real smell of decay about TIE? Am I a necrophiliac for still being in it, enjoying it and supporting it?
>
> > (Joyce 1992)

Two more long-term views come from practitioners each of whom has worked in TIE in three states for over twenty years:

> TIE is firstly a writer's theatre – but it is also experiential. It is the only form of theatre which is and has remained relevant to and written to its audiences.
>
> > (Preston 1992)

> TIE must be properly connected to the curriculum, or have real contemporary relevance, or be shit-hot art, if it is to have any place in schools.
>
> > (Haley 1992)

Though these two might appear to be having their cake and eating it, their statements perhaps convey best the ebullience which has characterized TIE in Australia.

THE BRITISH INFLUENCE AND ITS DECLINE

The term Theatre in Education came into general use in Australia round about the same time as in Britain, the late 1960s and early 1970s. It was consciously promoted in the same way, as a departure from previous traditions, and was certainly influenced by Britain's burgeoning movement. As in the UK, there had been travelling teams providing theatrical services in schools for many years, mostly 'to arouse enthusiasm for poetry [and Shakespeare] among secondary students and doing primary shows' (MacKenzie 1992). This long-established tradition still exists, with at least one obstinate survivor in Queensland (The Grin and Tonic Theatre Troupe) eschewing politics, purveying the Bard, Banjo Patterson and *Beauty and the Beast* in roughly equal amounts – it must be said with passion, theatrical skill and elegant form, and very popular with the schools, too.

In the 1970s Britain was very influential, in TIE as in DIE. One of the energies which led to major growth here too was excitement with Coventry Belgrade's initiative. In this growth period, companies were founded which have been continuously influential ever since. Some of these followed visits to the UK – such as Salamanca TIE in Tasmania and Sidetrack Community Theatre in Western Sydney. Major touring companies like Toe Truck and Freewheels in New South Wales absorbed the educational ideas and the language, while being consciously Australian in their concentration on performance and Australian content. Others were even more directly UK-inspired: one ex-Belgrade actor–teacher, Roger Chapman, came out and founded Magpie in Adelaide; another, David Young, has worked both in Western Australia and, until recently, as Director of Salamanca. In Queensland a Briton co-founded the Brisbane Early Childhood Drama Project (since transmogrified into KITE, much less of a mouthful), and Albert Hunt's visit to Australia was the spark for the now defunct Popular Theatre Troupe. Among the few direct interchanges between the two nations, Britain's David Holman has written programmes for both Magpie and KITE.

The Australian state-wide (and that means *very* wide) schools systems were much less responsive to the kind of LEA drama adviser-inspired initiative which produced so many of the

British teams of the period. However, a few education department funded teams did emerge, notably Salamanca, the Bouverie St team in Melbourne and its offshoots in Ballarat and
Benalla, Darwin's TIE/DIE and Brisbane's above-mentioned
Early Childhood team. Significantly, only the last survives with
its educational funding source intact. Ballarat gets help, but has
to pass the hat around; Salamanca is left stranded but surviving.
The others are dead, and most other education departments
pay only token alms. One Melbourne worker and observer
claims that 'a killer of TIE is the gradual abdication of education department funds from it' (Milne 1992). He identifies 1987
as a particularly bad year, when TIE/DIE and Bouverie St both
lost their funds and expired. The movement is by no means
unanimous that this is a bad thing, however. Another TIE
observer in the same city suggests that educational funding has
two major drawbacks. First, any increase has tended to create a
plethora of new groups of little substance or quality, leading
to general dissatisfaction, withdrawal of funds and recurring
cycles of boom and bust. Second, a sycophantic attitude to their
educational masters is engendered: 'As long as TIE accepts
educational rather than theatrical money and serves rather
than leads education, it will remain a peripheral learning tool –
a novelty rather than a vigorous force for change in the schools
and our way of life' (Galbraith 1992).

AUSTRALIAN THEATRE

The difference in funding sources is a pointer to other differences. Among these are Australia's geography and its educational systems, both of which will be dealt with later. Another is
Australia's post-colonial identity, which coincidentally was
undergoing a major maturation during the seventies, both
politically and theatrically. Following the long years of the
anglophile Prime Minister Menzies, British influence was dominant and largely unchecked in the arts. The local theatre was
not fully professional in all states. Not only play tours and
playscripts, but directors and academics too all poured in from
England, and were usually given jobs before the locals, who
were generally perceived as inferior or certainly less sophisticated (many quality locals had gone to England to pursue a
'proper' career, anyway). The early seventies saw the brief but

important accession of Gough Whitlam, much more restrictive immigration from Britain, and a deliberate artistic revolt against Australia's 'cultural cringe'. This was most noticeable in Sydney and Melbourne, where it coincided with a revolt against 'the museum theatre being dished up by the Melbourne Theatre Company and the Old Tote' (i.e. the state theatres) (Stevenson 1992), and crystallized into two aggressively Australian alternative theatre companies, the Australian Performing Group (APG) in Melbourne and Nimrod in Sydney, who provided a blaze of creative energy, a rash of new playwrights and directors and a significant proportion of Australia's current theatrical élite. They consciously created an Australian voice. Similar energies were at work in all other states.

This considerably complicated the TIE movement from the 1970s onwards. On the one hand, Australian theatre workers and educators were attracted to what they saw as participatory, popular theatre forms emanating from Europe, from the British fringe, from ASSITEJ and SCYPT. Most shared the dominant left-wing political and ideological orientations, too. On the other hand, these same people were struggling to find an identity of form and content independent of Britain's and Europe's cultural hegemony, whatever the political colour.

This is probably one of the several reasons why those classic British-style programmes with integral participation for small groups have never been generally popular in Australia, with only a few companies using participation regularly, and most workers either very wary or turning up their nose. For those who do still subscribe to the form, the geographical and financial exigencies have largely restricted their output to one-off projects or student tours from tertiary institutions. As early as 1981, we heard the slogan, oft-repeated since with apparent relief, 'the Coventry style TIE is obsolete, it's had its day' (Manning 1981) – which we took to mean participatory TIE with small groups; whether the relief was inspired more by financial considerations or theatrical philosophy is hard to say. Perhaps it also acknowledged that to do this well was often just too hard.

The truth is, there has been so little integral participation in Australia that few workers have actually seen it well done, and many have either only heard about it or seen the half-baked efforts which led to such perspectives as:

The more you move towards the notion of audience participation, the more you move towards the traditional participatory
lesson, being held in a classroom. Where is the magic of
theatre in that? Such experiences become simulation rather
than true experience.

(Galbraith 1992)

Drama teachers might be affronted by this definition of 'true
experience', but it holds true for many TIE workers. More
caustic still is this observation by one of Australia's most
respected adult playwrights, Alex Buzo (one of those 1970s
Sydney radicals), 'The TIE people do a great job educating
children, but it's not art and it's not entertainment' (Buzo,
1988: 44).

Australia's theatre profession is small and crowded. There is
a smaller gap between 'heritage/mainstream' and 'alternative/
community' theatre than in the UK. This means that actors,
directors and writers have to earn a crust where they can. In the
case of TIE this frequently means long and often rigorous city
or outback tours, in teams chosen by state theatre companies
with other funding priorities: cheap teams of young actors bent
on a potential mainstream career, working alongside dedicated
community theatre workers. Nor has TIE had the informal
umbrella of being seen as an eccentric but committed part of
the fringe. Rather, 'the prestige of TIE in the eyes of the
professional theatre was (and is) low' (MacKenzie, 1992: 47).

Buzo's baleful comment has been widely canvassed around
Australia, and very influential, though it is actually symptomatic
of a broader, very important concern of 'the TIE people' themselves. In fact, it has stung the really committed into proving
that TIE *is* real theatre, which can mix it with the best in actors
and directors, and is certainly not subservient to any narrowly
educational imperatives. This is expressed clearly by Magpie's
current Director: 'Schools are where TIE companies find their
audiences; it doesn't have to be where they find their form or
content' (Gration 1992). Though a contemporary comment,
this points to a major feature of Australian TIE, its development
as a writer's theatre that actually gives the lie to Buzo. The early
interest by adult playwrights like David Williamson in participatory forms, particularly group devising, was echoed in reverse
in TIE's growing interest in the playwright's contribution:

> I was seldom entirely satisfied with group devised shows. A good playwright is a person of special talent as well as skill . . . not always available among a small company of actors.

> [In group devised shows] . . . either the director or an actor fulfils the function of a writer, transcribing improvisations, editing, structuring, polishing or creating original material. The result of this process is that the writer's role becomes unacknowledged, invisible. This feeds into the concept that writers aren't necessary, a concept I feel that is less than honest.
>
> (both quoted in Fotheringham 1987: 44–6)

The first speaker here, Barbara Manning at Salamanca, was among the earliest of a long line of TIE directors to commission works, both from specialist writers like Anne Harvey, Pat Cranney (the second quoted), Richard Davey and Chris Dickins, and from some of Australia's most distinguished adult playwrights like Dorothy Hewett and John Romeril. New writers like Aboriginal playwright Jack Davis and Peta Murray cut their teeth on TIE shows. Some TIE shows have become all-age classics, like Davey's *Annie's Coming Out* and Davis's *Kullark*.

AUSTRALIAN EDUCATION

To fully understand this move towards adult theatre forms and away from those of drama in education, it is necessary to understand Australian systems of education, and the ambivalent attitudes of TIE companies to them. The same ambivalence may exist in the UK, but the systems here are very different, and, I believe, the gap in understanding between team and teacher wider.

First, the relevant external factors. As in the UK, Australian schools are divided into private and state, but with a smaller class divide. The state systems have traditionally had execrably poor funding by British standards. Each state has a single education department, which has been encouraging regional autonomy for only the last five years in over a hundred, and operates over tracts of land unthinkable in the UK, each with thousands of schools. They are a part of state governmental public service, headed by a minister, and the kind of direct government intervention in education which has been seen only in recent years in the UK is part of the landscape. Accordingly, syllabi and curricula have been traditionally very centralized and very conservative. The kind of humane scholarship of Dewey, Read, Bruner, etc. which drove British education when TIE was born, especially in the post-Plowden primary sector, was barely seen until recently; educational research and scholarship were overwhelmingly behaviouristic and have tended to reinforce the mechanistic and hierarchical administrative structures. Accordingly, odd things have happened, such as the growth of drama in education from the top down in some states (notably Western Australia and Queensland).

Second, within the schools themselves, traditional promotion by length of service also reinforced hierarchy, conformity and caution – along with a fear of nonconformity or enthusiasm. The teacher was not the monarch of the classroom, but rather the functionary of the Principal, who was in turn subservient to the education department and its inspectors. These traditionally have had a negative function, to ensure that the department's rules and policies are being correctly carried out by schools and teachers, and therefore absolutely not agents of encouraging innovation, like the HMI (Her Majesty's Inspectorate of Schools) in Britain in the 1960s and 1970s.

This was the school landscape into which Australian TIE teams attempted to insert themselves. Added to this, only in one or two states – notably Tasmania – had drama established sufficient status and acceptance, particularly in primary schools, for the team's visit to be consistently welcomed with an actively understanding staff response. All Australian TIE teams are very familiar with the Principal who greets them with the quip: 'Oh there's plenty of drama goes on in this school!' . . . i.e. there is none, merely lots of real-life initiatives from the students which he interprets as dangerous or disruptive to the even running of his school. This Principal invariably introduces the performance with a homily to the students along the lines of 'Now we're fortunate today to have some guests who are going to do a little play for you which I think you [not "we"] are going to find quite amusing, and you're going to show them how well-behaved you can be, aren't you?', equally afraid that the children will not be an appropriately passive, silent audience for the guests, and that the guests themselves might release some of those anarchic tendencies for which the arts are so notorious. Class teachers take their cue from the Principal's attitude and bring their marking into the performance or slope off for a coffee and a free period.

This picture of bleak ignorance needs of course to be contrasted with the excitement and enthusiasm which greets the same teams in more open schools – usually smaller schools, and often in the bush, where the team does provide a rare and deeply appreciated contact with the world outside. In such places, the team's visit becomes a whole community event (and some teams prepare for this with offerings for the adults, too). In this context, the normally terrible 'post-show discussion' – where the students do not ask penetrating questions about the programme's theme, but what it's like to be an actor, whether you get lots of girl friends and what do you do in real life – takes on a new and real meaning for people keen to know and starved of contacts. Even in these kinds of schools where TIE is welcomed, educational possibilities take second place to social imperatives, such as true Australian egalitarianism. Nearly all schools are fully comprehensive, with the advantages and disadvantages that entails. One of the authors has on occasion run foul of this, for instance when attempting to arrange a participatory programme for a limited audience, and a restricted age-range. The Principal is very likely to insist that all the year nine classes (14 to 15 year-olds) must have the programme – and usually the years eight and ten, as well as the year eleven class whose teacher is away today; it is not fair to discriminate, and if all the students can't have the experience then we don't want it, thank you. This has been embedded as official policy in Queensland, as we shall see.

However those two contrasting reactions to a TIE visit, the suspicious door-ajar and the welcome mat, have one common implication, that there has been very limited dialogue between teachers on the one hand and the TIE teams on the other. The British pattern of predominantly local teams, able to make regular return visits to the same schools and even classes, supported by the LEA drama adviser, with an advisory committee including teachers, has had much more opportunity to develop understanding in the schools of what TIE is about. Most Australian teams tour widely, and to recover their costs have to play to very large numbers of schools and children.

The educational advisory committee to an individual TIE

company, though not unheard-of (Salamanca and KITE both have one), is very rare. The programme preview for interested teachers is even rarer and geography often precludes it, anyway. Taking their place in most states, sometimes as the only organ of contact between TIE team and educational bodies, is some system of statewide assessment and/or quality control. That the administrative systems feel the need to control the product entering their schools is an implicit acknowledgement that the teachers do not themselves have discretion and sufficient access to knowledge or the time to make their own judgements.

CASE-STUDY 1: A TALE OF TWO CERTIFICATES

To paraphrase Dickens: it was the best of ideas and it was the worst of ideas. The attempts by education systems to control or at least harness any revolutionary tendencies of TIE have taken a number of forms, some more benevolent than others. In South Australia, for instance, all performance arrangements are channelled through the centralized Carclew youth arts centre, which acts as an informal information centre to schools and companies. In Victoria the education department's Drama Resource Centre, which itself included a TIE team, did much the same, until it was shut down in 1987, and produced a booklet for teachers detailing all the offerings – which vestigially survives, privately produced. Now form is reversed; TIE is the territory of the Ministry for the Arts, which jealously resents any interference from teachers, even journal reviews by the very active drama teachers' association VADIE. In defence of its territory, it is currently putting out a set of guidelines, not for teams, but for teachers.

This implied notion that educators should have no say in the arts being offered to schoolchildren is at an extreme opposite pole to the interventionist position taken by officialdom in New South Wales and Queensland – which themselves form a revealing contrast to each other.

Certificate A: New South Wales (NSW)

NSW has had far less co-ordination than Victoria or South Australia of its drama provision, inside and outside the school systems. In the mid-1980s, in the wake of the success of quality independent companies like Toe Truck, Freewheels and the Riverina Trucking Company, there was a proliferation of TIE especially in the Sydney area. The Department of Education became concerned at its variable quality and responsibility, and tended to intervene very conservatively, in ways often indicating incomprehension of how drama works, or the intentions of the programmes. A telling incident shows the depth of this incomprehension. *The Mathemagician* was a simple primary programme devised by Magpie TIE in South Australia, about a child who did not like mathematics; by the end of the programme, with the help of the participant audience and the lure of computers, the child was converted into a fan of mathematics. Harmless, even predictable stuff, one might think. Magpie at the end of a successful run sold the show lock, stock and props to NSW's Toe Truck, who rehearsed it with no qualms. It was not approved by the NSW education department, on the grounds that Toe Truck's team constraints meant that the maths-hater was a girl, therefore a poor role-model for the audiences. Fortunately, this misunderstanding of how drama works was not totally pervasive, and in 1985 their Drama Education Officer prepared a policy which the Director-General and TIE teams could both endorse. It was obvious that the autonomy of choice granted to South Australian schools was beyond the ken of the NSW bureaucracy, but the officer did want to stop the ignorant suppression of genuine enterprise and even genuinely contentious learning experiences.

> We are not into censorship – we know that for dealing with a controversial issue, like say AIDS, that's when you want to turn to TIE as the perfect medium for making it safe to handle in schools. On the other hand, schools don't have time to preview everything, and need to be protected from garbage.
>
> (Haley 1992)

Accordingly, after considerable consultation, NSW produced a policy statement incorporating a set of guidelines. These outline the procedures necessary to obtain department accreditation, involving joint advisory groups (including nominees from the companies), feedback forms and a two-year 'approval' period, as well as standardized systems for booking, information to schools, and so on. Non-accredited companies can still perform in schools, but only at the discretion of the Principal.

There is also, significantly, a set of appeal procedures for those who have been refused accreditation, involving consultation and second reviews.

The statement also incorporates a clear guide to what schools should be able to expect from TIE, such as (all quotations from Performances for Schools 1985):

A performance of high quality, presented by artists skilled in performing for and working with an audience of school pupils.

A well-planned performance with pre-performance material available if appropriate to all teachers to prepare the audience.

A performance in which the duration, cast and form are as stated in the publicity material and as evaluated by the advisory group.

Involvement of the audience appropriate to the performing arts experience being offered.

A performance that can serve as a valuable resource for pupils. It should be an experience which can be well integrated with the rest of the school's learning activities.

Enlightenedly, the policy also lays down to the schools the performers' expectations:

That schools will provide an audience of the agreed size and age range to view the performance at the scheduled time.

That the teachers have prepared the audience for the performance to be presented.

That school staff will co-operate with the performers to ensure that it runs smoothly and is an effective part of the school day.

That students will be aware of what is required of an audience. There will be adults present, from the school and community, who will provide models of appropriate behaviour.

The teachers will use the pre-performance and follow-up material, if provided, to maximise the effectiveness of the performing arts experience.

Seven years after its implementation, a TIE director's verdict is:

It's a great document – to have it to refer to – and the regional advisory groups too, they're very supportive, with the more timid schools. Like, we have this programme for six year olds where we use the words penis and vagina, and some of the schools are nervous, but we can turn round and say that it's the advisory groups, and the department, who instruct us to use those words.

(Joyce 1992)

Certificate B: Queensland

This is a far cry from Queensland, where the whole history has been and continues different, and by comparison, poverty-stricken. In this state 'moralysis' set in early, and did not lose its hold until rapid changes across the whole field of education accompanied political change in the late 1980s. Nowadays, regional autonomy, innovation and enterprise in education are valued as officially as they were once feared – everywhere, it seems, except in the Queensland Arts Council. This centralized and 'moralysed' body was originally set up to encourage adult performances in the bush, but was some years ago entrusted with the assessment of all TIE in state schools, and still controls all performers' visits to schools. Its policy document is a master-piece of patronage, which leads off with the significantly negative phraseology:

No programme is permitted to tour into state schools and charge a fee without written approval. All approved groups carry a certificate of authorisation signed by the Director General of Education and the General Manager of Queensland Arts Council.

A sort of quarantine certificate, but more pompous. Though there is an acknowledgment of 'the principle that access to the arts is not a luxury for the few but essential for all' and a set of commitments, nowhere amongst those commitments is any awareness of a connection between the arts and any kind of learning, or that one function of drama is to raise questions and provoke, at the very least, discussion. The document contains some extraordinary directives, such as (all quotations from *Your Questions Answered* 1992):

All programs should be approximately 50–60 minutes

duration. Preschool and lower primary programs should take into consideration the shorter concentration span of these students.

Primary companies do not offer workshops to schools. . . . Secondary workshops are usually of one hour's duration. All workshops conducted by touring companies require to be auditioned.

Artists who tour under the auspices of Queensland Arts Council [and remember, you can't tour any other way] provide programs for all students in either primary or secondary year levels. For example, a company with a program suitable for preschool to year 3 should also offer a program for years 4–7 inclusive.

The average audience size is 145 students.

The average number of artists in a company is two but some companies consist of up to four artists.

So much for participation, so much for variety, so much for artistic autonomy – and so much for the well-known ability of infants to concentrate for hours if they are interested. It makes one warm to the territorialism of Victoria's Ministry of the Arts. This written policy is administered quite as dogmatically as it is written. Some very talented drama teachers and consultants are roped in to view the fearsome 'assessment performances', and provide valuable professional advice. However, the council functionaries have the last word, and judgements sometimes exhibit a deep ignorance of the way both drama and learning work – as in the example given below of why *Grandpa Won't Budge* was knocked back. The number of TIE teams in Queensland remains small, the amount of quality work smaller, the amount of new work even smaller, and there is little evidence of growth of understanding of the potential of TIE among teachers or students. There are very few university students we speak to who can recall a TIE programme which stirred or moved them in school. It is a wonder, in fact, that any good TIE survives in Queensland. It does, of course, and parallels the rest of the movement across Australia, taking the initial impetus from Britain, then moving away from British terminology and tentative exploration of participation, towards a writer's theatre. The state theatre company team, like others, eschews the term TIE and sees itself as a community theatre which sometimes works in schools. Very untypically, the other main company, KITE, one of the last education funded teams in the country, is just discovering a new interest in participation and DIE forms.

This macro picture is clearly reflected in the following micro account, in her own words, of an individual TIE worker. Penny Bundy, a trained primary teacher with a background of drama in education, started a decade ago as an actor–teacher with the preschool TIE team KITE. It may be noticed that she lists, as those who have significantly developed TIE in Australia, writers, directors, performers and designers. Teachers are not included.

CASE-STUDY 2: FROM ACTOR–TEACHER TO TIE PLAYWRIGHT

One of my major influences in relation to KITE's work and TIE in general was David Holman's *Solomon and the Big Cat* in 1985. The concept of the whole venture was new in Queensland: this was the first time KITE had commissioned writer, designer and outside director. The show was performed in the imposing Queensland Performing Arts Centre. The money spent on the production was massive, compared to the normal possibilities of such a team. The public and media profiles were huge.

While these factors did affect the work, they were not the most influential ones on me. Rather, I became interested in the content and style of the script and the way the audience was moved differently by the material. KITE's previous work, similar to much Australian TIE, was directed by what I would call 'school issues' rather than a broader concept of 'educational value'. The characters in much previous work were little more than caricatures. Stories were simple, hardly challenging in an emotional sense. *Solomon and the Big Cat* was different. The 4 to 5 year-old children in the audiences responded with both laughter and tears. It reached beyond the shores of Australia and presented adult and child characters involved in a real-life issue, the slaughter of leopards for their skins. The audience was not shielded from the truth, but exposed to it. Theatre became a very powerful medium.

Was it possible to produce the same theatrical power away from that sort of venue, without those facilities and resources –

in a classroom or school hall? I believed it was. With KITE members supporting my desire to write a new show, rather than tour as a performer, in the following season I wrote *A Mugwump of My Own*. Though this was received well and is still in repertoire, it did not meet my expectations. The characters were still limited, the play shallow and one-dimensional.

I had lost interest in being a performer. To continue to explore the writing side meant leaving KITE and going free-lance. I hoped that by combining my skills and interests in directing and writing for TIE, and working in youth theatre, I might just about be able to live!

The first job I was offered was to direct a young people's performance at La Boîte Theatre, where the director had pulled out at the last minute. The play had been selected, the actors cast. Great, I thought . . . until I took the script home. I hated it. It was everything I thought young people's theatre/TIE should not be. I rang Jim Vilé, the theatre's artistic director, and told him what I thought. His response was: 'You write one then.' I had three weeks. The resultant play, *Rain! Rain! Come Again!* was based on an aboriginal dreaming story with a current setting. I played with masks, large stylized puppets and a soundscape of music to create desired moods. While these elements were effective, the characters and plot were still too simplistic.

With the continued backing of Jim and the Australia Council I was able to keep exploring. The result was *Grandpa Won't Budge*. For the first time I felt happy with the work. I had achieved more complex characters. The story was simple without being simplistic: Grandpa lives with his granddaughter Emma. On the day the local council comes to demolish their house, Grandpa won't budge. The play explored several issues: what it means to be old, and old in our society, the changing relationship between grandparent and grandchild, and ideas of magic and truth. Child, parent and teacher audiences reacted enthusiastically. Unfortunately the play did not get Queensland Arts Council approval, so was unable to tour in Queensland. The objection was to one line: Emma asked what would happen to her if Grandpa was put in an old people's home. The reply was: 'A nice foster home will be found.' This was apparently too brutal, and children should be protected from knowledge of such places. I thought the 'brutality' necessary and was not willing to change it.

The theatre and the Australia Council continued to support my work, and *Treehouse* was written the following year. I began with what others might term an educational aim – to explore the subject of deafness. To me it was broader. I saw it, as I see any good theatre, as an exploration of the human condition. I wanted to investigate how lack of communication leads to prejudice. (I wonder as I write this: was it a reaction to the censorship of the previous work?) I had observed among the children with whom I'd worked that these prejudices were beginning as young as four or five years old. Could I produce a piece of theatre which would be a powerful enough experience to shake their preconceptions?

After six months' research, the central character emerged: an oral deaf boy named Simon. The action takes place at Sarah's treehouse on the common ground shared by two flats, when Simon moves next door. Lack of communication amongst the characters, some of it provoked by deafness, leads to continual misunderstandings and moments both comic and emotional.

I felt I had managed to create complex, well-developed characters. From experience, I found that careful pacing of the action, particularly in relation to entrances and exits, kept the youngest children thoroughly involved. The play, forty minutes long with three actors and a simple portable set, met budgetary constraints as well as Queensland Arts Council's unique criteria for a touring show. The reaction in schools was fantastic. Typical feedback was, 'The play contained a range of emotions – anger, bewilderment, delight – and the timing of the action caused amusement in the audience. The story was amusing yet easy to follow. The children were intrigued.' Many teachers felt that this was a positive way to handle a concept they would find difficult to deal with in the classroom. A significant number of comments saddened me: some were surprised that children would be so engrossed in a show that was serious. Others felt that the show must have been successful because the children had laughed. This seems to me to be a poor criterion for judging success. The actors too found it necessary before the show to explain to the children that this would be different from previous theatre because they would not be asked to call out.

As I look back at my time in Australian TIE change can be seen. It has certainly developed in the quality (if not quantity) of experience it offers children. As I see it, this has been achieved through the dedication and growth of understanding of writers, directors, performers and designers who maintain a commitment to theatre for young people. If TIE is to continue to develop, the support of school personnel is necessary. This will only be achieved when more of these understand and value the medium. We have still got a long way to go.

NOTES

1 Special thanks to the following battle-hardened practitioners for their insight, much of which is incorporated, as well as from their verbatim quotes acknowledged below (from interviews and questionnaires, 1992):

> Chris Dickins, Director, Barnstorm Theatre, Ballarat
> Rob Galbraith, Education Officer, Victorian Arts Centre
> Steven Gration, Director, Magpie Company South Australia
> Jane Haley, now Senior Policy Officer, Queensland Division of the Arts
> Brian Joyce, Director, Freewheels TIE, Newcastle NSW
> Geoff Milne, Lecturer, La Trobe University Victoria
> Malcolm Moore, Coordinator, Theatre Administration, Western Australian Academy of the Performing Arts
> John Preston, Lecturer, Prahran TAFE College Victoria

and to the many other people who gave useful advice and perspectives, including:

> Bryan Nason, Director, Grin and Tonic Theatre Troupe, Queensland
> Paul Stevenson, an early member of Melbourne's APG
> Barbara Manning, Salamanca's founder.

BIBLIOGRAPHY

Buzo, A. (1988) *The Young Person's Guide to the Theatre and Almost Everything Else*, Melbourne: Penguin Books.
Fotheringham, R. (1987) *Community Theatre in Australia*, Melbourne: Methuen.
MacKenzie, D. (1992) 'A history of TIE in New South Wales', *Do It* 51, Sydney: NSW Educational Drama Association.
Performances for Schools: Policy Statement (1985), Sydney: New South Wales Department of Education.
Your Questions Answered (1992), Brisbane: Queensland Arts Council and Queensland Department of Education.

Chapter 8

Establishment or alternative?

Two Canadian models

Wayne Fairhead

BACKGROUND

Canada operates very much on a regional basis and this idio-syncrasy pervades all aspects of life. Education is a provincial matter, and thus there are great variations across the country. There is no national curriculum. As a result, the position of the arts varies according to the agenda of the provincial political party in power at the time. For drama educators this is a tricky business; for professional theatre companies who specialize in work for children and youth, it is a constant concern.

Learning through theatre is not a new phenomenon in Canada. There were individuals scattered across the country who were working in the medium in schools early in this century. Among them was Herman Voaden who created what became known as 'symphonic theatre'. A teacher and a play-wright, he saw an opportunity for young people to understand the land through their involvement with his plays and the theatre process.

He was very much influenced by what was happening in the visual arts, especially the work of Canada's 'Group of Seven', and his exposure to Appia and Craig, among others, in pre-World War II Europe also had a lasting influence. The pioneer-ing use of theatre by Voaden in the 1930s and 1940s in a large secondary school in downtown Toronto, complemented and enriched his writing and the staging of such plays as *Rocks, Earth Song, Hill-land, Murder Pattern* and *Ascend as the Sun*. In these works such elemental qualities as Canada's vastness, natural beauty and lurking dangers were explored.

Voaden incorporated his progressive thinking into his style of teaching, exposing students to new ways of coming at the learning process. In his time this early promoter of theatre, as both a distinct art form and a medium through which to learn, was considered somewhat eccentric by the education community. He was, however, a man ahead of his time. In 1974 Mr Voaden was appointed a Member of the Order of Canada.

During the first half of the twentieth century there was no professional theatre for young people; and it was not until the late 1960s that Dramatic (or Theatre) Arts was included, in some provinces, as an accepted subject in secondary schools. Up until the mid-1960s, with some exceptions, drama was still thought of by most educators as being 'acting' and 'putting on plays'! With the 1970s 'came the change in a big way' (Fairhead 1985: 236). The influence of such drama educators as Peter Slade and Brian Way from the 1950s and 1960s began to take hold, as did the impact of Dorothy Heathcote and Gavin Bolton later in the 1970s. These influential educators had a major effect on the role of drama and Theatre in Education in English-speaking Canada. Even though these same educators were known to Quebec and had some influence, 'unlike the rest of Canada, the development of drama in Quebec has been most strongly influenced by France' (Fairhead: 238). These influences must be considered in relationship to the realities of history: Canada is part of the 'new world' and has had to grow out of a colonial mentality that implies the belief that someone else always knows better.

Unfortunately much of the theatre for young audiences prior to the 1970s was coming from artists who were doing it in order to make ends meet and as a stepping-stone to the real thing – adult or what was termed 'legitimate theatre'. Even in 1977 a future artistic director of a now well-known Theatre for Young Audiences (TYA) company stated: 'Like most actors doing kids' plays, I would rather be doing straight dramatic roles' (Doolittle and Barnich 1979: 51). Because the first plays for young audiences had been done as add-ons by established theatres, there persisted this 'second-rate' attitude, which was also perpetuated by the types of plays presented.

With the onset of drama as a learner-centred process in education, juxtaposed against what had been a rather limited view of Theatre for Young Audiences, new opportunities and relationships between the two communities, theatre and education, began to evolve. This included a gradual comprehension of the drama–theatre continuum. In the 1970s and 1980s there had been a rejection of theatre by many drama educators – especially those working with elementary students. But with the partnerships that were developing, and with a better understanding by both teachers and TYA practitioners of the needs of students, the mutual benefits of the continuum were being experienced. It is, as Gavin Bolton states, necessary for a good drama teacher to 'move forward on all of these fronts simultaneously' (Bolton 1992: 108–9).[1]

As we move into the 1990s some companies are grasping the complexities of working within an educational framework and finding ways to do so with integrity. Effective drama teachers have always understood the need for providing meaningful theatre experiences for their students. In Canada, meeting this need is not easy due to the fact that it is an immigrant-based country and, consequently, multi-faceted in terms of differing values and expectations.

There are companies meeting this challenge and their work is respected both locally and internationally. A senior officer for the US National Endowment for the Arts, comparing various levels of artistic development in the US and Canada, quoted in an article by Christopher Wootten (former Artistic Director of Vancouver Children's Festival and former Executive Director of the Ontario Arts Council), observed: 'One area where the work done in Canada is way ahead of our own is in theatre and music for young audiences' (Wootten 1988: 1). And in the same article there is reference to the tenuous credibility within the theatre community which the efforts of artists for children and youth have:

> There still exists a bias that this work is less challenging and less prestigious than working for adult companies. There's still the notion that the work provides teachers and adults with time for a coffee break, while the children are entertained for forty-five minutes. Considering the work done recently by such companies as Green Thumb Theatre, Theatre Direct and Théâtre de la Marmaille, this attitude is preposterous.
>
> (ibid.)

One thing that Wootten suggests is that companies give public performances so that parents can attend with their children. New directions in Canadian education certainly encourage more effective partnerships between schools and their different communities. This is already being explored by many TYA organizations in various ways.

Although economically times are difficult and, as I write, the future political structure of Canada lies in the balance, the 1990s are proving fertile ground for renewed and strengthened relationships between TYA companies and educators. Barriers have been broken down, more teachers and artists understand the process–product continuum, and more also realize the need for change in terms of such socio-political issues as racism, equity of access to opportunities and the environment. These are unifying factors.

In 1991 fifty TYA companies responded to a survey from which a report called *The Status of Canadian Theatres for Young Audiences* was prepared. Significantly the data revealed that during the 1990–1 season these fifty companies anticipated playing to nearly 2.5 million people (or 9.4 per cent of the Canadian population). There were more than 200 productions being mounted, 84 per cent of which were of Canadian scripts. Thirty per cent of the productions were commissioned and 15 per cent of new works were shaped through a series of workshops by the company. The research also revealed a trend towards 'second productions' of Canadian scripts with a proven track record.

Obviously the number of companies across the country is too great for all to be mentioned, let alone discussed in any detail. So I will refer briefly to a cross-section of them, and then look in more detail at two quite different theatre companies – both in Toronto as these are the ones that I know best. One can be described loosely as 'establishment' and the other 'alternative'. But then these terms are somewhat inadequate in today's climate.

A CROSS-SECTION OF TYA COMPANIES

Founded in 1975, Green Thumb has had a profound influence both upon the genre of scripts for young people and upon the growth of non-patronizing theatre for children and youth. Based in Vancouver, British Columbia, its mandate is to develop original, topical Canadian plays for young audiences and to explore contemporary issues (illiteracy, immigration, family dislocation, native culture) with an emphasis on 'enlightenment, entertainment and education'.

Perhaps more than any other Canadian TYA company, Green Thumb's original scripts have both a national and international reputation; their work has been staged by 200 theatre companies worldwide and translated into Chinese, French, Spanish, German, Danish, Hebrew and Japanese. In addition, the company has toured extensively across Canada and the US, as well as to Australia, New Zealand, Hong Kong, Singapore, the UK, the Netherlands, Germany and Sweden. Particularly successful have been co-production ventures with such companies as Grips Theatre (Germany).

Special mention should be made of the outstanding work by playwright Dennis Foon, whose visions helped shape Green Thumb's philosophy. His plays include *Skin* which won a Governor-General Award for Drama as Best Published Children's Play in 1988, *New Canadian Kid* which won a British Theatre Award for Best Children's Play in 1985, and *Mirror Game* (1989) recently published by Blizzard Publishing (Winnipeg, 1992).

Green Thumb's emphasis upon building a supportive and interactive community as their home-base provides an example for all TYA companies. The lessons taught by the company through their insightful theatre are getting through to a wide cross-section of people, as illustrated by David (9) who was moved to say after seeing a Green Thumb production: 'I learned that some day a frog might be considered a treasure . . . and if we do not stop polluting that day may come' (Green Thumb 1992); and by Mr R. H. McLean (Public Relations Manager, Imperial Oil Limited): 'We feel that Green Thumb Theatre is providing relevant services to the children in our Canadian and world community through the production and presentation of plays dealing with real issues in an effective way' (ibid.).

In Quebec, as in English Canada, the first theatre for children was created by established companies. (Beauchamp 1985: 245) 'Newly formed collectives of the 1970s defined the theatre they would create for the young by refusing what was then produced, and especially all that spoke of magic, the marvellous and make-believe. They refused the worlds of fairies and dwarfs, of kings and princesses, of happy endings' (Beauchamp 1992: 15). One of the companies that grew out of this context was Théâtre de la Marmaille. Founded in 1973, it has created eighteen new plays and, like Green Thumb, has toured extensively across Canada and the US, to Australia, Central America, Africa and some parts of Europe. Co-founded by Daniel Meilleur, Monique Rioux and France Mercille, the company's work has always had a solid research component behind it. Also, especially during a production's formative period, children are themselves involved in validating the on-going process. In other words, they have the opportunity to respond to the work as it is being developed; and their responses influence the final product. La Marmaille's most recent work, *The Tale of Teeka*, examines the roots of brutality and the transmission of violence and can be viewed on many levels by children, youth and adults. 'We undertook to study one of the most obscure of the human soul's innate drives: violence,' said director Daniel Meilleur (Meilleur 1992).

Quebec companies have always placed an emphasis on authentic research as part of the learning process. Another major difference between Quebecois productions and those of English Canada is their imagistic and action-based qualities. Dynamo Théâtre, for example, places much emphasis on the acrobatic and visual image elements.

Hélène Beauchamp (1979: 180) observed that in Quebec: 'Since 1972, the mainstream of questioning has been related to the definition of "young audiences" and to the knowledge of children. It is now time to enquire into production techniques, into the theatrical translation of play contents as well as the use of specific styles.' Indeed that is just what innovative companies such as Marmaille (*Histoire de l'oie*), Dynamo Théâtre (*The Challenge*) and others have been doing.

The Prairie Theatre Exchange in Winnipeg, Manitoba, has within its statement of mission (1991) specifically: 'to operate a school to encourage appreciation of theatre and to provide accessible, high-quality, innovative drama education'. And in their value statement is included:

Our drama education program is committed to providing people with a healthy artistic expression to encourage them to grow to love and appreciate theatre as a dynamic art form and as an important aspect of their lives, an exciting and challenging medium through which they can communicate their hopes, their fears, their needs, their concerns, their ideas, their stories.

The goals of the PTE include involving people 'who have brought non-Western European cultural traditions to Winnipeg'. Specific goals for the PTE School include both the promotion of drama as a learning process and teaching method in the general curriculum, and the fostering of an appreciation of theatre as an aesthetic experience and an expressive medium. These are interesting goals, reflecting those of various provincial Ministries of Education written early in the 1980s.

On the east coast, Mermaid Theatre of Nova Scotia, with its home in Windsor, regularly tours schools. Founded in 1972, it also operates a respected puppetry school and a challenging youth program. This exclusively TYA company is one of Nova Scotia's major cultural employers. It regularly tours Canada and the US, and has represented Canada in Australia, Japan, Mexico and the UK.

Recently, an apprentice programme in puppetry was created, supported by funding from Employment and Immigration Canada and administered by the Canadian Conference of the Arts. The aim is to train a new generation of artists who can work in the multi-media style of presentation which is Mermaid's signature. It includes a blending of mask, puppetry, movement and music.

As well as touring their innovative versions of children's classic tales, Mermaid encourages young writers (Doug Curtis's *Black Ice and Red Adidas,* and the six-week summer New Play Collective for high school students) and brings in guest artists (such as Sirppa Sivori-Asp from Helsinki's Green Apple Puppet Theatre).

Other outstanding TYA companies across the country include The Globe Theatre's School Tour Company (Regina), Theatre-on-the-Move (Toronto), The Hour Company (Toronto), Carousel Players (St. Catharines) and Théâtre Petit à Petit (Quebec).

ESTABLISHMENT AND ALTERNATIVE

Two TYA companies that illustrate the powerful possibilities for learning on many levels are the well-established Young People's Theatre and the dynamic Theatre Direct Canada. These two companies are based in downtown Toronto.

As the country's largest professional theatre for young audiences, Young People's Theatre creates a wide range of work in two spaces – a studio and a mainstage. It also tours, maintains a school for elementary and secondary students, provides workshops for teachers, facilitates community forums and has originated a playwriting festival for young writers. What is unique about Young People's Theatre is the range of services offered to the education community and the public; what is very encouraging is the forward-thinking vision of its Artistic Director.

Young People's Theatre is primarily curriculum- and market-driven. Its staff is conscious of the perceived needs of students and teachers, and the theatre gears its work to meet these needs. A large organization with thirty-five full-time employees during the season and 468 seats to fill, there is always the danger of it becoming élitist due to rising ticket prices which tend to attract students and adults from higher economic brackets.

To address the needs of children and youth seeking more in-depth theatre experiences, Young People's Theatre offers classes on Saturdays and conducts a Summer Theatre School. Students work with professional teachers under the direction of Theatre School Director, Peter Gallagher. All classes use a theme (selected by the participants) as a focus for their work. Young People's Theatre's relationships with teachers is such that many educators plan thematically around the plays being offered.

In 1992–3 a series of workshops addressing changes in approach to education in Ontario was offered. Patterson Fardell (Director, Young People's Theatre Educational Services) invited well-known drama educators to lead workshops at the theatre in the following areas: conflict resolution, environmental concerns, arts integration and interrelationships, and storytelling.

Maja Ardal, the company's recently appointed Artistic Director, sees a need for developing new and deeper ties with the education community. Her vision is the creation of an arts centre where students, teachers and artists could come together in a variety of ways, through workshops, residencies, the creation of a museum of work by children and professional artists. Ardal's vision carries on from where the previous Artistic Director, Peter Moss, left off – namely, the desire to create a place accessible to all schools regardless of their socio-economic placement. In particular, she sees the need to make Young People's Theatre more appealing to adolescents by creating programmes and productions specifically for them.

The 1992–3 Season, Young People's Theatre's twenty-seventh, contained seven plays. The four mainstage productions included two newly commissioned adaptations of children's classics, Shakespeare's *A Midsummer Night's Dream* and the Canadian première of British writer David Holman's *Whale*. The three productions that toured schools, as well as having short runs in Young People's Theatre's Studio Theatre, were all issue-oriented pieces: Dennis Foon's *Mirror Game* which is about abuse and the cycle of violence; a new play from South Africa, *In Search of Dragon's Mountain*, about racism; and Marcy Rogers' *The Secret of Shhh*, a new Canadian script that explores the area of communications accessibility.

Young People's Theatre has a strong mandate to encourage family involvement through its family membership. Sixty dollars (for up to six members) entitles you to advance mailings, priority seating, a complimentary poster, an invitation to the annual family members' party and a tax receipt. This focus influences the plays chosen to be performed on the mainstage. Usually these tend to be adaptations of fairly conservative classics and productions of socially acceptable pieces such as David Holman's *Whale*, a wonderful celebration of the need to protect our environment. A quotation used by Holman in his Preface epitomizes the warm optimism Young People's Theatre is aiming for with its mainstage shows. It is a prophecy from a member of British Columbia's Kwakiutl tribe:

When the Earth has been ravaged and the animals are dying, a tribe of people from all races, creeds and colours will put their faith in deeds, not words, to make the land green again. They will be called 'Warriors of the Rainbow', protectors of the Environment.

(Holman 1989)

Whereas these mainstage productions are family oriented, the touring shows relate more specifically to the needs of children and youth.

On the other hand, Theatre Direct Canada is consistently on the 'cutting edge' with its work. It is, says General Manager Jessica Fraser, 'artist-driven, not market-driven' (in interview, 1992) – unlike Young People's Theatre. Consequently the productions are always powerful because they are expressions of the individual artist's values. The company's mandate is 'to engage youth through compelling, inventive and uncompromising theatre'. Its major focus is on the development, production and presentation of Canadian plays which provoke, challenge and question. This artistic honesty can pose financial hardships for the company when some educators refuse to book some of the shows.

Founded in 1976, Theatre Direct has mounted twenty-eight new Canadian plays for more than two million young people across the country. Its relationship with the theatre community is special in that it has consistently provided creative and challenging opportunities for both emerging and established artists. The company has maintained a youthful component to its artistic approach, allowing for an energetic and natural evolution of new theatrical forms.

Former Artistic Producer, Susan Serran, created quite a stir in the education community when she stated: 'Creating theatre that will resonate in the mind and heart requires a freedom of artistic expression that is not traditionally welcomed – especially in the corridors of our educational system' (Serran 1989: 4). The strength of Theatre Direct is that it has continued to create and provide meaningful theatre for young audiences regardless of some opposition; in so doing it has become more accessible and acceptable. This is partly due to efforts initiated by the company's management and artistic leadership, and partly because social values have shifted, especially in relation to issues such as racism, violence and abuse, the environment and AIDS. But the company's non-traditional approach is both courageous and necessary. At the same time, it continues to work towards a partnership with various sectors of the community (education, business), exposing young people to alternative ways of thinking and experimental presentation styles.

In the 1991–2 season Theatre Direct remounted *Flesh and Blood* by Colin Thomas. This important play about AIDS prompted current Artistic Producer Andrey Tarasiuk to comment: 'In the schools there are those educators who have chosen to bring their classes to see the play as well as to work honestly with their students to discuss such themes as prejudice and tolerance' (interview, 1992). Such statements in the press as: '*Flesh and Blood* is simply the latest in a long line of strong productions that are doing their bit to combat some of the more insidious side-effects of social conditioning. This makes it, as one colleague of mine puts it, "necessary theatre"' (Mira Friedlander, freelance arts journalist) and '*Flesh and Blood* can only enhance Theatre Direct's reputation as a consistently daring producer of theatre for young audiences' (Vit Wagner, the *Toronto Star*), are testimony to the artistic and social necessity of this company's work.

Whereas Young People's Theatre sees its mandate as being very much integrated with the education system, Theatre Direct Canada maintains an independence: it is in the business of creating powerful theatre as an art form that can stand alone. Concise, provocative teaching guides are provided by both companies.

Commenting on the 1992–3 season, Tarasiuk says it 'is a reflection of our continuing commitment to new Canadian play development which engages, provokes, questions and empowers a youth-oriented audience to reflect upon the social issues that affect their society'. And indeed it does, beginning with Ojibway playwright Drew Hayden Taylor's *Toronto at Dreamer's Rock*. This play was originally commissioned by the De-ba-jeh-mu-jig Theatre Group (Wikwemikong Reservation, Manitoulin Island)[2] and subsequently won the 1992 Chalmers Children's Play Award. It is about Rusty (an Odawa teenager living in the present), Keesic (from the past) and Michael (from the future). Rusty has made the long climb to the top of Dreamer's Rock, a large stony outcropping overlooking a beautiful valley. For thousands of years, this has been a sacred site for vision quests by his people. Here he meets Keesic and Michael, and together they debate questions about their cultural heritage and its place in the future.

The second production was Edward Roy's *A Secret Life*. This piece was testing the company's creative abilities as it was performed in two ways; the first production was environmentally staged, the second toured. The play focuses on three teenagers, each with their own 'secret'. It explores the themes of violence in schools, poverty, adult illiteracy and prejudice. Roy has written *A Secret Life* to be performed in specific school locations with the audience moving from scene to scene and interacting with the performers. To meet this demand, the first production was set in a school that is presently closed to students. The audiences were bussed in to this simulated high school location. The logistics of the subsequent tour certainly taxed the creative and human relations abilities of Theatre Direct Canada's crew and cast. These productions of *A Secret Life* continue Theatre Direct Canada's role of exposing youth to new scripts and new theatre forms.

Apart from these two major projects, the company also workshopped two 'plays in development'. The first one, in co-production with Green Thumb Theatre, was *Little Sister* by Joan MacLeod. This piece, by one of Canada's most exciting playwrights, deals with eating disorders, particularly as experienced by women. *The Girl Who Loved Her Horses*, based upon a short story by Drew Taylor, was the second 'play in development'. It was be directed and dramatized by Andrey Tarasiuk, Artistic Director of Theatre Direct Canada. The play is set both on a reservation and in the city. Taylor's new play deals with the issues of prejudice and identity, while celebrating the power of individual creativity.

Theatre for young audiences in Canada walks a tightrope between 'good theatre' and educational needs and directions. At times the space below is murky. But out of this very risky 'walk' have arisen some very definite attitudes and visions. Young People's Theatre and Theatre Direct Canada exemplify this on-going process of definition.

Young People's Theatre operates out of the 'traditional' venue of its own theatre, whereas Theatre Direct Canada is a floating company without a theatre space to call home. Maja Ardal, Young People's Theatre's Artistic Director, spent many of her formative years working in Toronto's first alternative theatre, the now defunct Toronto Workshop Productions. Many of her ideas (community involvement and universal opportunity to attend young people's theatre events and activities) and aspirations hark back to those days. Theatre Direct Canada operates a more independently minded operation depending for success upon artistic integrity and experimentation. These elements make it an 'alternative' company. However, the realities of the market place make dialogue with the community, especially the education sector, vital. Collaboration with teachers and involving students in new works development is an important aspect of Theatre Direct Canada's work.

Neither group is a TIE company in the British sense, but both reflect evolving approaches to learning by providing interactive theatre experiences for young people and permanent opportunities for artists to develop their skills within the unique genre of theatre for young audiences. The successful continuation of this process is dependent upon nurturing present partnerships and upon the creation of new ones with education, business, social agencies, community organizations and parent groups.

NOTES

1 The 'fronts' referred to by Bolton are content, personal growth, social development and the dramatic art form.
2 De-ba-jeh-mu-jig Theatre Group is an adult theatre company that also does work relevant to young people.

BIBLIOGRAPHY

Beauchamp, H. (1979) 'Theatre in Quebec', in J. Doolittle and Z. Barnich (eds) *A Mirror of our Dreams: Children and the Theatre in Canada*, Vancouver: Talon Books.
—— (1985) 'That "other" theatre: children's theatre in Quebec', in A. Wagner (ed.) *Contemporary Canadian Theatre: New World Visions*, Toronto: Simon & Pierre.
—— (1992), 'Forms and functions of scenography: theatre productions for young audiences in Quebec', *Canadian Theatre Review* Spring.
Bolton, G. (1992) *New Perspectives on Classroom Drama*, London: Simon & Schuster.
Doolittle, J. and Barnich, Z. (1979) *A Mirror of our Dreams: Children and the Theatre in Canada*, Vancouver: Talon Books.
Fairhead, W. (1985) 'Drama in education', in A. Wagner (ed.) *Contemporary Canadian Theatre: New World Visions*, Toronto: Simon & Pierre.
Green Thumb Theatre for Young People (1991) *Status of Canadian Theatre for Young Audiences Entering the 1990s*, Vancouver.

Green Thumb Theatre for Young People (1992) *Profile*, Vancouver.

Holman, D. (1989) *Whale*, London: Methuen.

Meilleur, D. (1992) *Festival of Theatre for the New World* (programme), Toronto.

Serran, S. (1989) 'Censored . . . schools' reaction to Theatre Direct's shows', *Canadian Theatre Review* Fall.

Wootten, C. (1988). 'Canadian Theatre for Young Audiences', *Directions* 1 (2), Toronto: Theatre Direct Canada.

Chapter 9

Unmasking the masquerades
The potential of TIE in Nigeria

Jumai Ewu and Tunde Lakoju

A BRIEF OVERVIEW OF THEATRE IN NIGERIA

Nigeria has a very vibrant theatre culture. Every rural community can boast of a performance tradition. Traditional performances, in which the masquerade phenomenon is most dominant, are mainly ritual based. Most of them have, however, now lost both their ritual bases and their spiritual functions. With urbanization and the attendant Western cultural penetration, through Christianity and education, most of our traditional performances have been sapped of their ritual essence. They have either been forced to move from their socio-cultural rural contexts in search of new roots within the urban cultures or have willingly moved in search of economic patronage and social visibility. This inevitable development has its consequences. For instance, outside of their traditional rural roots they become mere entertainments. Their ritual essence is lost on their new audiences, who are mainly interested in the exotic elements and moments of the performances. To such new audiences the solemn moments communicate no message or meaning. Also in such new settings the medium of performances must inevitably shift from the original 'native' idiom to an adulterated idiom that the new audiences can comprehend. These are the inevitable consequences of modernization.

The urban centres are the meeting points of many performing traditions. Every state has its Centre for Arts and Culture whose most important mandate seems to be the commodification of the various traditional performances of their respective states. These are 'refined' and made available to a national audience via the annual Festival of Arts and Culture. After each of such festivals the television stations spend the rest of the year exchanging video tapes of the various performances recorded during the festivals.

At such festivals it would be quickly noticed that the mask has persisted as a central image in Nigerian traditional performances. The masks are usually of different shapes, colours and sizes, but they all perform approximately the same symbolic functions. They are either vehicles of transition or effective shields through which important social or political comments may be made without giving away the commentator. When worn, masks are not just mere costumes, they become metaphysical mechanisms through which ancestral spirits courier to our objective world, on visits to their living offsprings. The human body of the mask-wearer is assumed to have dissolved to allow the ancestral spirit to inhabit him. He or she then becomes a medium, whose voice becomes the unmistakable voice of the ancestral spirit. The awe a particular mask conjures is determined by the venerability of the ancestral spirit itself. Every masquerade, by the mere look of it, has its unique identity, which all initiated members of the community recognize.

But the masquerades are being rapidly unmasked or demystified. The masquerades encountered during state or national festivals perform very little or no ritual or spiritual functions. Away from their traditional cultural roots, they do no more than entertain. The colour and sophistication of a masquerade are, therefore, no longer determined by the stature of the ancestral spirit of which it is a medium, but are now rather an index of the relative affluence of the owner. The masquerade culture has responded to market forces. Whoever has the means can now own a masquerade, as opposed to the cultural imperative that communities, through their various cults, own masquerades. In a few rural communities, however, masquerades are still communally owned and still perform their diagnostic and prognostic ritual functions.

As has been observed above, the urban settings are the melting pots of rich but adulterated traditional performances. These find expressions through the live stage and the electronic media, radio and television. But by far the most vibrant of the performing traditions in our urban settings is the itinerant or travelling theatre, dominated by the Yorubas (Adedeji 1981).

This theatrical form borrows very largely from traditional performances, especially its elaborate use of costumes, music, dance and songs, that allows the audiences full mental and physical participation. Like its antecedent, the traditional theatre, the travelling theatres build their performances around the talents of the best performer, usually the owner of the theatre, who plays all the major roles. The medium of performance is usually one of the major languages – Yoruba, Igbo or Hausa – or Pidgin English, which is the urban working-class language and Nigeria's unacknowledged lingua franca. Most of the plays in the repertoire of these theatres are not based on any written scripts. They are collectively devised around some current gossip picked up from local customary courts, beer parlours, market places or interpretations of myths and folk tales. The plays are usually of topical relevance even though treated superficially. The beauty of the performances is in the form rather than the content of the plays. In modern Nigeria the travelling theatre movement was pioneered by the late Hubert Ogunde, Duro Ladipo and Kola Ogunmola. By the last count there were over a hundred and fifty such theatres in the Yoruba dominated western states of Nigeria.

Of great importance also is our rich harvest of literary theatre. Following the pioneering examples of Wole Soyinka (the Nobel laureate), J. P. Clark and Ola Rotimi, the terrain now witnesses radical playwrights like Femi Osofisan, Bode Sowande, Segun Oyekunle and Bode Osayin, to name but a few. Apart from their exploration of traditional motifs, these playwrights all borrow profusely from traditional forms in their use of music, dance, songs and costumes. In their dramatic techniques, however, as a result of their education, they borrow extensively from Western classical traditions of play-making. In their plays one notices a rich blend of Western artistic canons and traditional forms in the exploration of current social and political realities.

Worthy of note is the popular theatre tradition now fast gaining ground in Nigeria. This unapologetically Marxist-based theatre tradition started in the mid-1970s at the Ahmadu Bello University, Zaria.[1] The tradition has since been embraced by many of the universities and colleges of education in the country. Essentially this is a theatre form anchored on the principle that theatre should be taken to the people rather than wait for the people to come to the theatre. It has for its content the immediate reality of the people – their fears, anxieties, crises, aspirations – it incorporates the familiar performing traditions which, along with the dominant language of the audience, form the main means of expression. Because it deals with the reality of the audience which is dynamic, the emphasis is on the process rather than the final performance. In a sense, therefore, it is a rehearsal theatre, involving the people as the actors of their own experiences. From data gathering to story-making, through scenario-making, rehearsals and final productions, the people are very involved. Usually the plays are deliberately designed to admit 'interruptions' and interventions – by any members of the audience who feel that actions are not unfolding in the 'right' direction. Its subversive potential makes this theatre also a favourite of the working-class and radical youths, mainly university students. The ruling class has never been comfortable with this theatre form and has taken consistent steps to check its growth and spread.

Although they are addressed mainly to an adult audience, all these theatre forms have serious implications for the emergence of TIE in the country. A viable TIE movement must not only recognize the active presence of the various theatre traditions previewed above, but must borrow from and build on the strengths of all the above traditions.

THEATRE FOR CHILDREN

While child audiences are not deliberately excluded from the venues of performances, the performances themselves are not particularly addressed to them, though there are of course a few exceptions.

Storytelling performances

From a cultural standpoint, the storytelling performance is the most popular and influential performance tradition for children. Children everywhere love stories. They love them even more when the telling of the stories is accompanied by dramatic activity, which further vivifies the experiences narrated. The storytelling performance is a mixture of various art forms which include drama, narrative, poetry, music and dance. These, in addition to masks and costumes, are utilized as vehicles of expression while spectacle and colour provide a means of sharpening the aesthetic feelings and talents of children. Such performance is the most effective and the most subtle instrument of educating and socializing the child, and because the stories are performed mainly by adults, the themes usually reflect the anxieties of adults for children. Thus performances are geared towards inducting the unsuspecting children into the dominant values and cultures. Usually both the narrator and his or her audience, in their different roles, are drawn together in creating meaning which orders and perceives the society in a particular way. The flexibility of the performances, the relaxed and free atmosphere of the settings, unhampered by unnecessary structural forms such as prescribed buildings, platforms or auditoria, create an atmosphere in which both the performer and the audiences are hardly conscious of the potency of the activity in which they are actively engaged.

The performances function as a means of communicating, recording, preserving and giving meaning to tales or legends. Apart from passing on the history of the society from one generation to the next, the more ceremonial storytelling performances also serve political and religious functions. They are often performed to reaffirm, reconsolidate and justify existing power structures.

Storytelling performances generally have considerable educational and entertainment values for both children and adults. The two values always overlap. There is entertainment in the characterization of the various characters, the twists of the plots, the fantastic settings, the irony of situations and the rendering of the narrator. There is entertainment also in the cathartic quality of some of the tales.

Improvisation is a characteristic feature of storytelling performances. The performer has to be able to compose or substitute new material derived from his or her environment. The ability to adapt the performance to the circumstances of the immediate environment, in order to suit audience, time and place, distinguishes the talented performer from his or her less talented counterpart. This usually makes the tales contemporaneous and more acceptable. The tales must have meaning for the here and now. This way the children are in time taught to be observant of what goes on around them.

Puppetry

The art of puppetry is not as common in Nigeria as it is in some other regions of the world where it has been part of a long-established entertainment tradition, especially for children.

By far the most sophisticated and most popular folk theatre of its kind is the Kwagh-hir puppet theatre of the Tiv. It is still to be found existing in communities settled in Gboko, Makurdi and Katsina Ala of Benue State. Kwagh-hir is a relatively recent performance form dating from the early 1960s, although its roots lie in the more ancient tradition of the storytelling performance. According to reports, the origins of Kwagh-hir can be traced to the violent riots of 1960 and 1964. It is an art form that emerged to challenge an oppressive political party, the NPC (Northern People's Congress) and the type of feudal government it imposed on the people (Hagher 1981: 10). As a mouthpiece for the political protests, the function of Kwagh-hir was to offer social criticism against the ruling administration and to counsel the audience on correct social behaviour. This function combines the traditional educational function of story-telling performance with the new function which the tradition has been called to serve as a result of changing socio-political circumstances. As Etherton verifies, the Kwagh-hir is

a performance dynamic which combines the various tradi-tional artistic elements to depict that change metaphorically. The Kwagh-hir lies in the interstices between the traditional and essentially rural arts inherited from the past, and the fully fledged urban theatre performances of travelling theatre com-panies like the Ogunde Theatre Company which are grassroots artistic products by urban folk for their own communities.

(Etherton 1982: 40)

In its present form the Kwagh-hir is a composite art form involving music, song, mime, dialogue and poetry. The various characters are drawn from the animal, human and supernatural worlds while the performers include the various puppets backed by a musical orchestra. The puppets in use vary in size and style, ranging from the very simple rod and string puppets to the large masquerade puppets which require more than one person inside each to animate its movable parts.

The narrator is a must in every performance, which comprises short vignettes. It is the narrator who provides the vital links that clarify the meanings of the sketches. He or she motivates both puppets and audience, urging the latter's participation. The narrator's jokes, versatility and flexibility are said to add to the celebratory mood of the performance. The orchestra, which is supported by the audience as chorus, provides the music for the dances, mimes and interludes.

Although historically Kwagh-hir is an art form created deliberately by adults to articulate their protests against an oppressive system, children are not altogether left out of its existing repertoire. But here again the intentions of the adult performers are clear. There are sketches that are used to frighten children into obedience and conformity. Among the masquerade puppets is the Gaga Nyam (hippopotamus). It is an animal masquerade puppet that is believed to swallow children who refuse to work. With the aid of two men crouched in the belly of the costume, the masquerade is animated to scare children among the audience. Another masquerade puppet, Anyamagurugu, is used to evoke fear in crying children to silence them (Hagher 1981: 208).

Puppetry is fast developing as a compelling theatre form for children in Nigeria. The Nigerian Television Authority (NTA) in Jos, Plateau State, has popularized puppetry for children's education and entertainment. Its one-hour slots every Sunday have been taken over as a national network programme watched by over thirty million viewers across the nation. Many other television stations have come up with their own versions of the Jos pioneering programme.

TIE IN NIGERIA

At this point in time we can only discuss the potential of TIE in Nigeria because the movement is still in its formative stages when compared with the highly developed British model. The first national debate on the subject took place in Benin city, Edo State, in 1986, with the presentation of a paper at the annual conference of the Nigerian Educational Research Association (NERA) (Lakoju 1988).

Since that historic debate TIE as a discipline has found its way into the curriculum of teacher education in Nigeria. At the Nigeria Certificate in Education (NCE) level, TIE is now available both as a compulsory and as an optional course. It is an optional course for teacher trainees majoring in Science or Social Sciences, while those specializing in English Language and Literature in English take it as a compulsory course. It is also compulsory for all those majoring in Theatre Arts Education at that level.

Nigeria is moving rapidly towards professionalizing teaching. Towards this end, 1998 has been given as a deadline when all practising teachers in Nigeria must possess as a minimum the Nigeria Certificate in Education. The NCE will therefore become the minimum entry qualification into the teaching profession in Nigeria. At present there are about fifty-six colleges of education producing NCE teachers to staff the primary and junior-secondary classes in Nigeria. The National Teachers' Institute, some universities and a few colleges of education are also licensed to train NCE teachers on sandwich, correspondence or part-time courses.

All of these institutions utilize the same standard curricula produced by the National Commission for Colleges of Education (NCCE), the body charged with the responsibility for producing the minimum standards for training teachers at that level.[2] With the inclusion of TIE in the curriculum of the NCE programme, it means that sooner than later all the teachers in the nation's primary and junior-secondary schools will be able to engage in or participate actively in TIE programmes. Naturally not all those who go through the course will wish to practise it but at least they would all know what TIE is all about and might be less hostile to the movement and its practitioners.

A proposed Nigerian TIE model

The TIE model being proposed for Nigeria is not radically different from the British model. To some extent it shares the same radical ideological backdrop, but it will, we hope, benefit from and transcend some of the problems which the British movement has been facing in recent times.

Philosophical Background

Essentially the British model of TIE has drawn predominantly upon Marxist philosophies of one kind or another. Until recently most of those involved in the movement have been either left-wing or at least have had such inclinations. We are aware, of course, that within the movement there is an ideological struggle between the orthodox Marxists, the neo-Marxists and the liberal and some right-wing elements. This inevitable but unfortunate internal struggle within the movement, as exemplified by the ideological struggle for the leadership of SCYPT, has made the movement very vulnerable to attack and cuts by the establishment who see the movement as a threat.

Due to its own peculiar circumstances, the Nigerian model of TIE would adopt a liberal philosophy on the understanding that even the most reactionary education system has the potential for producing radicals. Considering that Nigeria is a peripheral capitalist state we are aware of the hidden agenda that education or the school system is expected to serve – to produce socialized rather than educated individuals. Socialized individuals would be more willing to accept the dominant values as given, while educated individuals are likely to be more critical. We are aware that a truly revolutionary educator is not one who recites Marxist liturgy before his or her students but one who succeeds in provoking disturbances in their minds which lead them to question existing facts or knowledge, in the hope of creating new facts or knowledge.

Considering that the average child is confronted by many and varied conflicting ideologies, and considering that the child spends more time outside the school than in, and considering also that TIE experience takes only a minute portion of the child's school time, we see the futility in trying to feed children with slogans they may never fully digest before they are countered by the realities of their life. Having managed to get TIE into the school curriculum where many converts are waiting we see a danger in posing it as a radical alternative to the dominant ideology.

Aims and objectives

Culturally children and women are to be seen and not heard. What Paulo Friere described as the culture of silence is a living reality in the upbringing of children in most developing countries, of which Nigeria is one. In a typical school setting the teacher, whose words are infallible, commands the image of authority. Not even a more enlightened parent can convince a child that it has been misinformed by its teacher. Above all, the printed word is believed to be a gospel fact, which even the infallible teacher cannot contest.

TIE will seek to show the children that every so-called fact can be explored beyond its boundary. It will attempt to give to children the tools for asking questions and for exploring alternative possibilities to any fact or area of knowledge. Like the British model the Nigerian TIE model will not aim to serve any school subject directly but would attempt to explore the matters arising from the facts of the subjects being taught. Propaganda or indoctrination would not be on the agenda; rather the actor–teachers would seek to provoke disturbances, at the affective level, in the minds of the children, of a kind that leads them into a deeper reflection about a particular reality that is unfolding before them, and possibly action too.

Content

The education system insists that abilities shall be tested through examinations, and examinations are based on prescribed syllabuses, which teachers must cover and pupils must learn. Our model of TIE will seek to support the teacher in assisting children to learn facts critically since they may utilize the knowledge in real life, which is far more unpredictable than the secure atmosphere of the classroom. But above all our model of TIE will attempt to explore the human aspect of knowledge.

Form

We have already briefly analysed the various manifestations of our rich theatrical heritage. We hope that our TIE model will borrow unapologetically from all these robust traditions. We shall utilize to the full our potentials of dance, song, music and mime. We shall explore the potential offered by masks and puppets. We are fascinated by the powerful role played by the narrator in our storytelling performances. We will de-emphasize the proscenium arch and play more in the round to motivate audience participation, as is the case with our traditional performances. However, actor–teachers will be more animateurs than actors.

Structure and process

We consider the structure of the British model as ideal. Likewise the process will involve research and data collection, story and scenario-making, then play-making. We also consider preproduction and post-production workshops as crucial stages of the process.

Funding

This is where we hope to learn from the mistakes made by many British TIE companies in the past. A form that claims to be antiestablishment cannot honestly expect adequate patronage from that system. As the English saying goes, whoever pays the piper must inevitably dictate the tune. As of right the Nigerian child is entitled to a balanced education. That is what our model of TIE will attempt to give. Whatever type of government the country has, whether socialist, communist or capitalist, our model will not seek to confront it. It will seek to assist the child in understanding the true nature of the system, its vital strengths and weaknesses.

From such a position we shall canvass support from government, corporate bodies and individuals. More importantly we shall canvass to make TIE an integral part of the school system; hence it may not require any special funding outside of the normal budgetary allocations to education.

Administration

It will be unrealistic to adopt the egalitarian style of the British model where all actor–teachers are equal in status. Our observation is that this style of administration is not conducive to group discipline. Some kind of hierarchy of authority is necessary for effective management. Also the registration of companies as limited liability companies is, in our view, counterproductive. It makes them vulnerable as they are forced to operate within the framework of an intricate legal system which most company members either may not fully comprehend or even care to read. The authorities can easily evoke the provisions of the law to deal with 'erring' companies.

The Nigerian model shall operate within the school system. All actor–teachers shall be employees of the state or local government education authorities and their salaries and conditions of service shall be determined by the appropriate education authorities based on their qualifications and experiences.

The drama

In Britain there is an on-going debate about the relative advantages of a group-devised play over a commissioned script. In Nigeria both methods are currently in use. The subject-matter of the production and the complexity of available data will dictate which approach to adopt. If the subject is complex the group will brainstorm and feed a playwright with the facts to create a script. A playwright is better able to explore the depths of a complex subject and come up with viable conflicts, characterization and effective dialogue. If the subject is straightforward the group can deal with it collectively and come up with a good production.

We may now examine the first known TIE programme in Nigeria. Our hope is that our theory will inform our practice and that practical experience will help to strengthen, modify or expand our theory. The experiment reported below is our first tentative step in that direction.

AS YOU MAKE YOUR BED

As You Make Your Bed was funded by the Family Health Services Division of the Johns Hopkins University, Baltimore, Maryland, USA. In Nigeria it was co-sponsored by the Kaduna State Ministries of Education and Health. A consultant and a staff member of the Family Health Services project in Nigeria, and two staff of the Kaduna State Ministry of Health, were assigned to work with the theatre company to produce the programme. Kaduna State was going to be used as pilot. Based on the success of the programme, it may be either sponsored for a nationwide tour or filmed for national and international distribution.

The funding body dictated what was required. Between June and July 1990 they had commissioned a study on adolescent fertility in Kenya and Nigeria (Barker and Rich 1990). The primary objective of the study tour was to meet with organizations and individuals with an interest in the issue of adolescent fertility in Kenya and Nigeria to gather their perceptions on the following:

(a) the scope of adolescent fertility in the two countries;
(b) the perception of the issue of adolescent fertility, i.e. is it perceived as a problem?
(c) early marriages and the consequences of teenage pregnancies.

To collect information the study group carried out the following activities:

(a) interviewed key individuals working on the issues of family planning, sex education and youth development;
(b) visited projects working in adolescent pregnancy prevention and interviewed peer promoters working with some of the projects;
(c) interviewed and observed youth in formal settings, including discos, movie theatres and public beaches;
(d) conducted focus group interviews with youth in Mombasa, Kenya, Zaria and Ibadan in Nigeria; and
(e) conducted a literature search on teenage pregnancy in Africa.

The most revealing findings of the Nigerian group included the fact that in the predominantly Muslim northern Nigeria, girls can legally marry as early as the age of nine, and that both religion and culture strongly sanction early marriage – primarily to guard against the social disaster of out-of-wedlock pregnancy and also to preserve the purity of young girls. The attendant early childbearing in this part of the country has the biomedical outcomes of vescovaginal fistulae (VVF), maternal mortality and infant mortality. VVF is caused by obstructed labour in young girls or by 'gishuri' cuts inflicted by traditional midwives during difficult deliveries. Education for girls was noted as being the prime variable in early marriage, but the precarious economic situation in Nigeria was also noted as a contributing factor to early childbearing, forcing many young girls into situations of sexual exploitation such as accepting the offers of 'sugar daddies', older men who offer to pay the school expenses or provide other gifts to young girls in exchange for sex. Young people interviewed by the group talked about the lack of information on sexuality and family planning, and the taboos associated with talking about sex with the immediate family. The interviewees also mentioned that their main sources of information are equally misinformed peers, locally printed 'adult' comic books and magazines which offer skewed and sexist messages, and 'adult' foreign movies. High rates of illegal abortions and sexually transmitted diseases (STDs) were also mentioned as concerns. Young schoolgirls who get pregnant often resort to back-room abortionists and a good number either get killed or have their wombs damaged. As in most societies, sex is powerful and mysterious in African culture. Parents are extremely embarrassed to talk about sex and leave their children clueless about the mechanisms of reproduction. While some are just plain shy to talk about it, others feel they do not know much about it, and some believe that if youths are aware of sexual matters, they will begin experimenting. The full report of the study group was made available to the TIE specialists after an elaborate exchange of ideas about the subject of adolescent sexuality and teenage pregnancy,[3] and a script was commissioned that would highlight the critical findings of the study group.

The dialogue began in November 1991 between the Nigerian consultant to the Family Health Services and the playwright.[4] The final script entitled *As You Make Your Bed* was completed in December of the same year.

As You Make Your Bed is cast within the storytelling tradition. The narrator, an old woman approaching her eighties, tells the story of two families in the imaginary semi-urban town of Maradi. Each of the families had a pretty daughter. The relatively wealthy family had a daughter called Hauwa, while the poor family had a daughter called Amina. Both girls were about fifteen years of age and were classmates in the first year at the senior secondary school. Hauwa's father Alhaji, was a successful business man and her mother was a chief executive in a bank. They had a housemaid who did all the cooking and household chores. Hajiya, Hauwa's mother, over-indulged Hauwa. Hauwa did nothing at home besides eating her food (cooked and served by the housemaid) and going out in search of sugar daddies with her best friend Binta. Amina on the other hand came from a poor but very caring home. There was an intense rapport between her and her parents, who showed much concern for her development and progress at school. Amina grew to be a very successful person. She did well at school, got a scholarship to read medicine at university and later became a very successful medical doctor. She was also a happy wife and the proud mother of four beautiful children. She set up her private medical practice in the town of Koko. Hauwa, on the other hand, was a pathetic failure. She dropped out of school, having lost her parents in a car crash. She lost her best friend Binta, who died of some strange venereal disease. Hauwa had two children but could not be sure who were the fathers. By the time the play ends Hauwa was in a private hospital receiving treatment for a complicated third pregnancy. The doctor treating her was none other than Amina, her former classmate. Recognition came at a critical moment during the diagnosis and there was a freeze. The pathetic image of Hauwa holding back tears, and a successful Amina, had a very powerful emotional effect on the audiences. Two songs ended the play. The first, *Too Late*, came while all the characters were still in a freeze, and it ran thus:

CHORUS: Too late, too late, too late, too late.

REFRAIN: One certain morning when the sun was shining (*twice*)
Hauwa left her parents after men
We tried to talk to Hauwa but no use
Hauwa kept running after wealth
We talked, we begged
Oh Hauwa . . .
Oh oh oh oh oh oh oh oh.

CHORUS: Too late, too late, too late, too late.

The second song came when the characters came out of the freeze and Hauwa was being led away by the doctor and nurse who had brought her to the hospital. The song, *Life is a Cycle*, ran thus:

Life is a cycle
What you plant you reap
It is not always rosy
Please be careful

From the synopsis above the play would appear to be a simplistic moral tale, but characterization and conflicts were manipulated to make simplistic moral statements difficult. Until the last scene, when Hauwa was broken, she attracted much admiration from the audience, most of whom tended to identify with her fast life. Rather than condemn Hauwa for being a bad girl, the young audiences, during the post-production workshops, blamed her parents for not giving her the right education and guidance.

The structure of the play was episodic to admit the intervention of the powerful narrator who compelled the audience to look beyond the action of the play. At critical moments she called in the dancers and singers to create the right atmosphere for the next episode. In all, seven songs and three different cultural dance movements were used for the seventy-minute production. Music from traditional instruments and the very colourful costumes of the dancers and actors gave a richness to the production.

There was a total of six productions in five zones. The zones were Saminaka, Zonkwa, Zaria, Soba and Kaduna. There were two productions in Kaduna. In each zone the group played to audiences drawn from about six schools. At least six hundred students and their teachers watched each performance.

The group spent two days in each zone – Fridays and Saturdays. Fridays were spent on workshops with at least one hundred and twenty students from six schools. During the workshops, which were conducted by five actor–teachers, efforts were made to investigate and explore the students' perspective of the problems highlighted in the report of the study panels. Issues, such as sexually transmitted diseases, abortion, early marriage, sugar daddies, blue films, sex magazines, attitudes of parents, peer influences, etc. were explored through open discussions, debates and short improvisations. All the songs to be used during performances were taught, rehearsed and thoroughly enjoyed by the students who joined the actors in singing the songs during the performances. The workshops turned out to be the most memorable occasions because of the intense rapport that took place and the level of openness in the exploration of the issues. Towards the end of the workshops each actor–teacher worked (out of role) with a group of at least twenty-five students (boys and girls) to explore in greater detail the critical issues raised by the play.

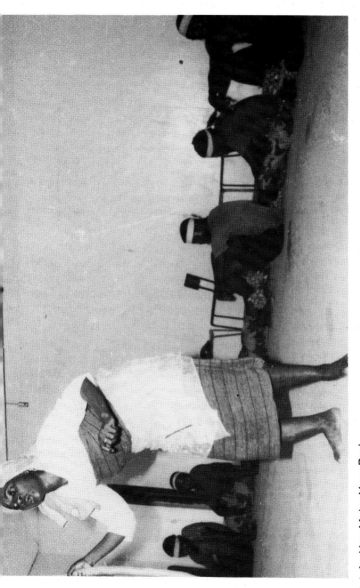

Plate 9.1 As You Make Your Bed
As You Make Your Bed by Tunde Lakoju (1992). The Narrator begins the play.
Photo: Tunde Lakoju.

Among the strengths of the play was the number of thematic and theatrical issues which it raised for questioning, debate, objection, exploration and re-creation by the students. At the workshops conducted immediately after the production, the level of understanding shown by the students was amazing. Some students criticized Amina (the good girl) for being a bookworm. Some preferred Hauwa's extrovert nature, but thought she went too far. Some thought that the old woman was too much of a gossip, but generally she was a very likeable character. When necessary the actors were called back on stage to re-enact particular scenes or moments which the students found problematic or engaging to enhance discussions. The songs and dances were greatly enjoyed, perhaps so much so that there were no questions asked of the manner in which they were used in the play.

Ten boys and ten girls were selected from two schools for the project. Two boys and three girls joined four of the actor–teachers to do the acting. The others formed the dance troupe. Three of these were in control of the musical instruments. For them as well as for us, the experience was memorable. Using the students as actors and actresses was extremely effective. Their mates identified with them very easily everywhere we went.

The major weakness of the programme was the lack of provision for any sustained follow-up work. Professional evaluators are in the field now to assess the impact of the programme on the audiences.

Whether or not an awareness of social issues which have become health issues will lead to practical action still remains to be seen. The hope is that TIE will develop to provide an effective forum for exploration, debate and expression and for involvement in these and similar issues by young people.

NOTES

1   It was introduced as the main focus of the university's Drama Programme by Michael Etherton, a Marxist theatre practitioner. He came from Zambia where he had popularized the tradition through the Chikwakwa Theatre movement, which he founded. Practice was anchored on the theories and experiments of Brecht. Augusto Boal and Paulo Friere were also very strong theatrical influences.

2   Fortunately Tunde Lakoju who first proposed a model of TIE for

Nigeria is now the Director of Planning, Research and Statistics of the Commission. He proposed TIE to the Commission and it was included in the curriculum that was approved by the Honourable Minister of Education.
3 Members of the panel included Christine Adebajo, Deji Popoola, Faith Ekwempu, Bayo Akintobi, Grace Delano and O. A. Ladipo.
4 The Nigerian consultant was Mrs Data Phiod, herself a theatre specialist. The playwright is Tunde Lakoju.

BIBLIOGRAPHY

Adedeji, A. (1981) 'Alarinjo: the traditional Yoruba travelling theatre', in Y. Ogunbiyi (ed.) *Drama and Theatre in Nigeria: A Critical Sourcebook*, Lagos: Nigeria Magazine.
Barker, G. and Rich, S. (eds) (1990) 'Adolescent fertility in Kenya and Nigeria', Centre for Population Options and Population Crisis Committee, Johns Hopkins University.
Etherton, Michael (1982) *The Development of African Drama*, London: Hutchinson University Library for Africa.
Ewu, J. R. (1990) 'A proposal for the development of children's theatre in Nigeria', Ph.D. thesis, University of Leeds, Leeds.
Hagher, I. (1981) 'The Kwagh-hir: an analysis of a contemporary indigenous puppet theatre and its social and cultural significance in Tiv land in 1960s and 1970s', Ph.D. thesis, Ahmadu Bello University, Zaria.
Illah, E. (1983) 'The performing art of the masquerade and its changing status in Igalaland', MA thesis, Ahmadu Bello University, Zaria.
Lakoju, T. (1985) 'A critical evaluation of the nature and function of Theatre in Education in Britain and a proposed model for Nigeria', Ph.D. thesis, University of Wales, Cardiff.
—— (1988) 'Towards a Theatre in Education model for Nigeria', in Ehimetalor, E. T. (ed.) *Education and National Development*, Benin city: Nigerian Educational Research Association.

Chapter 10

TIE in Scandinavia

Tove Ilsaas and Torunn Kjølner

GENERAL INTRODUCTION

In the late 1960s and early 1970s the traditional concept of theatre in Scandinavia was challenged by the emergence of what was known as a group theatre movement. A variety of small theatre companies were established with the aim of breaking down the traditional hierarchy of theatre production. Drawing on a range of personnel – teachers and social workers, many with no formal theatre training, as well as actors from the small avant-garde theatres that had developed in the early 1960s – they wanted to debate contemporary issues and make room for new life in the theatre. Building a 'free' group theatre company challenged accepted theatre practice and political life alike.

A new political awareness in the ''68 generation' also triggered a search for a new audience. It became an explicit aim to reach people who had normally not been consumers of theatre. Children and teenagers were among those who had so far been deprived of theatre experiences, and therefore became an obvious potential audience. The term 'opsøgende teater' was coined; it literally means 'a theatre in search of an audience'. By investing in big vans and mobile settings rather than in well-equipped theatre studios, an assertive 'ready to act' profile was created. To produce theatre with themes and problems that the new audiences would identify with became paramount. In many cases a unique didactic theatre developed from these endeavours.

When the TIE format was tried out on a small, experimental scale in the late 1970s and the early 1980s, the British term Theatre in Education was translated into the term 'theatre in teaching' ('teater i undervisningen' – abbreviated into TIU). Today the concept of TIE has come to comprise a diversity of different participatory theatre forms and activities; what they have in common, however, is that they are more or less clones of the 'classic' British TIE concept. The instigators who introduced TIE were actors and directors of the so-called 'free groups' as well as drama and theatre educators in colleges and universities who launched pioneering projects with students, sometimes in conjunction with 'free' groups.

Because the legal framework for publicly funded theatre has differed in the Scandinavian countries, the strong upsurge of group theatres in the 1970s developed differently in the three countries. However, ideologically the developments have taken similar paths: a very experimental phase was superseded by a very political phase, which again slowly grew into a more 'aesthetic' phase (giving priority to developing the art form). Although the Scandinavian social democracies on the surface may seem fairly homogeneous as far as educational and cultural politics go, the situation concerning arts in schools and theatre for children and young people in fact still varies a great deal from country to country. Diversity, in content and in form, marks the didactic theatre which is now offered by professional companies to schools in Scandinavia. By way of introduction to the two following articles from Norway and Denmark, let it suffice to make some sweeping remarks.

Sweden for many decades has had a high quality, innovative children's theatre movement, spearheaded by Unge Klara (Young Klara – the municipal theatre in Stockholm), and implemented too by a number of professional regional theatres and independent companies with a strong dedication to young people's theatre (YPT). Publicly funded theatres also have a long-standing tradition of touring the schools. A state-appointed consultant co-ordinates public efforts in this field and organizes a national outreach to provide children of all ages with theatre experiences. Such theatre, moreover, will frequently reflect, in exciting ways, controversial issues. This well-organized and high-profile policy may be part of the reason why the idea of participatory theatre so characteristic of 'classic' TIE does not seem to have caught on in Sweden in quite the same way as in the other two Scandinavian countries.

In Denmark, Teater Centrum – an agency for the numerous

'free groups' that are involved with YPT – provides schools with ample opportunities for visits from appropriate age-geared productions. When TIE evolved in the late 1970s, the initiative came from actors and directors who sought to find new ways of stimulating and engaging their audiences. The development of TIE in Denmark is seen here in the context of an on-going debate on art and education taking place among many of the YPT companies and in drama in education circles, and is discussed, therefore, in terms of the challenge it offers to dramaturgical as well as to educational thinking.

Whereas Denmark and Sweden were remarkably willing to support the growth of YPT advocated by the small independent companies, Norway has been less willing to do the same. On the other hand, Norway has developed an impressive drama in education tradition in that drama departments have been established at most teacher training colleges. In Norwegian classrooms, drama as a learning medium is accepted and respected. And as classroom drama practice is rooted in a theatre tradition, theatre as an art form is about to gain a new footing in schools. This process has been inspired by visiting British drama practitioners and theoreticians as well as by specialists from other Nordic countries. Lately, varied method-ologies (from drama therapy to Boal's Forum Theatre) have provided burgeoning TIE companies with models that enable them to offer a repertoire of different approaches and aesthetic forms. The following essay holds that the long-time dichotomy between theatre and pedagogical drama is about to disappear and discusses what seems to be a current positive development for Norwegian TIE.

The section on Norway is by Tove Ilsaas; the section on Denmark is by Torunn Kjølner.

NORWAY: NEW DEVELOPMENTS IN TIE

1991: a watershed for theatre for young people?

In the spring of 1991 the Norwegian Arts Council and Council for Teacher Education jointly published a most significant report. This 'Action Paper' reviewed the state of the arts subjects in Norwegian schools and in teacher training and made a number of recommendations for improving the poor state of affairs in arts and crafts, dance, drama and music in the school system. Already there are signs that this document will have a positive effect in the classroom, and the new emphasis being put on the joint efforts of school and professional theatre is proving favourable for TIE as well as for developments in drama in education.

This section will make an effort to explain why – in Norway, in the course of the last five years – TIE seems to have caught on as an appropriate and exciting teaching tool.

Recent developments in the field of YPT

Let me remind you that Norway is an extremely sparsely populated country of a mere 4.2 million inhabitants, with a rugged coastline and mountainous inland regions. Ways of life may be different in the rural and the urban areas, but on the whole drama and theatre activities in schools exist only by chance – if, that is, the school happens to have a trained drama teacher. With the 1987 National Curriculum Plan for the primary and middle schools, drama as a learning medium became one of the recommended methodologies in several subjects (such as Norwegian, History, Religion and Ethics). But as a school subject in its own right drama (and theatre) exists only in the occasional school, and the responsibility for dramatic learning has been left willy-nilly to the individual and lonely drama specialist as an extra-curricular activity. Among secondary schools, only a very few offer drama and theatre courses, and drama as a learning medium is even less practised than in the primary school.

The 1970s and 1980s saw an upsurge of independent theatre companies dedicated to children's and young people's theatre, but expansion has been much slower and more modest in Norway than in Denmark and Sweden. Many of these small companies managed to stick it out for a few seasons supported by public funding, but many of them had to pack up as they were axed from the local or national budgets. Only very few have survived as full-time professional touring companies. The lack of public interest in children's theatre – as evidenced by no special funding, no public support structure, no formal agency to provide consultants or training – left even the established theatres with few incentives to undertake performances for children. With strict labour regulations and strong actors' guilds, such performances just added extra cost.

However, with the 1991 effort on the part of public agencies to upgrade the arts in schools this complacent attitude may well change. Although at first sight TIE may seem to be a fairly expensive and exclusive kind of theatre, it offers itself as an appropriate model in the new climate, especially as the theatres seem to be increasingly successful in finding allies willing to share the cost, not only in the schools but in the arts funding councils too.

So, paradoxically, Norway's former 'backwardness' in the field of YPT may in the longer run turn out to be an advantage for the promotion of TIE work within the professional theatres. Because relatively little children's theatre is offered on the main stage of the institutional theatres, involving as it does high costs, low box office income and low profit, the wish and the obligation to do YPT can now be channelled into TIE.

What we witness is a combined 'push and pull' process. In the 1990s it appears to be easier for theatres to be accepted into the schools; the market is opening up, so to speak. During the last ten years or so the number of drama and theatre teachers has increased at an accelerating pace, especially now that some colleges and universities have introduced courses in TIE. Although few and far between, these courses have produced a handful of outstanding TIE programmes. And as exciting TIE work forces its way into schools, demonstrating to the grassroots teachers how theatre may work as a learning tool, the institutional theatres all over the country have begun to show increasing interest in devising TIE programmes.

Over the past few years, several of the publicly funded regional theatres – of which there are five in the country – have been hiring TIE or drama specialists to coach their actors and persuade their marketing people to give TIE a try. In some cases, the impetus to do TIE comes from the actors themselves as they advocate TIE as an exciting alternative theatre experience for young people. They realize that TIE offers a chance to develop their own communication skills in new and exciting ways, and find this a challenge. To relate to a participating audience, stimulating and responding to their contribution in the exploration of an issue, is both an artistic and a human challenge.

This interest on the part of the theatres is indeed promising.

After the first experiments in TIE at the National Theatre School in 1982, practical TIE work in Norway has been developed within several academic institutions, or as a joint effort by academics and theatre artists, and pioneer projects have been launched by both teacher training colleges and university drama/theatre departments. A few of these institutions offer one-year drama specialist courses in drama in education, and two – in Oslo and Bergen – have offered drama diploma courses especially geared towards TIE (at Bergen Teacher Training College and the State Teacher Training College for Arts and Crafts, Oslo). As a result of a two-year TIE course at the State Arts College in Oslo, two TIE companies (TIU-Teatret and HeraTeatret) have emerged, serving schools in the southern part of Norway with professional TIE programmes.

Examples of Norwegian TIE

The subject-matter for these programmes is chosen from among pressing contemporary social conflicts, in particular those afflicting multicultural schools and towns, and from traditionally controversial themes, like racial discrimination, hooliganism and sexual abuse. In a one-day programme called *Where Are You?* (1989–90), TIU-Teatret told the story of an Asian immigrant girl who was forced to run away – and possibly take her own life? – due to the discriminating behaviour of ignorant and prejudiced pupils in her class. After the play the spectators were invited to explore the concepts of prejudice and racism. Participatory activities such as still-image depictions, structured role-play, hot-seating and forum theatre were just some of the techniques employed in this session. The forum theatre in particular offered exciting opportunities for the youngsters to demonstrate alternative paths of action to the actors/characters.

In the first TIE programme of the company HeraTeatret (1991) the sensitive issue of sexual violence and incest was beautifully treated in a programme for older teenagers, students in college nursing courses, police academies and social work courses, parents and teachers. It began with a poetic and surrealistic theatre piece in which the abuse scene, in an incestuous father–daughter relationship, was depicted through the metaphor of a small bird and a larger bird of prey, using masks and dance. This one-hour play was followed by a structured two-hour programme of drama work, in which the participants were invited to explore their own attitudes as well as the fears and needs of the characters in the story, and to express alternative communication strategies – in the roles of mother, best friend, teacher, psychologist – to the victim, the young teenage girl.

In a forthcoming TIE programme called *Sprit* (in English 'Spirits'), on alcohol abuse among parents – presented by the regional theatre Teatret Vårt ('Our Theatre') in Molde, a small town on the west coast of southern Norway – the situation of an 11 year-old girl, Tilla, in relation to her hard-drinking and helpless mother is treated with warmth, humour and sensitivity. The play is a hard-hitting piece, but with lots of comedy too. The participatory section of the programme follows the play and invites the children (9 to 12 years old) to explore their roles as helpers and friends; it also imparts factual information about the help Tilla can get from the adult world. Teatret Vårt has managed to raise the interest of schools and arts councils in the region, and teachers as well as school advisers, psychologists and parents have been invited to the one-day workshop to be held two months prior to the tour of schools. Led by a university drama specialist, the adult workshop will provide in-service training to teachers on how to use drama as a learning medium to prepare for the theatre programme, and how to structure the follow-up work. The participation of the youngsters involves them in role-play, in-role writing and still-image depictions. The questions to be explored are:

> Why is Tilla afraid of telling anyone about the secret (her Mum's drinking)?
> Whose fault is it when grown-ups are unhappy?
> What does it mean to show responsibility? – concern?
> What is friendship?

TIE as in-service training for teachers

Another example of a forthcoming project that combines theatre work with teenagers and both pre-service and in-service training of drama teachers is planned for Autumn 1993 at the University of Oslo. Here the Centre for Teacher Training (SLS) will offer a course to the drama students and to teachers in schools, hopefully culminating in a TIE programme on parent–children relationships. The material to be used as a starting-point is to be found in Henrik Ibsen's plays. In weekly seminars teachers and drama students will explore Ibsen's plays through drama and improvisation, to learn a classroom methodology to be implemented in their own classrooms. The teenagers will likewise come to weekly workshops to explore themes and characters from these plays and in turn make their own plays. The outcome – a one-day TIE programme – will tour the participating teachers' classrooms, performed by students and teacher together: the students as actors and the teacher as the facilitator for the learning process.

Why this change in public attitude towards TIE?

What are the mechanisms and tendencies that apparently have changed the mentality towards TIE? What reasons do official school and arts agencies have now for apparently being willing to spend money on TIE?

It is important to ask this question about motivation, so as not to adapt uncritically to the wishes of the sponsorship. There is always the concern that this market demand, so to speak, may lead to 'watered down' TIE – simply because bureaucrats, business people, theatre directors and teachers are not yet acquainted with the theories behind TIE and therefore do not know what high quality TIE can – and should – be. Dramatic competence is by and large not adequate among teachers, let alone among the general public, to enable them to distinguish the good from the mediocre. The interest in the arts expressed in the previously mentioned 'Action Paper' from the Arts Council has not yet resulted in an across-the-board strengthening of the drama component in the general training of teachers.

The question we must ask is whether this new interest in TIE on the part of the professional theatre companies is genuine or merely tactical. No doubt, in some instances the attraction towards TIE is to be found in the local money available for art in schools and in the community. Especially for those companies that are required by their charter to tour their region, to do TIE may be a way of obtaining sponsorship. To combine public performances at the local town hall or 'culture house' with sponsored visits to the school gyms or classrooms, may be a roundabout way for the theatres to fulfil their obligation to provide entertaining and worthwhile theatre for young people without jeopardizing box office income.

Another incentive for what appears to be a growing interest in TIE may be discerned in the general 'back to basics' trend that is so pervasive in public debates on education in Norway. In the general quest for clear goals and clearly delineated objectives, and in the new willingness to accept assessment and product-oriented teaching, there is the obvious danger that TIE programmes will be judged by the measurable amount of factual knowledge they communicate. However, in the educational community there is a critical awareness of the concepts of knowledge and learning, which will ensure, I think, that TIE programmes will produce interesting theatre as well as a diversity of learning strategies. To employ theatre as an instrument for communicating mere facts or pat answers to standard questions would be 'a nail in the coffin' for Norwegian TIE.

What is the challenge for the future?

The most important challenge at this point therefore seems to be to educate the actors and the public alike as to what TIE is and can be – on the basis of its theory and practice so far. This presupposes an interest within the theatre in educational ideas and learning theories. Does such an interest exist? I think the answer is a definite yes. The traditional antagonism between theatre professionals and drama pedagogues is slowly but surely withering away as a result of efforts within the theatre as well as within academia. Drama specialists with both a theoretical and a practical/artistic knowledge of the theatre have worked with the theatres to develop appropriate material and workshops for teachers on theatre methodology for the classroom. Actors have been met with a respect for their profession and their art that has taken away some of the old prejudice against teachers. With growing confidence theatre artists have ventured into the schools to do TIE – helped by experienced drama teachers to structure exciting ways of exploring issues and to relate appropriately and effectively to youngsters. Thus a few but successful TIE programmes in recent years have actually demonstrated to actors as well as to schools that both pedagogy and the art of theatre have an important role to play in education. We should not underestimate the serious work that remains to be done on both sides to train first-class actor–teachers. But if the professional actor is willing to learn from the professional teacher – and vice versa – they can, quite literally, play that part together!

TIE: A DANISH PERSPECTIVE

Every year between fifty and sixty companies gather at a unique national Children's Theatre Festival in Denmark. For a week their latest productions are presented in schools, libraries, halls, theatres and streets to thousands of children and teachers, and during the weekend eighty to a hundred performances are given to a public of 10,000 people or more. At the 1992 festival, two critics from abroad, Michael Fitzgerald and David Johnston, were invited to report on what they had seen. They praised the general artistic quality, the energy of the performances, the design and the ability to share experiences. On the other hand, they missed workshop activities and an educational policy. The aesthetics of the theatre seemed to them to be emphasized at the expense of ideologically focused issues. Nevertheless they applauded Danish companies for having developed theatre forms that achieved a fair balance between social perspectives and pure entertainment (Fitzgerald 1992, Johnston 1992).

From a Scandinavian point of view it is interesting to note what they missed. The constant questioning of aims, issues and political values that constituted every agenda some years ago is certainly absent today. Most of the debates within Danish YPT used to revolve around political practice and theory, and radical analysis dictated the terminology of the questioning. But as political Denmark has undergone many changes since the 1970s, so too has the theatre. Today political engagement is no longer the common point of reference. So a fundamental and explicit change of perspective seems necessary if we are to re-examine theatre for young people. It is part of my argument that perspectives are changing, but that this is not yet happening very explicitly.

When Marxist politics and terminology ceased to dominate production processes, the idea that theatre as an art form was good for children in its own right saw a renewal. A considered debate on the educational value of theatre could have supported this change, but, as it happened, 'pedagogical' became just another word for bad or boring theatre. However, remnants of political discourse are still to be found in the language and practice of many of the companies. One example is the belief that things exist in opposites: theatre versus education, fiction versus facts. Theatre and education seem to be viewed as an impossible combination. Indifference towards debating educational philosophy as part of producing theatre for children was perhaps one reason why TIE never caught the general interest of Danish children's theatres when it was first introduced in the 1970s.

So TIE in Denmark has been a story of occasional experiments. In constructing the story I hope to challenge 'oppositional' thinking as well as looking at TIE as something essentially experimental.

Some starting points

In 1976 Preben Friis, a director and former teacher who knew TIE from England, mounted a TIE programme with the children's theatre company Rimfaxe. This experiment gained considerable recognition, but nobody seemed prepared to develop the possibilities. Soon afterwards Friis initiated a debate in the *Children's Theatre Journal* (Friis 1977) where he maintained that, in terms of their importance in schools, the established small theatre companies were losing ground. The idea of 'opsøgende teater' had originally been an exciting alternative to traditional theatre. Enthusiastic and progressive teachers had been part of the fight for something different, and the touring companies often created great excitement and discussion due to the controversial issues they brought into schools. Now, however (Friis argued), stagnation and adjustment to the school system had crept in. Neither artistically nor educationally were the groups able to offer the children anything really new. Starting out to fight the idea of theatre as something that happens on a big stage in a big theatre, the touring companies had arrived at another deadly concept: forty-minute pieces with three actors and a multi-mobile stage set in a gymnasium hall. Children's theatre was in Friis's opinion becoming an institutionalized phenomenon, an undangerous theatre that diverted the children once or twice a year. The

theatre form that had developed had derived from sound
theatrical and educational knowledge, but neither was now
being fully exploited. So Friis asked why an explicit wish to
involve children did not lead to theatre forms where children
were part of the dramatic fiction.

Critical questions about the touring companies were also
raised by school teachers. What was the actual value of theatre
visits? An investigation carried out by Gert Allan Hansen concluded rather harshly that theatre visits in schools mainly meant
a prolonged break for children (Hansen 1981). This statement,
together with his suggestion that TIE was a way to renew
children's theatre, was unsurprisingly greeted with some hos-
tility by the theatre companies. This is no more than an
anecdote told to explain how tensions between education and
theatre can so easily develop within the circle of children's
theatre. The fact that many theatre workers were trained
teachers or social workers did not lessen the tensions. Theatre,
in their view, represented an important alternative to the school
system, and this was one reason why they engaged in it. It was
also important to fight for their own professional status: clear
borderlines between their artistic work and teaching in schools
needed to be maintained. This schism between acting and
teaching, education and theatre, became, in my view, deeply
embedded in the Danish children's theatre scene from an early
stage. Years later the companies still criticize each other's
tendencies to be 'too pedagogical'. Usually this means that the
message is too obvious and the performance is lacking in
artistry. Questions about the dichotomy of theatre and education were raised in various articles in the *Children's Theatre
Journal* in the 1980s, at meetings and at the national festivals,
and so became part of an on-going discourse (e.g. Szatkowski,
1984). Nevertheless, one has to search hard to find arguments
that really attempt to change theatre practice.

1534: an early TIE experiment

In the early 1980s, Preben Friis, Gert Allan Hansen and others
gathered to set up a TIE project which was carried out in 1983–4
in Odense. The local children's theatre company did not want
to collaborate mainly because they believed that to engage in
TIE might jeopardize their existence as a theatre company.

Local school authorities might see theatre as an educational tool, and expect the company members to teach as well as act in order to obtain public financing. Another argument was that theatre's true artistic role was to offer subjective statements to an objective school system.

The TIE project *1534* aimed at breaking down traditional barriers between actors and spectators and exploiting the potential of a theatre form that combined acting *for* children and *with* them. The basic educational philosophy was that TIE could deal, in fictional terms, with issues that teachers in schools would probably find difficult to tackle – those involving feelings, empathy, understanding of history as lived experience, for example.

1534 comprised two performances, the first in schools and the second on location: a monastery outside Odense. Research, class preparation, and follow-up ideas were all part of the devising of the programme. It became an enormous undertaking which many people still remember. But rather than becoming a breeding ground for new TIE experiments the most noticeable result was a three volume report (Hansen, 1984). However, many actors gradually came to recognize that touring schools with forty-minute performances was problematic, particularly in terms of educational value. One way of dealing with the problem was to overcome the teachers' lack of appropriate preparation by offering workshops on how to prepare for a theatre visit. A good idea, no doubt, but a solution that mainly soothed the immediate problems of the theatre workers, and a poor substitute for developing more appropriate forms of theatre for children in schools.

Parallel to these discussions and experiments, a debate on aims and methods in drama in education also took place, as a result of which teachers' awareness of what to expect from theatre as a tool and as an art form increased. Barriers between drama and theatre began to be broken down.

New attempts: TIE in the early 1990s

In 1990 a one-day seminar on TIE took place at the National Children's Theatre Festival. Two companies had, quite independently of each other, produced programmes with strikingly similar approaches. One was *Tændstiksbørn* ('Match-children'), written and directed by Preben Friis. The other was Filuren's *Børn af landet* ('Children of our land'), which I had directed. The former was set at a match-making factory in Copenhagen in the 1870s, the latter used a margarine factory in Aarhus in the 1890s as the setting for a battlefield of dilemmas. In both cases children of 10 to 12 years 'worked' in the factories. Anyone with merely a faint knowledge of TIE will immediately recognize these frameworks, which is why I will return to them later. A third contribution was made by a more established TIE team Terra Nova who have combined language teaching with issue-based theatre followed by workshops. Nothing concrete resulted from the seminar, but one saw a definite will to discuss theatre and education anew, and things have certainly started to happen. New TIE programmes have been initiated both by Terra Nova and Filuren. While the view of theatre and education as complementary concepts was still provocative for some, for others it constituted an understanding of role work they wanted to be involved with and challenged by.

Match-children was done as a two-and-a-half-hour programme in a theatre space. Specially invited classes participated as children in the factory. (Unusually, a paying audience was also present.) Preparation work was based on character descriptions. The story was acted out lineally, but loops in the storyline were made possible through improvisations with the children so that on the surface level they could make important inputs. One argument for doing it this way was that the actors, who were not teachers, would not have to take or claim responsibility for the educational process. The important objective was to give the children a *feeling* of the story and its context, and to put the audience in some social and emotional conflict situations that needed to be solved.

Children of our land was the culmination of a desire for renewal on the part of the company Filuren, who had for some time dramatized classics for large stages and produced small-scale pieces in their own studio theatre. As none of the actors had experienced either TIE or teacher-in-role work in the classroom, big investments were required from everybody. A devising group consisted of the dramaturg, Janek Szatkowski, a drama teacher, Claus Jantzen, and me. Having trained in Britain, I knew of TIE, but my main experiences stemmed from teacher-in-role work and involvement in two TIE programmes in Norway in the early 1980s. I had visited Greenwich Young People's Theatre and was inspired by their thinking and their devising models.

The local school authorities and the cultural affairs office contributed money and prestige to the project. For better or worse this resulted in a very comprehensive programme. Twenty financially supported teachers were invited to participate in the process. Lectures, workshops and discussions with the actors were arranged. Six actor–teachers were involved in the production. The result was a full-day programme for forty pupils (aged 10 to 13) in a gymnasium hall. The set was lit and completely surrounded the action; there was live music; the actors wore specially made costumes; the children wore 'aprons' when they were in the factory.

Devising *Children of our Land*: a dramaturgical challenge

Some early decisions provided a framework for the devising process. We wanted a local 'true-life' story to work from, and the actions had to take place in a specific period of time. Given the choice between 'the Viking Age', 'the 1890s' and 'the 1950s', the teachers decided that the metaphoric value of 'a hundred years ago' had the biggest appeal. I insisted that Filuren as a whole working group should decide which concept to work from. After much discussion around our dilemmas as adults in a fragmented and constantly changing society, we came to the concept of justice and punishment. What does it mean to be just, when questioning the rules has become an integral part of our consciousness?

We searched for stories from Aarhus a hundred years ago, with justice or punishment as potential themes, and preferably with children involved. A story we found made such an impact on us that it seemed impossible to let it go. On the morning of Christmas Eve 1898, two farmworkers, husband and wife, returned from their morning duties to their little cottage to find all but one of their six children poisoned by the smoke of a fireburner in bad condition. The editor of the social democratic newspaper in Aarhus, Peter Sabroe, also known as a fighter for children's rights, turned the accident into a political case. He summoned all workers from Aarhus to march to Skejby to participate in the funeral in order to show their solidarity with the farm workers and their conditions. On a freezing cold December day more than 1,000 people walked the eight miles to the funeral.

We did not want to dramatize the fatal accident as such. To turn it into a case history would have meant bringing Sabroe to the centre of the action, which for several reasons we did not want to do. We did not see an adequate educational challenge in debating whether it was right or wrong to do what he did, nor did his political career have the necessary metaphorical power or contemporary relevance. The political situation in Denmark today is not one of class struggle. Heavy progressive taxation, a developed unemployment benefit system and housing support mean that 90 per cent of the population virtually have the same amount of money to live on when tax and rent are paid. I am not saying that there are no social problems in Denmark; there are serious ones, but they are not British.

Looking back it is clear that devising a programme in the 1990s from a TIE philosophy which is basically British made us realize something about Danish reality. In the 1970s 'everything was political'. Today radical language has almost lost its meaning. Political discussions from party-specific affiliations do not happen very often. Many young people, whose childhood was one long learning to know right from wrong in political terms, are fed up with it all, and have found other ways of fighting for their existence.

A contemporary TIE programme in Denmark could possibly use historical events to construct a political debate based on Marxist philosophy. But we could not see that such an undertaking would have made for an effective TIE experiment. It should be added that this is more a conclusion reached with hindsight than something we explicitly argued for in the devising process. Today I am convinced that the construction of meaning in a much broader sense must guide the devising of a programme. This, of course, could be done from historical events as well as from anything else. It seems to be a vital dramaturgical challenge to deconstruct stories and find theatrical ways of demonstrating their construction to the children. In *Children of our Land* we sensed the problem, I think, but we were not able to carry it through within the frameworks we had chosen. We constructed the story so that the children could experience how the three main characters made decisions from three different socio-political positions and in changing contexts. We could not, however, bring the children to see these larger perspectives within the fictional construction. In other words, without the help of the actors out of role, the children were not really able to see the perspective of each of these characters beyond their personal stories. We had wanted the children to gain such a meta-perspective through empathy and involvement in action. Wishful thinking! To look for identification and distance at the same time is an advanced task. The programme was coded in a psychological realistic mode. Through their empathy with the three characters the children were confronted with difficult choices, complicated by what they knew of the characters' past actions, or what the children saw in several small plays within the programme.

A short summary of the programme is now needed to continue the discussion: Karl, a farmer's son, goes to town to become a journalist on the social democratic newspaper. The young maid Elisabeth has left her place because the squire has made her pregnant. She gives birth to the child and moves in with her cousin Johanne, who is a widowed factory worker. To get work Elisabeth leaves her child at an infants' home. She meets Karl and gets work at the margarine factory through her cousin Johanne who exploits the fact that the foreman has proposed to her. Elisabeth counterfeits a document to get money from the squire. The call for a demonstration to participate in the funeral of the five children initiates a conflict at the factory. Johanne goes, Elisabeth does not. The foreman wants Johanne fired, but under pressure he asks the children to choose between the two adult workers. Karl is brought in as a journalist who covers the conflict. The children decided how to solve the actual conflict, but they were not able to change the end of the story because of what had already happened between the characters outside the factory. In the end Elisabeth's crime is discovered: she is sentenced to three years in jail. Meanwhile Johanne and Karl get married. The programme ends with Elisabeth meeting Karl and Johanne as she is about to start her 'free' life again.

The children developed both empathy and dissatisfaction with the way the three characters acted, and many were strongly against Elisabeth as she went back to the factory when all the rest had left. The children would sometimes decide to express their views (in role) by working in slow motion, sometimes they would try to talk to the foreman, sometimes they decided on a strike or other actions. But whatever happened, and however angry they had been with Elisabeth, her sentence in the end was still too harsh. Nobody considered the reason why she acted the way she did, some would say very egoistically. A strong feeling of injustice was expressed and many questions were raised after the programme ended. Each character's line of action had been given a representative function to make it possible to reflect on the decisions that were made. We had tried to build the educational concept and the conflicts into the development of three characters. The result was a complex story that made it necessary to reflect on it afterwards in order to be able to see it clearly.

The dilemma of dilemmas

What had become too complicated was to expose the conflicts so that it would be possible for the children not just to influence the dramatic fiction, but actually decide the end of the play. It did help a bit to distinguish between dilemmas that can be solved and dilemmas that cannot be solved – unless, one should add, they are accepted as pure dilemmas, or even paradoxes, and dissolved. To dissolve a problem means that the children on a meta-level must be able to identify the nature of the paradox. When they faced the choice between the two women who were given 'equal empathy', it was important for us that the children could discover the 'constructed' dilemma the cunning foreman had presented them with. Dissolving the dilemma was necessary to clarify the real conflict and to choose ways of action. Several attempts taught us that if it was difficult for the children to reach this in the situation itself, the actor–teachers could either (a) in role help them spell it out, or (b) let them decide and then reflect on what had happened out of role later.

Different kinds of energy

Looking back, we learned that to make it possible for the children to participate in the deconstruction and construction of a story, they should have been given the opportunity to influence the action line of each individual character and bring in new characters, new actions. With inexperienced TIE actors this is perhaps more of a challenge than they can be expected to undertake. It would probably question character-based acting techniques as well as improvisational skills. There were already challenges enough for our actors. First of all it was unusual to start working from a concept, and to be involved in giving educational thinking theatrical form. It is easy enough to understand that you have to think about the children's learning process and act at the same time. It is less easy to find a way to do it, especially if you have no teaching experience. On the intellectual level the actors were asked to be ahead of things and constantly pick up on the children's and other actors' input. But everybody knows how crucial it is to anticipate the action on an acting level. An attempt to solve this constant inner fight on the floor was the introduction of different acting energies, which attempted to make it easier to change modes during the programme. In this we saw four levels of communication at work: (a) the 'I am me' level (before and after the performance, including attitudes towards children in general); (b) a story-telling level, used during the programme simply to further the story; a 'transitional level' mediates to level (c) the role level, where the improvisations with the children would take place; and (d) the character level, which more or less was restricted to the theatre pieces in the programme. As to pace, timing and theatrical awareness it became important to work with different energies. The role level necessarily puts the educational concept at the forefront; at the character level acting techniques rule the energy. A fluctuation between these energies helped to build up to the dilemmas and turning points.

Reflecting on these questions naturally leads to reconsidering the importance of dilemmas in TIE programmes and teacher-in-role work altogether. Is it still an educational must to build up moral dilemmas, or is it time to develop new production 'models' that bring the making of meaning to the centre of the fiction – a process that involves the children in deconstructing or constructing stories rather than making decisions about problems posed by us? Such a development would mean reconsidering in what way theatre is educational. We also have to discuss what it means to produce meaning in educational terms. No doubt these questions open up fields of research waiting to be explored, practically and theoretically. These, to me, are the real challenges of TIE today.

BIBLIOGRAPHY

Arts Council (Norway) and Council for Teacher Education (1991) *The Arts in Norwegian Schools: An Action Plan*, Oslo.

Børneteateravisen (The Children's Theatre Journal) (1972–) Danish Association of Children's Theatres.

Fitzgerald, M. (1992) 'There is nothing rotten in *this* state of Denmark', *Børneteateravisen* 81.

Friis, P. (1977) 'Børneteater – kunst eller underholdning?' ('Children's theatre – art or entertainment?'), *Børneteateravisen* 18.

Hansen, G. A. (1981) *Børneteater i folkeskolen* (Children's theatre in schools), Odense.

—— (ed.) (1984) *Teater i undervisninger: en rapport om et forsøgsproject* (Theatre in Education: a report about an experimental project), vols 1–3, Odense skolevæsen.

Johnston, D. (1992) 'Teaterliv i top' ('Top of theatre life'), *Børneteateravisen* 18.

Szatkowski, J. (1984) 'Er dramapædagogik nu blevet teater?' ('Has drama in education now become theatre?'), *Børneteateravisen* 44.

Chapter 11

The Creative Arts Team in the United States

Mark Riherd with Gwendolen Hardwick

INTRODUCTION

The Creative Arts Team (CAT), the professional educational theatre company at New York University's Gallatin Division, has been innovative in the uses of theatre for educational purposes in the United States for the past eighteen years. By presenting original theatre performances and participatory drama workshops, CAT aims to motivate urban youth to examine pertinent curricular themes and social issues, including race relations, HIV/AIDS, child abuse, teen pregnancy, violence, multiculturalism and the environment. CAT currently comprises nearly fifty full-time employees, including actor–teachers, workshop directors and arts administrators, serving, through four programmes, approximately 35,000 young people annually in the five boroughs of New York City.

CAT's funding is unique in that less than 5 per cent comes from arts related organizations; the rest is provided primarily by various government social service agencies, including New York City Department of Youth Services, New York State Division of Substance Abuse Services, New York State Division for Youth, New York State Department of Health/AIDS Institute and the New York City Board of Education. Additional private and corporate funders include United Way of New York City, Diamond Foundation, Bristol-Meyers, Squibb Foundation and Primerica Foundation.

The philosophy and methodologies of CAT are firmly rooted in the British Theatre in Education movement. During the summer of 1975, a group of graduate students who were participating in a study abroad programme in England, sponsored by

New York University's Program in Educational Theatre, were introduced to the concepts and practices of TIE. Inspired by this unique approach to learning, their task upon returning to New York University was to translate those practices to fit a different educational system and population, a challenge which is continually being confronted. The projects described in this chapter are intended to exemplify that principle.

The New York City Board of Education consists of thirty-two separate school districts. Even though there are certain mandated policies overall, each district has its own unique regulations and procedures as well as student populations. CAT's primary audience consists of young people who have been identified as at risk of dropping out of school for a variety of reasons. Most of them are from poverty-ridden inner-city environments where positive adult role models are scarce and children learn as best they can to survive in a world fraught with crime, violence, substance abuse and welfare dependency. Too often these young people have given up on an educational system and a society that they feel have abandoned and betrayed them.

In 1990, upon the occasion of CAT's fifteenth anniversary, Lynda Zimmerman, Executive Director, stated:

> The 15th anniversary celebration of the Creative Arts Team is time to reflect on the choices that influenced our success in creating innovative, exciting programs that engage students in learning through drama. It is also time to realize that once in a great while, through the confluence of chance, determination, passion and perseverance, one can create something that truly matters in the lives of young people.
>
> (Creative Arts Team 1990: 2)

This chapter will examine the work of CAT, including its history and a brief description of current work; it ends with a case study by Gwendolen Hardwick from *It's What You Do . . .,* an HIV/AIDS Theatre in Education workshop series for 'at risk' high-school students.

THE FOUR PROGRAMMES

CAT is currently comprised of four programmes, Drama Unlimited, Special Express, Project Communication and Conflict

Resolution Through Drama. Each programme maintains its own staff of a workshop director, who is responsible for designing the curriculum, training the personnel and sustaining the quality and integrity of the programme; and actor–teachers, the professional artists who implement the performances and workshops in the schools. Each curriculum design is age-specific and incorporates drama in education and/or Theatre in Education methodologies appropriate to the populations being served.

Drama Unlimited

In 1984 Arts Partners, an arts-in-education programme for New York City schools, was initiated through a unique collaboration of the Office of the Mayor, the New York City Board of Education, the Department of Cultural Affairs and the Department of Youth Services. The thirty-two school districts of the city were each offered the opportunity to forge collaborations with a variety of arts agencies in order to meet, through the arts, specific educational objectives to be determined by the districts themselves.

CAT responded by developing Drama Unlimited, a drama in education workshop series designed for elementary school students, grades 1–6 (ages 6–12). The programme fosters a partnership among students, classroom teachers and actor–teachers to enhance communication, critical-thinking and interpersonal skills, while addressing a specific social issue through the process of drama.

Drama Unlimited provides several curricula models yearly, each created by the programme's workshop director in collaboration with the actor–teachers. Each curriculum design is population specific such as elementary, grades 1–3 (ages 6–9) and upper elementary, grades 4–6 (ages 10–12). All residencies are ten sessions in duration and generally occur once a week, providing actor–teachers with time to meet the classroom teachers to assess the programme's success as well an opportunity for the students to implement follow-up activities, assigned by the artists and guided by the classroom teacher.

During the residency, each classroom teacher is offered two staff development workshops led by the actor–teachers. These sessions provide teachers with knowledge and introduce skills they can use to incorporate drama in education strategies to meet pre-determined educational objectives.

Curriculum design: Common Ground, *grades 4–6 (ages 10–12)*

Through a series of one-hour participatory drama in education workshops, students, their teachers and two CAT actor–teachers explore the theme of human relations and cultural diversity. The first six sessions of the residency concentrate on a continuous drama created with each class which concerns the building of Common Ground, a new community where the residents will live and act identically. All decisions will be democratic and the community will advocate non-violence. The establishment of Common Ground comes about because the residents have been forced to leave their previous homes, having been marked out as 'different' from the other inhabitants. These differences are determined by the students and most often include race, clothing, speech and even hair-style! In response to their previous treatment, the residents now pledge to ameliorate their diversity.

They are content until the Henryites move into Common Ground. These new residents wear strange masks, have unusual houses, sleep during the day and work at night, and they refuse to honour the Common Ground pledge or sign the constitution. Tension ensues and the Henryites are accused of various mishaps and crimes. Through a series of events, established throughout these initial six sessions, the residents of Common Ground realize that their judgement of the Henryites has not been based upon factual information. Eventually, they invite them into their community, ultimately respecting and accepting the differences among them.

In Sessions 7 to 10 the students explore the issue of human relations and cultural diversity through a series of conflict scenes depicting situations relating to their lives.

Special Express

CAT's relationship with the New York City Board of Education Division of Special Education began in 1978 when a citywide arts-in-education programme was inaugurated for special education students. Since that time, CAT has been able to meet the particular needs of learning disabled, emotionally disturbed, hearing and visually impaired as well as other categories of students with special needs by developing appropriate drama curricula.

In 1989, Special Express was created as a full-time CAT programme designed to meet the needs of early childhood (ages 6–9), elementary (ages 10–12) and junior high school (ages 13–16), special education students and the paraprofessionals or full-time teaching assistants who work with them. Students at various levels are actively engaged in a five-session residency during which they explore through drama the theme of multiculturalism with emphasis upon such aspects as prejudice, racism, co-operation, peer and family pressure and self-esteem.

Staff development is a vital component of the Special Express programme, enabling teachers to explore the uses of drama in education to address curricular goals as well as to develop lesson plans for their specific populations. Several models are offered, from a single two-hour session to a two-day weekend residency.

Curriculum design: The Sea Kingdom of Friends, *early childhood (ages 6–9)*

Through a series of five one-hour drama in education workshops, special education students focus upon learning to accept differences in others and developing self-esteem. In Session 1 the participants, having been invited to tea with the Queen of the Underwater Kingdom, practise skills necessary for their journey.

In Session 2 the actor–teachers present each child with a magical medallion inscribed with his or her name, which must be worn in order to find the Queen's castle. After swimming through the sea, using movements practised in Session 1, they arrive in the Sea Kingdom. The Queen welcomes them by saying something special about each child (information learned during the residency conference with the classroom teacher). After everyone has pantomimed having tea and cookies, the Queen teaches the students a song.

'The Sea Kingdom' (by Evie Hantzopolous)

Let's swim, swim down to the sea
Through the blue, blue ocean so blue

We'll have fun, fun just you and me
In a world exciting and new.

The Queen will be there (clap, clap, clap)
And she wants to have tea (clap, clap, clap)
We'll show her we're friends (clap, clap, clap)
And how nice we can be (clap, clap, clap)

When tea is finished, the children begin to swim home. Suddenly they hear an unusual sound. Opie the Octopus (a hand puppet) appears but quickly hides when he sees the children. Encouraged by the actor–teachers, the students speak to Opie and discover that he is sad because he has never been invited to have tea with the Queen. The reason, he believes, is that he is different; he is unattractive, he doesn't know any songs and he has no manners. The session ends with a discussion among the children and the actor–teachers about the drama.

During Sessions 3 to 5, the participants encourage Opie's self-esteem by emphasizing his positive attributes and by convincing the Queen to invite him to tea.

Because both Drama Unlimited and Special Express incorporate drama in education methodologies, the classroom teacher is vital to the success of each programme and instead of being a passive observer frequently enacts a specific role in the drama, thereby becoming an active participant in the workshop. The teacher also aids by maintaining class order, questioning students' responses, encouraging the completion of follow-up activities and assisting the actor–teachers in the implementation of the drama activities. The success of these programmes relies upon this collaboration.

A teacher orientation session for each programme is provided prior to the residency, during which objectives of the project and the role of the teacher are defined. Classroom resource guides, which include suggestions for furthering the examination of the residency's theme through various curricular activities, are provided at the end of the residencies.

Project Communication

Intended to enhance the oral and written communication skills of junior high school students (ages 13–16), Project Communication combines an original theatre performance with classroom participatory drama workshops. The scripts, written specially for this programme, focus upon a specific issue relevant to the population being served and include *Last Year* (teen suicide prevention, 1991), *Show of Force* (consequences of the use of weapons, 1989), *The Divider* (racially motivated violence, 1987), *Home Court* (drug abuse, inspired by the cocaine-induced death of basketball star Len Bias, 1986), *I Never Told Anybody* (child abuse, 1984), *Joe Louis: The Brown Bomber,* and *Rosa Parks: Back of the Bus,* (the denial of civil liberties, 1982 and 1980 respectively).

Each play is intended to motivate students to explore a particular issue through an examination of the choices made by the characters. In a discussion immediately following each performance students confront and challenge the characters regarding their decisions and the possible consequences, affording the participants an opportunity not only to reflect upon their own reactions to the play but also to act through immediate response.

Workshops in the classroom for selected classes both precede and follow the performance. Students participate in drama activities including role-play and improvisation actively to examine the issues presented in the play. As with other CAT programmes, classroom teachers attend an orientation session prior to the residency and are provided with resource guides and follow-up activities.

Curriculum design: Last Year, *junior high school (ages 13–16)*

Last Year, by Jim Mirrione, identifies factors contributing to suicide among teenagers and examines possible strategies to assuage problems before they become so overwhelming that suicide becomes an option.

The play contrasts the lives of two teenagers, Tyrone and Felicia, during one school year. As the play begins, Felicia is recovering from a suicide attempt. With the support of her boyfriend, Tyrone, she begins to recognize and acknowledge conflicts which she has with her mother, a single parent who is frequently absent, and her friend, Sheena, who encourages her to drop out of school.

As Felicia begins to come to terms with her life, Tyrone faces mounting pressures including his father's high expectations, an alcoholic mother, falling grades and Felicia's suspected involvement with his best friend, Breece. Tyrone is finally devastated when his mother announces that she and his father are separating.

Scene from *Last Year*

(Tyrone is sitting on the edge of the roof, going through the contents of his duffel bag. Felicia enters. Music fades.)

FELICIA: Tyrone . . .
TYRONE: (*surprised*) What are you doing here?
FELICIA: Looking for you.
TYRONE: (*angrily*) Well, you saw me. OK? Now, get lost.
FELICIA: What's up with you anyway, Tyrone? I've been calling you for two days and you're never home.
TYRONE: Yeah, I've been out.
FELICIA: You mean up here.
TYRONE: Look, this is my roof, so step off. Besides, how did you find me here in the first place?
FELICIA: Breece told me.
TYRONE: I don't appreciate the spy routine.
FELICIA: What's in the bag?
TYRONE: None of your business.
FELICIA: Yeah, well, I'm making it my business.
TYRONE: Look, don't do me any favours, OK? You don't need to squeeze me in between you and your squeeze, Breece.
FELICIA: Breece? Do you think I've been hanging out with him? We've been worried about you since you freaked out on your geometry test. What's going on with you?
TYRONE: Nothing.
(He attempts to leave. As he goes, he drops the duffel bag and the contents spill out.)
FELICIA: What is all this?
TYRONE: (*defensively*) Stuff I'm getting rid of.
(Tyrone attempts to put the objects back into the bag.)
FELICIA: You expect me to believe that? Look at this stuff: your football jersey . . . your CDs . . . your baseball hats?
TYRONE: Since you're so worried about it, then take it. Go on, take it all!

FELICIA: (*stopping Tyrone and grabbing him by the wrists*) Tyrone,
I know what you're doing. (*she shakes him*) What's
wrong?
(Tyrone pulls away. There is a pause. Tyrone then turns to
Felicia and speaks slowly and directly.)
TYRONE: Things are wacked at home, and I don't think they're
gonna get much better.

It was not just Tyrone's decision to take his own life, but
Felicia's ability to see the early warning signs and her attempt to
prevent the suicide, that gave the play its momentum and
energized the workshops that followed.

Conflict Resolution Through Drama

The oldest of CAT's programmes, Conflict Resolution Through
Drama, grew out of a 1979 request from the New York Urban
Coalition for CAT to create a series of drama workshops for
high school students (ages 16–19) to channel their negative
behaviour into more positive directions. The series of twenty
workshops addressed such issues as parental and peer pressure
as well as drug and alcohol abuse.

The Conflict Resolution Through Drama programme continues to work with at-risk high school students characterized by
high truancy, low academic achievement and involvement with
family and/or criminal courts. Since 1979, the programme has
been expanded to serve not only the New York City Board of
Education high schools but also alternative schools, drug treatment centres, juvenile detention facilities, prisons and community social service agencies. The four components of the
programme currently serve students in more than a hundred
facilities annually throughout New York City with the goal of
developing, through drama workshops, their decision-making
skills while addressing a specific social issue.

Regardless of the issue being examined, the methodology of
all Conflict Resolution Through Drama workshops remains
constant. Participants observe a series of scenes which build to
a point of conflict; the scene freezes; the students examine the
sources of conflict and identify alternative methods of resolution. Students are then actively involved in creating improvised
scenes based on those suggested resolutions. The workshops

serve as a catalyst for examining choices, decisions and consequences of actions and at all times the aim is to elicit strong responses from the students.

Curriculum design

Prejudice and Racism workshops: a two-day workshop series during which the participants recognize and identify the types of prejudice motivating various conflict situations. Within each session the distinctions between different causes of prejudice, including class, gender, physical disability and age, are explored, with an emphasis upon race.

Youth Employment Video series: a four-day workshop series (incorporating CAT's professionally produced videotapes) that explores the attitudinal skills necessary for success in the workforce.

Intensive Drama module: a three-day residency which examines a variety of issues not explored in the programme's other projects, allowing CAT the opportunity to tailor the content to the students' immediate needs.

HIV/AIDS workshop: a two-day workshop series addressing attitudinal and behavioural issues surrounding HIV/AIDS infection. The case-study that follows is taken from this workshop.

CASE-STUDY: *IT'S WHAT YOU DO. . .*
Gwendolen Hardwick (director)

8 a.m. Monday morning. An unusually large crowd of students is gathered at the school's entrance. What's happening? I nudge my way through students milling about on the sidewalk and open the door to make my way to the security desk. Oh, no! Lines and lines of students are queued up at 'checkpoints'. They are emptying their pockets and putting the items on plastic trays which they hold out in front of them. Security guards move something shaped like a large square lollipop up and down each student's body. Every schoolbag and purse is opened and poked through, eyes peeking into corners between books and personal items. The team and I have, until now, been spared the random 'weapons check' at various high schools the city deems 'dangerous'. Today we will be screened along with

the students. While waiting in line, I hear that today's bell schedule has been changed. Our contact person later informs me that the class period will be shortened by eight minutes. 'Can the team get into the room to set up before . . .?' I barely get the question out when she interrupts: 'I'm afraid not.' The actor–teachers all make it through the inspection. When the bell finally rings, we enter and quickly begin to rearrange the space. After a few minutes, students straggle in, surprised and curious as they notice the desks pushed up against the walls, chairs in a semicircle two rows deep and an actor–teacher seated 'onstage'. Some sit quietly observing the actor–teacher. Others continue conversations with friends, intermittently glancing toward the 'stage'. Still others comment aloud:

STUDENT 1:   Yo? (Speaking to 'Victor'.) What are you doing? ('Victor' does not answer. The student turns to someone next to him.) My man is bugging.

STUDENT 2:   Looks like he's watching something. (The two students watch 'Victor' for a moment, then burst into laughter.) Yeah, he making like he got a remote. He's watching TV or a video.

VOICE (from back of the room): Miss Hanks? What's this about?

TEACHER: Tasha, just be quiet and you'll find out.
(Suddenly, the opening scene begins)

NURSE: Good morning, Victor. What a beautiful day out. I'll open the blinds for you and let some sunshine in. So, how are you feeling today? (Victor does not answer.) Victor? (Still no response from Victor.)
What programme is that you're watching? It looks interesting. (Victor changes the channel.)
Would you like me to walk you down the hall to the lounge?

VICTOR: No.

NURSE: There's going to be a counselling session for . . .

VICTOR: I said no!

NURSE: Okay. I'll take the i.v. needle out of your arm, now. (She sits in a chair beside him and mimes removing the i.v. needle.)
I see you'll be discharged in a couple of days. Will someone be coming to take you home? If you like, I can make a call for you at the nurse's station, since you don't have a phone.

VICTOR: No. No. Just get out of here, you're bothering me.

NURSE: I'm sorry, Victor. I don't mean to bother you. But, it would be better if someone could accompany you home and stay with . . .

VICTOR: Can you leave?

NURSE: I'm not finished yet. I still have to give you your medication.

(As the scene continues, Victor remains rude and unco-operative. The nurse attempts to give him his medicine and he knocks it to the floor.)

Oh, so now you're not going to take your medicine?

VICTOR: Get out of here and leave me alone!

NURSE: (Angrily.) Like it or not, Victor, you can't go throwing medicine on the floor.

OFFSTAGE VOICE: FREEZE!

Processing the opening scene

All action and dialogue stops. The actor–teachers drop character and formally introduce themselves. Students are asked to identify the characters in the scene and their relationships, as well as the conflict and its possible cause. These initial questions are brief and initiate the process of critical thinking. There is some discussion about Victor's response to the nurse and what he might be feeling. The students are asked why Victor is in the hospital. Though they suggest a number of possible reasons, when probed to support their answers they realize they do not yet have enough information.

Scene Two

Victor has been discharged from the hospital and is hanging out on a street corner engaged in a popular urban hustle – washing car windows of drivers stopped at the red light. Another actor–teacher, 'Fresh Jeff', enters and crosses the street to where Victor is now resting on a milk crate:

JEFF: Victor. Didn't you hear me calling you from across the street? I thought that was you sitting over here. I was on the phone, trying to hook up this job Forty told me about. I turned around and saw you. Yo, man, I haven't seen you . . . how long has it been?

Plate 11.1 It's What You Do . . . .
The character Victor confronts the student audience in the HIV/AIDS awareness programme *It's What You Do . . .* (Creative Arts Team), as presented in classrooms in high schools and prisons in New York, 1991–2.

VICTOR: I don't know, a few months.

JEFF: Naw, man. It's been almost a year, damn! Where you been at?

VICTOR: You know me, just hanging.

JEFF: Why don't you come hang out with me?

VICTOR: Okay, that sounds chill.

JEFF: Matter of fact, I'm on my way to Forty's. Yo, man, I got some stuff on me. Wanna do some?

VICTOR: No, man. I don't do drugs no more.

JEFF: What? You ain't doing drugs? You kidding? Since when?

VICTOR: For a while now. I'm clean . . . just trying to get myself together.

JEFF: Clean and sober, for real?

VICTOR: For real.

JEFF: That's cool. (During this conversation, Jeff has been continually scratching himself.)

VICTOR: What's the problem, man?

JEFF: Victor, you know the girlies are on my jock! So, I get a little something every now and then . . . it goes along with the territory.

VICTOR: Just use a 'jimmy hat'.

JEFF: (Laughing.) Vic, you know me, man, I got to have that natural feeling! Besides, I can go over to the clinic and get it taken care of in a minute. Man, I got to get over to Forty's, I'm late. Why don't you come walk with me over there, that way we can hang for a while. Forty'll be glad to see you. Hey, that's the last time we saw each other, remember that night?

VICTOR: What night?

JEFF: We were at Forty's doing mad drugs, getting busy with the girlies, then we left to go chill in the park . . . that's when you split.

VICTOR: Yeah, I needed to break out, that's all.

JEFF: I better get over to Forty's. You coming, right?

VICTOR: No. I ain't going to Forty's.

JEFF: I thought you said you wanted us to hang. We go to Forty's we can chill. Forty'll hook you up with some cash flow. You don't need to hustle cars, Vic.

VICTOR: What? You ain't listening? I said I ain't going to Forty's. I . . . I don't ever want to see his face again!

JEFF: Victor! Chill! Why you gotta dis Forty? You know he always looking out . . .

VICTOR: Looking out? Forty ain't looking out for no one. I remember that night, the night you was just talking about. Do you remember that dude Ted came in?

JEFF: Oh, you mean the guy Forty said was Five-O![1]

VICTOR: He ain't no Five-O, Jeff. (Victor's voice becomes loud and angry.) He's a social worker or something like that . . . he came in the joint . . . we was doing drugs. I was shooting up with some dudes in a corner. Ted came in and was passing out information about cleaning the works, the needles we were using. He's the one looking out . . . trying to save people from getting AIDS.

JEFF: Man, that's all hype . . .

VICTOR: Oh yeah, well how you think I got it? (There is a momentary pause for the audience to take in this piece of information. Victor then regains his composure.)
            I'm sorry man, I'm getting loud. It's just that . . . it ain't easy . . . never mind . . . so let's hang out, okay? (He moves toward Jeff.)

JEFF: Back off, man! I ain't going nowhere with you! (Another argument ensues as a result of Jeff's misinformation and misconceptions about HIV transmission.)

VICTOR: What's the matter? (Still moving toward Jeff. Jeff backs away.)

JEFF: You breathe your AIDS on me and I'll beat you down!

VICTOR: You don't understand . . .

JEFF: I understand you better not touch me, Victor! (In the midst of this dialogue, Kim, Jeff's girlfriend, enters. The exchange between them reveals that Jeff has not been home in two days, angry about their disagreement over the use of condoms. Their continuing argument verges on a near violent confrontation.)
            You gonna bring up my business out here on the street, Kim?

KIM: Jeff – I was just telling you what the clinic doctor said about my infection. Maybe if you use condoms . . .

JEFF: What's wrong with you? I said I ain't using condoms! What I gotta do? Smack you down out here? (He raises his hand to hit Kim but Victor grabs Jeff's arm in mid-air. Jeff breaks away from Victor's grip, moves 'downstage' and speaks directly to the audience:)

Jeff: (Directing his dialogue to a male student sitting in the front row.) You see what I gotta go through? These girlies are crazy! She gonna loud me in the street. I should smack her, right?

Boy: Yeah, hit her. (Some of the other boys laugh.)

Girl: What you gonna hit her for? She was just telling you she don't want to get your infection.

Jeff: Infection from who?

Girl: From you, 'cause you nasty! Digging in your pants, you probably got crabs. (Girls nod and laugh in agreement.)

Boy 2: He got it from a dirty girl, too!

Girl: How you know that? He could've gotten it some way else.

Boy: 'Cause he said so. You weren't listening.

Girl: I was listening. Just 'cause he said so don't make it true. You boys lie all the time. (This issue has apparently struck a nerve between these two students. The actor–teacher playing Jeff tries to draw others into the discussion.)

Jeff: Whatever I got, it ain't what Victor got.

Girl 2: How you know that?

Jeff: You trying to say I got AIDS? I don't shoot up and I ain't no homo!

Girl 2: You don't have to be gay to get AIDS.

Jeff: I don't know why I waste my breath talking to you girls. You think you know everything. (He incites two girls in the back to respond at once.)

Girls: She should leave you . . . you ain't that cute. (Jeff waves his hand at them and crosses to a male student wearing sunglasses who has been quietly slouched down in his seat.)

Jeff: Yo, my man. (Jeff holds out his hand for the student to slap five, but gets no response.) You know where I'm coming from? You get AIDS from people who breathe or cough on you. That's why I told Victor to keep away from me.

Boy: (Quietly.) Naw, man.

Jeff:	What you mean, naw?
Boy:	Naw, you can't get AIDS like that.
Voice:	FREEZE!

Processing Scene Two

Victor's revelation that he is living with AIDS acts as a catalyst to inform students that HIV/AIDS risk reduction and prevention is the topic of the workshop. Information regarding HIV/AIDS transmission is presented and written on a chalkboard for students to copy and use as a reference during discussions. Students are asked to determine, based on the documented modes of transmission and information presented in the scene, how Victor may have contracted HIV. Are other characters at risk? Jeff uses drugs but is not an intravenous drug user. Is he still at risk? In a subsequent scene, Kim learns she may be pregnant. Determining her risk for HIV often sparks a discussion about male–female relations and what constitutes a healthy relationship.

During the final portion of the Day 2 workshop, students are provided with an opportunity to identify support systems, from hotlines to social services agencies and community based organizations that provide HIV/AIDS services to young people. In addition, a health professional employed by CAT addresses students' concerns regarding the specifics of the disease, including transmission and prevention.

It's What You Do . . . is an aggressive, straightforward Theatre in Education project, which, because of its realistic characters and relevant situations, initially allows students simply to observe but eventually compels them to become actively involved (through role-play and improvisation) in the critical-thinking process. Moreover, each of the actor–teachers possesses strong teaching ability and experience mingled with an almost uncanny sensitivity to this delicate issue.

CONCLUSION

CAT's success may most concretely be measured not only by the consistency with which the programmes are requested by the same districts and schools year after year, but also by the continually positive oral and written evaluations from teachers and administrators, indicating that, ultimately, the work speaks for itself. In addition, since 1985, CAT has employed independent evaluators who, through a variety of strategies, measure the effectiveness of all the programmes, the findings of which are presented in a year-end report. These on-going evaluations have assisted CAT in assessing, refining and, often, restructuring programmes. The 1987 report, for example, highlighted the importance of the work for teachers as well as the students:

> The actor–teacher brings a vitality and enthusiasm to the children as well as a repertoire of activities that are not only educational, but exciting and innovative as well. All the programs presented by the team are well thought out and carefully tailored to meet the needs of individual districts and classes. Thus, the workshops are not only beneficial to the students, but serve to provide teachers with dramatic techniques that they can implement on their own.
>
> (Jacobowitz and Meyers 1987)

However, one of the weaknesses indicated by these findings is that due to the brief duration of most of these programmes, generally lasting from two to five sessions, a change in students' behaviour is improbable. This is a situation that CAT is attempting to alleviate by establishing a drama in education project with elementary school students, meeting once a week for a minimum of one academic year, thereby providing sufficient data for a long-term study.

For eighteen years, the Creative Arts Team has employed theatre performances and drama workshops to serve as catalysts for examining a plethora of themes and issues with thousands of young people in New York City. While our work will necessarily change in response to changing needs, it will always be designed to empower young people with the intellectual and social skills to make appropriate, constructive choices relevant to their lives.

NOTE

1 Five-O: Police.

BIBLIOGRAPHY

Creative Arts Team (1990) *Fifteenth Anniversary Booklet*, New York.
Jacobowitz, T. and Meyers, R. (1987) *Report*, Arts Partners: New York.

Part IV

TIE in the 1990s and beyond

Introduction

Almost all the chapters in this book could have justified a place in this section, for most look forward as well as back. The chapters that follow, however, have a particular claim to be about the future directions that TIE may take or may need to take.

Steve Ball discusses one of the main growth areas in TIE over the past ten years and reminds us that health education, while it has moved fast up the social and political agendas of most countries because of the rapid spread of HIV/AIDS, covers a wider range of concerns than many realize, and that this important area of work needs approaching with some rigour if it is not to be reduced to the level of walking/talking slide shows. There are of course other developing areas in which TIE methodology is playing a growing part, some of which (theatre in museums, in prisons and for the disabled) have been mentioned earlier. Two further brief examples here will help to underline the diversity of opportunities for TIE in the future.

One of the companies Ball discusses, Age Exchange, has recently expanded and developed its educational theatre programmes, particularly those in which young people interact with professional 'senior citizen' actor–teachers. During 1993, designated 'European Year of Older People and Solidarity Between Generations', the company will be touring two of its plays to six European countries and running workshop exchanges with theatre companies and arts organizations in Germany, Belgium and France. Clearly, the projected rapid increase in the numbers of the elderly in society over the next few decades makes the need to bridge traditional gulfs between young and old all the more pressing – and could mark another significant path for exploration by TIE companies.

Also alert to the opportunities offered by the 'new Europe' as it expands, as borders disintegrate and as different problems present themselves in the process, is the Spiral Theatre Company, based in Southampton but now offering multi-lingual educative theatre across the continent (their brochure is written in four languages). The aim is not only to spread the use of TIE methodology through its plays and workshops, but to 'celebrate difference between regional and ethnic cultures and languages' (Spiral Theatre Brochure, 1992). The hope must be that Britain will benefit from similar visits of educational theatre companies from abroad who will in turn enrich and cultivate British TIE practice.

The final three chapters all share a broad concern with 'evaluation', though it is approached in a variety of ways. Lowell Swortzell provocatively poses some questions about TIE and how – if – it is to move forward: questions that not only echo some of the objections to TIE that were heard in the early 1970s, but are being reformulated now, more uncomfortably, at a time when practitioners are having to take stock and rethink their role in a changed economic and cultural climate.

Ken Robinson's chapter on evaluation (reproduced with only a few small amendments from the 1980 edition) looks head-on at the whole vexed question of evaluative methods as applied to the arts and TIE in particular. Companies are having to be accountable far more frequently and extensively than ever before; but how the accompanying evaluation is conducted, and the pitfalls that are to be avoided, are matters of which TIE teams need to be fully aware. To leave evaluation to others, the 'experts', could well prove to be a recipe for self-destruction. Once again, a matter that seemed pressing in 1980 proves only too immediate and unresolved a concern thirteen years later.

Finally, from a different standpoint altogether, that of the receiving institutions, Geoff Readman urges a wholesale rethink about how TIE goes forward and especially how it develops and extends the partnerships that will increasingly be vital to it in an economically more hostile world. Although his discussion is framed within the context of the recent upheavals in the British education system, his concerns and the questions he poses will have relevance for the discussion of how TIE is to progress in any country where state educational provision is undergoing (or has already undergone) substantial change.

Chapter 12

Theatre in Health Education

Steve Ball

One of the most provocative and exciting developments in Theatre in Education and Community Theatre in recent years has been the emergence of Theatre in Health Education (THE). This chapter will consider the wide-ranging nature of THE and raise some questions about its future role.

A class of secondary school pupils is watching a play about HIV and AIDS; a group of young parents is using Forum Theatre techniques to explore problems relating to parenthood; and a cast of elderly people is performing a play about keeping warm in winter.

These three different experiences, for three different audiences, have one thing in common: they all use theatre as a medium for learning about health. They serve to illustrate the wide-ranging and eclectic nature of Theatre in Health Education. THE encompasses a broad definition of both 'theatre' and 'health education' – that is, theatre in its widest sense, involving a diverse range of styles, form and content, and 'health education' in keeping with the World Health Organization's definition of health as 'a state of complete physical, mental and social well being, and not merely the absence of disease or infirmity' (WHO 1948: 1).

REASONS FOR THE EMERGENCE OF THEATRE IN HEALTH EDUCATION

Theatre in Health Education has not evolved in a social and artistic vacuum. Rather it is the result of a number of factors and developments in both health education and TIE.

(a) We live in an increasingly health conscious society where health promotion and the prevention of ill health are no longer the sole concern of the medical profession. An emphasis on preventative health and 'care in the community' has resulted in new roles and responsibilities for members of the caring professions. In this relatively new environment it is less surprising that theatre workers and health educators have started to work together to develop THE.

(b) There has been a growing interest amongst TIE companies in issues relating to personal, social and health education. In 1988 57 per cent of all TIE companies that replied to a survey reported that they had recently been involved in, or were about to embark on, a health related programme (Ball 1992).

(c) There has been a growing awareness amongst health educationalists of the value of and potential for using theatre and educational drama in health education. This has coincided with the realization by many in TIE and health education that both fields of work share common philosophies and approaches.

(d) A number of organizations have set up procedures aimed at facilitating and encouraging the use of Theatre in Health Education. Yorkshire Arts (now Yorkshire and Humberside Regional Arts Board) produced a set of guidelines in 1990 to help health authorities and theatre companies work together to produce good practice, good theatre and good relations (Burgess 1990); the Health Education Authority, which has a statutory responsibility for the promotion of health in England, is about to produce a similar set of guidelines on the use of theatre in HIV and AIDS Education (Harris 1993). The Theatre in Health Education Trust, established in Birmingham in 1988, aims to provide an information service about THE, attract funding for THE initiatives and encourage and facilitate good practice.

(e) However, the most significant factor in the development of Theatre in Health Education has been the emergence of HIV and AIDS. The threat which the AIDS virus presents to the health of the nation brought a new sense of crisis and urgency to the health education movement. Many newly appointed 'HIV officers' who were keen to take risks and try out radical strategies commissioned a plethora of performance-based pieces which desperately tried to 'get the message across'. In 1991 there were at least fourteen programmes by

English companies (McEwan, Bhopal and Patton 1991: 155) which addressed the issue of HIV and AIDS. These ranged from *Dreamdate?*, a participatory TIE programme co-devised by Language Alive! and New York's Creative Arts Team, to *Body Talk*, a play followed by a workshop by Big Deal Community Theatre Company and *Throwing Stones*, a play performed by a group of unemployed young people who worked with a writer and director from the Royal Court Young People's Theatre. The sheer quantity of work has left many to assume wrongly that Theatre in Health Education and AIDS are virtually synonymous.

THREE EXAMPLES OF THEATRE IN HEALTH EDUCATION

Help! I've Got a Toddler

This was devised in 1990 by Jaswinder Didially, Hilary Pearce and Iain Smith of Language Alive!, a Birmingham based TIE company that uses drama and role-play to stimulate language development across the curriculum. Since 1986 over forty participatory TIE programmes have been devised on a range of themes and issues from shape and colour with infants, to local history and bullying with juniors, and the solar system and the media with secondary school students. THETA, its Theatre in Health Education wing, devises participatory THE programmes and tours schools, colleges, youth clubs and community groups nationally.

Help! I've Got a Toddler, which was sponsored by the National Society for the Prevention of Cruelty to Children (NSPCC), aimed to explore parenting skills and strategies with parents of pre-school children and to promote positive attitudes towards parenting. The ninety-minute programme, which was researched and devised with young parents, toured to parent and toddler groups, family centres and maternity hospitals. It included elements of performance as well as drama in education conventions such as Hot-seating, Still Image and Forum Theatre.

The programme began with a performance extract in which a television presenter introduced 'Parents' Hour', a daytime TV programme. Her patronizing style cut no ice with two 'toddlers' in the audience who took over the programme and, through the use of extracts of their own and their parents' diaries, presented five scenes each highlighting problems between parents and their young children. These included pestering, tantrums and bedwetting.

The performance element of the programme was followed by small group work, based on Augusto Boal's Image Theatre. The participants produced a still image (or tableau) based on their perceptions of one of the worst aspects of being a parent. They were then asked to produce a second image which showed an ideal way of solving the problem. A third transitional image illustrated the way in which the parents could move from the 'worst' to the 'ideal' image. This still image work provided an accessible and economic form for expressing ideas and acted as a stimulus for discussion about different parenting strategies.

This was followed by a repeat of the different scenes. The parents hot-seated (questioned) the characters from the scenes and were then given the opportunity, through the use of Forum Theatre, to take on the parent's role themselves. Follow-up interviews, conducted by the NSPCC one week and six months after the programme, suggested that by providing young parents with a supportive environment in which to share ideas and try out different strategies, the programme helped to reduce the sense of isolation which many parents of pre-school children experience. Although many of the parents were unfamiliar with the use of theatre, and some felt inhibited by the participatory elements, the evaluation suggested that the programme had been successful in meeting its initial aims of exploring parenting strategies and providing positive images of parenthood (Hayes 1991).

The Inner Circle

This is a play followed by a workshop which was originally devised through improvisations with teenagers led by Ed Decker of the New Conservatory Children's Theatre in San Francisco. The play was scripted by Patricia Loughrey and adapted by Nigel Townsend for Y Touring, a performance company which is part of London Central YMCA. They have toured *The Inner Circle* nationally to schools, colleges and youth clubs since 1989 and, in keeping with the peer group education model of the American programme, have used young professional actors (aged 17 to 23). *The Inner Circle* aims to help prevent HIV infection amongst young people by providing information about AIDS and the transmission and prevention of HIV infection. It also seeks to help prevent and break down prejudice and to create opportunities for young people to clarify their own attitudes toward sexuality, drug taking and related issues and to help them decide how best to protect themselves, their partners and their friends.

The sixty-minute play tells the story of four friends, all secondary school students, and their responses when one of them, Mark, becomes infected with HIV and develops AIDS. The play opens after Mark's death and begins when his three closest friends return to the flat where he had hidden when he first learnt that he had been infected with HIV. Through the use of flashbacks the audience meet Mark and trace the path of his illness. They learn that Mark became infected with HIV through one experience of skin popping (subcutaneous drug injection). The three friends all bring different human perspectives to the story: Danny's realization that he is gay raises questions about sexuality and the media's attitude towards the 'gay plague'; Sarah's memories of Mark draw attention to heterosexual transmission and Cathy's response challenges misinformation and irrational fears of HIV and AIDS.

The play incorporates information about HIV and AIDS and includes facts about prevention. The follow-up workshop brings the three friends back together and through hot-seating encourages the students to examine how the characters have come to terms with Mark's death. It also provides students with the opportunity to clarify their own thoughts and feelings about HIV and AIDS and consider how the existence of the virus will affect their own behaviour through the three different views and opinions which the characters present. Cathy doesn't want to have penetrative sex until she is married, Sarah believes that she can carry condoms without being labelled a 'slag', and Danny confronts the issues and prejudices surrounding his sexuality. At the end of the workshop the facilitator leaves the students with a series of open questions concerning HIV and AIDS. The workshop is limited in what it can achieve, not least by the short amount of time devoted to it and the fact that it usually takes place with one whole year group involving up to 120 pupils. However, the company views the workshop as a 'bridge' between the performance and the follow-up work which teachers and health education officers can develop back in the classroom.

The feedback which the company has received suggests that *The Inner Circle* strikes a chord with young people. There are a number of reasons for this: the play is a captivating piece of theatre and it involves clearly drawn characters who are readily identifiable with young audiences. The use of young actors, usually only two or three years older than the audience, is supported by research (Redman 1987: 150–1), which suggests that peer group teaching is an effective way of educating young people about HIV and AIDS (Y Touring 1991).

Keep Warm, Keep Well

This was devised and performed by pensioners (senior citizens) in association with Age Exchange, a theatre and publishing company which aims to improve the quality of life of older people by giving them a voice through the production of plays and books (Age Exchange 1991). Their Reminiscence Theatre work involves interviewing people, transcribing the material, putting it into dramatic form and giving the stories back to the pensioners in the form of plays performed by teams of professional actors. While it could be argued that all of the company's work contributes indirectly to the health of older people, some projects have had a specific Theatre in Health Education focus. *Can We Afford the Doctor* (1985) sought to remind people of life before the National Health Service at a time when its very existence was under threat. The show included songs and sketches which explored traditional remedies and examined the close relationship between bad housing conditions, unemployment and ill health.

Age Exchange have also been involved in projects in which elderly people themselves produce their own theatre. *Keep Warm, Keep Well* was devised by pensioners through improvisation with Age Exchange's director, Pam Schweitzer, to launch the Department of Health's 'Winter Warmth Line' (telephone service). This aimed to raise awareness amongst older people of the importance of keeping warm in winter and the dangers of hypothermia. A scenario was developed based on the story of a person who stopped attending a lunch club. Some of her

Plate 12.1 Keep Warm, Keep Well
Keep Warm, Keep Well (Age Exchange 1991). TIE play presented by older people from the Age Exchange Reminiscence Centre, directed by Pam Schweitzer. Photo: Alex Schweitzer.

friends who were concerned about her called at her house and, finding her drowsy and cold, warmed her up, gave her some food and let her know of sources of help. The short play, which toured to groups of older people, was followed by a discussion, led by the actors out of role, in which the issues raised in the play, including the status of old people in society, levels of benefits and the reluctance which many old people have in claiming benefits, were explored. These discusssions provided anecdotal evidence that the play had succeeded in raising awareness of the importance of keeping warm in winter.

Although these three programmes have been devised by three different companies for three different audiences, they serve to illustrate some common features of THE. The work usually involves relatively small homogeneous groups – parents, young people or the elderly – in closed environments: a community centre, school or home for the elderly. The three projects also share common aims which could be said to characterize Theatre in Health Education. All are concerned with using theatre to encourage self empowerment and explore attitudes and values. They all involved, to different degrees, the active participation of the audience, and all three programmes were devised in consultation with members of the health or caring professions and regarded as a stimulus for, or an integral part of, a wider health education programme.

Just as the three programmes share common aims, so too they experienced similar problems. The principal problem, experienced by all three companies, relates to funding. Limited and threatened financial resources create problems, by no means exclusive to THE, which require companies to engage in complex balancing acts in terms of cast sizes, production budgets and audience numbers. *Help! I've Got a Toddler*, for example, was originally intended to have a cast of four, but the company were financially restricted to using three teacher–actors. The workshop following *The Inner Circle* is ideally suited to a class unit of thirty pupils but in order to make the tours financially viable it had to take place with whole year groups involving up to 120 pupils at a time. The length of the *Keep Warm, Keep Well* tour was restricted by lack of funding. These financial restrictions also limit the amount of time and resources available for evaluation, whether they be internal company evaluations or external reports.

THE FUTURE

It is difficult to predict whether THE will continue to develop and become a major force in education and the arts. It would however be wrong to assume that there is universal agreement between arts workers and health educationalists about the use of THE. Anecdotal evidence suggests that health educationalists are rightly suspicious of those theatre companies that they perceive to have 'jumped on the bandwagon', exploited funding opportunities and produced poor work. Other health workers are generally sceptical of the claims made for drama and theatre. Some regard it as an expensive use of limited resources, others are concerned with the difficulties surrounding evaluation procedures and some believe it encourages noisy, aggressive behaviour in children and young people.

Likewise there is a significant number of TIE practitioners that share reservations about the use of drama and theatre in health education. This largely stems from a general prejudice, especially prevalent in the wider young people's theatre movement, about using theatre as a learning medium. This is partly a reaction against much of the issue-based TIE and young people's theatre of the 1970s and 1980s and a general concern that the emphasis on personal development, self empowerment and problem solving, which characterizes much THE work, fails to recognize drama as an art form with an aesthetic dimension. Some theatre workers are concerned at what they see as the relegation of theatre performance to a single component in a wider educational package. There is also a concern about the extent to which sponsors and funding bodies can compromise the work. Whilst this is a common concern for all those involved in the arts it is especially pertinent when commercial sponsors want to be associated with a healthy image, through using a theatre company to promote a particular product, or when funding bodies seek to use theatre to 'get their message across' at the expense of the aesthetic dimension.

The future success of THE depends on a number of factors:

(a) It is generally recognized that THE is principally concerned with empowering children, young people and adults by providing them with information, opportunities to examine attitudes and values and the chance to practise skills so that they can make informed decisions about their own health and lifestyle. However, if THE is to develop it must move beyond an exclusive concern with self empowerment and recognize the wider structural and political factors which affect health. Account must therefore be taken of the complex social, political and environmental influences which affect individuals and communities. It must also go beyond a functional, utilitarian mode and recognize that the full potential for using drama and theatre requires a respect for and recognition of the aesthetic dimension inherent in theatre as an art form. Otherwise THE is likely to be reduced to the status of an expensive audio-visual aid, rather than regarded as a worthwhile drama and theatre experience in itself.

(b) THE needs to move away from its almost exclusive pre-occupation with HIV and AIDS in order to address other personal, social and community health issues. This is not to deny the importance and seriousness of the HIV/AIDS crisis, but to suggest that theatre which examines HIV and AIDS needs to place this concern within a wider context and recognize the potential for using drama to examine a broad range of health-related themes and issues.

(c) The collaboration which has so far taken place between health authorities and arts organizations needs to be enhanced and developed. Serious consideration must be given to establishing and developing collaborative approaches which enable teachers, health education officers and TIE practitioners to work together. The role which major bodies including the Arts Council, Regional Arts Boards and the Health Education Authority can play in this needs to be addressed.

(d) As THE involves the use of active learning methods, and an emphasis on decision making and the exploration of attitudes and values, those teachers and health educationalists that have regarded their role exclusively in terms of information giving may feel threatened by THE. There is therefore a serious need for training opportunities, both for health educators and teachers, in the potential for using THE. Such training could also involve skill sharing so that teachers, health educators and drama workers exchange skills and working practices. Such training opportunities would help to increase the understanding between drama workers and health educators which is essential if THE is to develop.

(e) The continued low status of TIE and health education with politicians, funding bodies and senior managers in education and health authorities needs to be addressed. Neither Drama nor Health Education are foundation subjects in the National Curriculum and as such have to compete with core and foundation subjects for resources and space on a crowded timetable. The values often expressed in these areas, such as encouraging children to question established views and attitudes and challenge many of the values inherent in the society in which we live, are not necessarily in line with government opinion on education, the arts or health.

(f) There is a continued lack of consistent evidence concerning the effectiveness of THE. At a time when THE is being compared in cost effectiveness terms with mass media campaigns (McEwan, Bhopal and Patton 1991: 159), it is essential that clear criteria are established which illustrate the effectiveness of the comparatively expensive medium of THE. These evaluation procedures must of course be acceptable both to those involved in THE, some of whom are rightly suspicious of scientific evaluation methods, and funding agencies who often regard THE as an expensive luxury. It is important to recognize that scientific evaluation methods, with their tight controls and systematic objective-oriented procedures, may be appropriate for testing routine operations of a cognitive nature but are unsuited to the complex human interactions inherent in a THE programme. The challenge remains to find evaluation procedures which are sensitive enough to measure the often subtle shifts in the attitudes of participants, the complex mixture of cognitive and affective intentions within a single THE programme and the way in which a THE programme can change and develop during the course of a tour.

CONCLUSION

Recent reports have suggested that the emergence of Theatre in Health Education has influenced health education officers working in HIV and AIDS and has begun to influence health promotion in general (Harris 1993). This not only involves health educationalists drawing upon TIE and community theatre companies as a health education resource, but includes a growing number of health educationalists that use TIE and drama in education methods and strategies in their day to day practice. THE has also provided a focus for a number of TIE and community theatre companies who have examined themes and issues relating to personal, social and health education.

However, if THE is to develop beyond the novel and firmly establish itself it has to move away from an almost exclusive concern with HIV and Aids and examine other areas of health education. It also requires individuals and organizations involved in the arts and health to examine crucial issues such as collaboration, networking, training, evaluation and the continued low status which health, education and the arts are generally accorded.

BIBLIOGRAPHY

Age Exchange (1991) *Annual Report 1990–1*, London: Age Exchange.

Ball, S. D. (1992) unpublished Ph.D. research, Manchester University.

Burgess, G. (1990) *Let's Get This Show on the Road*, Yorkshire Arts.

Harris, S. (1993) *Theatre in HIV/Aids Education for Young People in Schools and Informal Settings*, London: Health Education Authority.

Hayes, E. (1991) '"Help! I've Got a Toddler" Evaluation', unpublished report, NSPCC.

McEwan, R. T., Bhopal, R. and Patton, W. (1991) 'Drama on HIV and Aids: an evaluation of a theatre in education programme', *Health Education Journal* 50 (4).

Redman, J. (1987) 'Aids and peer teaching', *Health Education Journal* 46.

WHO (1948) *World Health Organisation Constitution*, Geneva.

Y Touring (revised 1991) *The Inner Circle Project: Information and Action Pack*, London: Central YMCA.

Chapter 13

Trying to like TIE

An American critic hopes TIE can be saved

Lowell Swortzell

Leafing through the earlier edition of this book I was amused to come upon a pencilled entry made when I first read Tony Jackson's declaration in the Introduction stating that: 'No one who has seen good TIE in action will need much persuasion of its potency as an educational resource, nor of its value as a medium of theatre.' My marginal note exclaims, 'Oh, yeah?' And this impertinent expression of doubt may be the right place to begin a discussion of several characteristics that in my view keep TIE from realizing its full 'potency' and 'value'. Yet let me state that however strong or harsh some of these opinions may be, they originate from a deep belief in the potential values of TIE as well as from a hope to see it hold an established place in both education and theatre. As an American professor of educational theatre, I have watched the TIE movement from its beginnings in England; as a researcher, I have studied earlier efforts in other parts of the world, including the impressive 'Blue Blouse' companies playing throughout the Soviet Union in the 1920s and the excellent programmes of the Federal Theatre Project in the United States in the 1930s. In editing *The International Guide to Children's Theatre and Educational Theatre* (1990), I collected information about TIE as it was practised around the world through the 1980s. And I have advocated the adaptation and advancement of TIE in the United States ever since our first efforts in this direction at New York University in the early 1970s. Still, for reasons that follow, I am not convinced that after all these years TIE can yet be called 'a medium of theatre'. And one of the questions to be examined here is: 'Should it be?'

This question certainly is not new, for as far back as 1974 an

American publisher expressed anxiety about the movement in words that, for me, still remain cruelly pertinent. Sara Spencer who had seen TIE in England wrote, 'While in general I found its content rich and exciting and contemporary, in my judgement the scripting was often of poor quality, scenery scuffed, costumes grubby. TIE has many values. I would just hope that our children would not grow up to think this was theatre!' (Spencer 1974). If not theatre, what, then, *should* they think it, or, for that matter, should we who make, teach and write about it? Let us base our examination here in these same three crucial areas of concern: scripting, production and mission.

THE TIE SCRIPT

The usual practice employed in writing TIE scripts, at least until recently, came about as a result of the age in which the movement started. With various social revolutions afoot in the early 1960s, and with rebellion rampant everywhere in the lifestyles of the young, the communal concept of creativity prevailed in many of the arts. Where once there had been traditional companies, the avant-garde theatre world soon experienced the emergence of collectives, and sometimes even cults. We witnessed the advent of Grotowski and his followers and their dedicated deconstruction of texts; we read of Peter Brook's retreat into the desert with his polyglot disciples to forge the mythical meanings of ritual. And later we saw a group turn *Hamlet*, of all plays, into a machine and a number of other things Shakespeare never envisioned. But this sort of 'revisionism' scarcely mattered since the directors had declared themselves and not the playwrights to be the quintessential theatre artists of the day. Their resolute pursuit of improvised visual and physical imagery only served to encourage loyal actors to make cannon fodder of scripts, if indeed they bothered to employ the written word at all.

Understandably, then, in the development of TIE, 'team' identity took hold as a principle although not necessarily with the 'guru' figure at its head. Designed instead to be true democracies in action, TIE teams closely worked together to research, devise, write, stage, produce and act their offerings as well as to participate in pre- and post-performance school and classroom activities. Whether members had abilities in all of these areas did not seem to matter as long as each was committed to the team. But art, of course, cannot be created by committee, a fact that became particularly apparent in the task of scripting, where artistic merit suffered the most. Often sounding like the assembly-job constructions they were, texts tended to lack individual dramatic voices that audiences could hear in performance or later could recall. Few evidenced dramatic distinction, and, with only a handful of exceptions, scripts seldom played as effectively in the hands of teams other than those that originally had devised them. It is little wonder they came to be called 'programmes' rather than plays.

In recent years a few individual playwrights have emerged in Great Britain but the most impressive of these, David Holman, Paul Swift and Noel Greig, now tend to create full-fledged plays rather than TIE programmes. In America, too, of the early 1990s, Laurence Yep has come forth with *Dragonwings* and James Still with *Amber Waves* to prove what enormous contributions real playwrights can make to those educational companies willing to produce real plays. But after thirty years of weak TIE scripts, this rather tardy appearance of genuine dramatists may prove to be too late, for today, as never before, established dramatists in both professional and amateur theatres for young people are focusing on social themes. Even a playwright as long planted in the traditional American repertoire as Aurand Harris now uproots himself from time to time to write a play like *The Arkansaw Bear*, dealing head-on with the subject of death, or, as in his most recent and realistic work, *The Pinballs*, dealing with the psychological adjustment of children in a foster home. Prize-winning playwrights Susan Zeder and Joanna Halpert Kraus have employed such serious themes and issues as prejudice, peer pressure, Asian–American adoption, children of divorce, outsiders and loneliness. Brian Kral has tackled 'big' subjects in his use of teenage suicide in *Apologies*, the environment in *Troubled Waters* and problems of the handicapped in *Special Class*. These plays and authors are widely produced in the United States in theatres by established companies, but not in schools by TIE teams. With the help of study guides, teachers can prepare their students for these performances and for the company-conducted workshops which follow performances and foster discussion and related dramatic activities. So what was once TIE's exclusive terrain is now increasingly and highly effectively encroached upon by professional companies for young people.

Nor is this invasion limited to British and American dramatists and theatres. The Unga Klara of Stockholm and the GRIPS of Berlin, among dozens of others, have been moving in the same direction in recent years. Suzanne Osten, one of Sweden's leading directors, film makers and playwrights, has attracted international attention with works like *Medea's Children* (written in collaboration with Per Lysander), in which she deals with the subject of divorce. The play's children feel separated from their parents, so much so that they speak in contemporary idioms and wear modern clothes while their parents quarrel in classical dialogue and dress in ancient robes. Unga Klara's *Hitler's Childhood* by Niklas Raadstrom, advertised as 'a drama about hidden cruelty in child rearing', is based on the book *For Your Own Good* by psychologist Alice Miller. And even when this company takes on a classic such as *The Tempest*, they find a way to be at once contemporary and controversial (it was a sex-charged production with one scene of male nudity), yet true to Shakespeare. Here their attention centred upon family relations, and in particular upon those situations in the play dealing with factors of dependence and separation (see Swortzell 1990a). The GRIPS Theatre, no less daring, claims to be 'emancipatory' in its aims to empower young audiences to exercise their full political rights. Volker Ludwig, the dynamic director and author or co-author of numerous GRIPS works, likes to address specific problems familiar to his audiences, such as oversized classes that prevent students from learning or the mistreatment of immigrant labourers pouring into Berlin in search of work. Their plays have been televised nationally and have also been produced by other theatres in Europe and America. *Line One*, a GRIPS musical about teenage survival in Berlin, became a commercial box-office hit that also produced a best-selling original cast recording.

Why should such successes constitute a threat to TIE? For one reason, they can provide a better product (I do not suggest that they necessarily do!) but, put most succinctly, they can offer genuine works of theatre that also have strong educational implications. Because their playwrights are not restricted by time limits imposed by school officials they can plot stories step-by-step and develop characters stage-by-stage and thereby gain the dramatic weight needed to support an issue which gives the play a life of its own. But in TIE, more often than not, the writer with only an hour or so to command must assault the problem as directly and quickly as possible, which results in a script that draws its power from the issue itself rather than from the lives of its characters. And so the work becomes polemical, tending to be politicized rather than dramatized. The best most TIE writers can do is to provide an outline, often sketched in a series of short scenes, with the hope that the actors will flesh out the characters through their own personalities and performance skills. Luckily a few are able to do this, but most appear in programmes in which the problems of the play matter far more than the people who possess them. And because the characters can seldom be known very deeply, they have little lasting effect beyond the duration of the performance.

Another reason these theatres threaten TIE programmes stems from the fact that their plays have a beginning, middle and end that together provide a complete dramatic experience, almost always resolved in some artistically satisfying way, even when it turns out to be tragic and emotionally harrowing. TIE, on the other hand, normally avoids endings in order to allow its audiences the opportunity to discuss issues and to come to their own conclusions. When 'problem solving' and 'decision making' became buzz words in the educational jargon of the 1970s and early 1980s, TIE with its 'hot-seating' and other participation techniques emerged as a perfect vehicle for simulations in which audiences could determine the outcome of a situation. Teachers were urged not to vote or to sway opinions of their classes so that students might experience the full responsibility and power they had been given. But an open-ended per-formance will remain an unfinished one, and potentially frus-trating to audiences anticipating resolution, unless, that is, the team returns and plays the possible conclusions and thereby allows students to discover their preferences by experiencing them. When this happens, viewers are both reflectively re-warded and aesthetically fulfilled.

THE TIE PRODUCTION

'Scuffed' scenery and 'grubby' costumes were the images that lingered with Sara Spencer after viewing productions in the early years of TIE, and, unfortunately, they remain apt for much of the work to be seen today, at least in America. I am told that many British TIE companies have addressed the widely acknowledged problem of production values by engaging resident or freelance designers who in recent years provide impressive scenic elements of professional calibre. American actors, on the other hand, often appear in contemporary clothes that look as if they had been bought off the rack at the nearest discount department store. Some performers actually wear their own clothes and walk on stage in the same outfits they arrive in at schools. Grubby? Yes. Costumes? No, at least not in the usual theatrical meaning of the word. And scenery is often reduced to compact units made to fit into a van or into the back seat of a car, which can be assembled and disassembled in short order and which looks cheap as well as no doubt being so. Certainly, underlying budgetary reductions prevent some companies from creating elaborate settings but, economic cutbacks notwithstanding, teams still face the artistic responsibility to present theatre of high visual appeal. They often excuse themselves by claiming there is little point in transporting set pieces and lighting equipment to schools devoid of technical resources and where they may have to play in the cafeteria or in the gymnasium. But we all know that every space, be it hallway, closet or classroom, can become theatrical if a true theatrical mind decides to make it so. Today most companies seem to prefer to pour their production budgets into portable sound systems, boom boxes and keyboards that make their work loud, if little else.

In the case of TIE, 'scuffiness' always has been less a question of money than an aesthetic statement, made as if some essential correlation links being serious with being tacky. Indeed, sometimes the more urgent the topic the more shabby the production is likely to be: child abuse somehow equals theatre abuse! This practice may derive its inspiration from the example of Bertolt Brecht who is said to have applied dirt daily underneath his fingernails in order to intensify his identification with the causes of the great unwashed. But even dirty old Brecht demanded and received money for his productions which in their intended simplicity were also costly, especially in the use of lighting designs. No one knew better how to make spectacle out of bedsheets strung as a curtain on a wire across a bare stage. No one was more aware that this was a political statement but also, and as important to him, this was a theatrical statement! As also would be two folding metal chairs placed in a chalk circle drawn on the floor of a classroom if these were all that were available to him. TIE designers readily recognize the political statement inherent in a programme but they may not always find the equivalent theatrical expression that proves they are artists as well as educators.

Despite great odds, a few TIE companies have managed to offer audiences productions that look professionally designed because in fact they have been, usually by someone who has been engaged from outside the team to perform this function. And sometimes even costumes of historical periods look authentic, as they did in the Leeds TIE Team production of *Raj* in which there was a designer at work who knew what he was doing. But this should be true of every TIE production, rather than the exception.

When it comes to acting, TIE teams often demonstrate professional standards to be proud of, especially in the established companies in England and in the Scandinavian countries, where high levels of performance are maintained. On the other hand, in those instances in which TIE is presented by amateur and student actors, and even the less experienced professional teams, the quality is bound to vary from production to production and there can be no guaranteed level of artistry from year to year. TIE as a training ground, however, has proved to be an extremely effective discipline for students in colleges, universities and educational theatre programmes. And the work that goes on in these courses feeds into the professional companies which in the United States often offer internships for college credit that provide valuable experience in all aspects of administration, fund raising, production, performance and assessment. The university as a training ground for future teams is solidly in place in at least half a dozen American institutions.

It must be clear by now, however, that I cannot advocate 'future teams' modelled on past or even most current examples, simply because I am convinced that the team concept should have been abandoned ages ago, along with the rest of the 'collective' culture of the 1960s. What TIE needs now is what theatre has always needed: the best qualified artists for any given project, which means one writer, one director, as many actors as the script requires, one designer for sets and one for costumes (and if there is to be stage lighting, as I hope there will be, then a third designer), a stage manager and technical support. If the playwright cannot research and devise the script alone, then the producers should find one who can. It's as simple as that. There never was a need for everyone to do everything and the artistic progress of TIE has been stunted long enough by this naive and foolish notion.

THE TIE MISSION

When I read that a teacher is only interested in the educational value of the programme visiting her school and could not care less about the theatrical values, I know something has gone awry, no, seriously wrong, in the creation and marketing of TIE (Scott 1982: 25–6). And this opinion is confirmed when a script states:

> It is also crucial that the teacher at no time tells the children that a *play* is coming to school. If the children think it is just a *play*, it makes it very difficult to get the necessary involvement as there is a security in knowing it is just a play that a child can cling to to avoid any real questions or problems.
>
> (Belgrade TIE Team 1980: 21)

Just a play! Indeed, if a child could perceive exactly that, how fortunate for both TIE and the child! This is what TIE should be and often was all about, a theatrical experience which forced children to confront real questions and true problems.

By now the direction away from TIE's theatrical roots in Artaud, Brecht and Piscator may indeed be difficult to halt. The TIE movement in England originated not only in education and theatre but also in politics, so from the outset teams sought subjects they held to be important, urgent and controversial. TIE made its reputation as a power that could address social conditions and define current problems in communities or school districts. By provoking thoughtful discussion from audiences on how these ills could be recognized and perhaps cured, TIE programmes involved young people in areas of concern that schools were often reluctant to investigate and sometimes in causes they traditionally avoided altogether. TIE proved to be so effective at this sort of latter-day agitprop presentations that 'issue-based' programmes became its speciality, its trademark, its purpose. Titles flourished such as *Our Streets, Our Lives; In Your Own Backyard; Unemployment: An Occupational Hazard* and *Ways of Change.* Much of this work was vigorous, moving and often intensely political, yet still theatrical, the kind of presentations we came to say TIE does well. Theatre directors and educators from all over the world arrived in England to see what the excitement was all about. Even now, TIE can still explore expertly the arenas of dissent, although seldom with the same flame of commitment it generated in the 1970s when the cause often literally leapt from the stage to demand our attention and reaction.

But this impressive achievement is only one type of presentation and only one approach to education, and the fact remains that TIE has not moved into other areas with equal success. For in pursuing the 'big' issues in its desire for change, TIE has ignored topics of other sizes to make them moving and powerful as well. Claims once were heard that through TIE we could teach and learn all subjects, yes, even mathematics and the sciences; we were assured teams could breathe life into the most abstract disciplines and codes of critical thinking. But instead of revitalizing the curriculum most teams looked to challenges outside the classroom as their areas of concentration; attempts to teach algebra and biology never progressed much beyond the level of conference demonstrations and weekend workshops.

Yet what for me remains one of the most successful programmes I have seen did exactly that: it taught children to read. Wanting to devise a non-controversial topic of interest to all schools and curricula, the Newham Drama Team in the East End of London developed an infant programme, *The Biggest Nursery Rhyme Book in the World*, in which the cast and audience together had to reassemble a huge twelve-page book that had collapsed and scattered all about the performance area. Each page demonstrated a different reading problem and a page could not be turned until every child had mastered it. Most important in this process, the children could not be manipulated by the actors who had to proceed at the speed of the audience. The reassembled book became both the script and a remarkable theatrical metaphor, extending its animated style to the costumes and performances which conveyed warmth and informality. The programme required no post-performance discussion inasmuch as learning already had taken place entirely within the course of the action itself. After the performance a teacher near me remarked, 'If you had told me you could get 5 year-olds to read for an hour, I would have said you were crazy.' But that is exactly what had happened and something more besides, because a theatrical event had also taken place (see Swortzell 1989).

My enthusiasm for this programme should not be misconstrued as a vote against issued-based TIE but as an endorsement for TIE in the full spectrum of education, as well as in the park and playground, in religion and recreation, and in the teaching of the performing arts, including theatre itself. For here, in our own form of expression, TIE has scarcely begun to recognize its opportunities as it steadfastly clings to basically realistic styles of presentation. This practice is not surprising when most scripts strive to be contemporary, depicting graphic conditions in true-to-life language, settings and costumes, often accompanied by the latest vogues in teenage music. But what of other forms of theatre at our disposal? When are we going to explore what TIE might gain from techniques of the circus, vaudeville, mime, puppetry, mixed media, musical comedy, clowning, improvisation, the living newspaper and so on? When will theatre be seen in all its manifestations so that students learn not just the subject of the programme but also come to appreciate the imagination of the form it takes? Indeed, when will students come to think that TIE *is* theatre? Only when its creators do, and so far they seem far from convinced.

James Thurber, the American humourist, essayist and playwright, in a letter written in 1953 stated: 'People never learn that there is 1,000 miles of desert between a good cause and a good play. Few people cross it alive' (Thurber 1953). And he was right, especially in the case of TIE which, clearly, is a good cause, one that can vitalize learning through the dynamics of living theatre. Equally evident is that TIE is not yet very often a good play. Several reasons have been given here for its lack of well-written scripts and high production values, but for me an even greater problem keeps TIE from travelling those thousand miles: TIE has forgotten that it is theatre. Just as each year we hear someone crusade to put Christ back into Christmas, I am here to plead that we put theatre back into TIE – before it dies

in the desert. And it has already run out of water and is crawling
on its knees!

BIBLIOGRAPHY

Belgrade TIE Team (1980) 'Pow Wow', in P. Schweitzer (ed.) *Theatre in
Education: Five Infant Programmes*, London: Methuen.
Scott, A. (1982) 'Frills or fundamentals', *SCYPT Journal* 10.
Spencer, S. (6 August 1974) letter in Child Drama Collection, Arizona
State University, Tempe, Arizona.
Swortzell, L. (1989) 'Biggest Nursery Rhyme Book in the World', *TYA
Today* (Theatre for Young Audiences Today) 4 (3), published by
ASSITEJ–USA.
—— (1990a), 'Stormen (The Tempest)', *TYA Today* 5 (2).
—— (ed.) (1990b) *International Guide to Children's Theatre and Edu-
cational Theatre*, New York: Greenwood Press.
Thurber, J. (21 March 1953) letter in James Thurber Collection, Ohio
State University, Columbus, Ohio.

Chapter 14

Evaluating TIE

Ken Robinson

In this chapter I want to discuss three questions: How are TIE programmes to be evaluated and by whom? What are TIE companies accountable for? I want to look at these general questions by considering first some characteristics of TIE and some of the functions of evaluation. I then want to look at what is involved in evaluating an arts-based programme in general and TIE in particular, outlining an approach.

THEATRE IN EDUCATION

The activities of TIE companies have become very diversified. Teams work not only in schools but in community centres, clubs and institutions, theatres and so on. I want to look particularly at work in schools and how it can be evaluated since this is where issues of accountability can be most sensitive. It is useful to compare some of the general characteristics of current TIE practice with those of school-based teaching to indicate some of the particular issues in evaluating TIE.

TIE companies vary enormously in composition, in their views of what they are doing and why, in where they work and in terms of employment. The structures of programmes vary according to their objectives, content and the intended audiences. Performance is often only part of a TIE programme which may include any combination of workshops, discussions and simulations. Despite the diversity there are some general observations which hold good for most if not all programmes.

1 They are devised for a wide range of schools and for general groups of children – say 10 to 12 year-olds – whom the

company do not usually know, even if they know something about them. School-based teachers work with the same groups of children on a regular basis and know considerably more about them.

2 Contact time is short – half a day, or a couple of days. Companies have a short-term commitment to particular groups in contrast to the teachers' long-term commitment.

3 TIE companies do not have the same range of educational responsibilities as teachers. The teachers are involved in the development of particular skills over a long period as well as exploring a wide variety of subject-matter. TIE programmes are primarily content-based. Broadly speaking, TIE companies are committed to affecting children's understanding of specific issues – that is, their work is focused on ideas and attitudes. This is as much a matter of choice as of necessity.

4 Companies can research specific issues in greater depth than teachers because of their working as a specialist team. They can provide a powerful and vivid presentation of the material beyond the resources of a particular school.

Given the nature and circumstances of the work how is TIE to be evaluated and who is to do it?

WHAT IS EVALUATION?

Evaluation is a multi-faceted process. How it is tackled depends on: (a) who is doing it and to whom; (b) what is being evaluated and why. In essence, evaluation is a process of arriving at understanding the worth of something. This means recognizing the multiple dimensions and the differing perceptions of its worth. Evaluation is not the same as assessment. In broad terms the purpose of assessment is to provide information about pupils' abilities and attainments in education: the purpose of evaluation is to provide information about the quality of educational opportunities they receive. Evaluation looks at the teaching, not just at the children.

WHAT KIND OF EVALUATION?

There is no single method of educational evaluation. During the last twenty years the assumptions of many conventional approaches have been fundamentally challenged. There is one approach which needs to be discussed here because it is especially suited to some of the demands of public account-ability. This is generally known as the objectives approach or 'objectives model'. There is a common tendency when thinking about evaluation in TIE or elsewhere tacitly to accept the assumptions and methods of this approach because they seem on the face of it to be just common sense. In more ways than one the objectives model is inappropriate for evaluating a TIE programme.

OBJECTIVES AND OBJECTIVITY

According to the objectives model there are three main steps in an educational programme. First, the team agrees on its objec-tives. Second, it devises and operates the programme to try to achieve the objectives. The third step is evaluation which is essentially a matter of finding out to what extent the objectives have been achieved. This model was set down in general terms in a key paper by Ralph Tyler, who argued that, since educa-tional objectives aim 'to produce certain desirable changes in the behaviour pattern of the student, then evaluation is the process of determining the degree to which these changes in behaviour are actually taking place' (Tyler 1949; reprinted in Hamilton et al. 1977: 106).

In the 1950s Benjamin Bloom of the University of Chicago built on Tyler's initiative and produced, with others, a *Taxonomy of Educational Objectives* (Bloom, ed. 1956) which helped to trigger a search for effective ways of measuring the correlation between objectives and outcomes. This drew heavily on the research procedures of social science and psychometrics. If objectives could be specified clearly enough, it was argued, the changes in behaviour could be measured and the success or failure of the programme accurately recorded. Standardized tests of skills learnt and attitudes acquired could be statistically analysed to help establish 'scientifically' whether or not the programme had worked.

An important feature of this approach to evaluation is the emphasis on 'objectivity'. In designing the 'evaluation instru-ments' – the questionnaires and so on – it is important to find out, says Tyler, to what degree two different persons . . . would be able to reach similar scores or summaries when they had an opportunity to score or summarise the same records of behaviour. If the scores or summaries vary markedly . . . it is clearly a subjective kind of appraisal and requires improvements in its objectivity in order to be a more satisfactory means of appraising a human behaviour.

(Tyler 1949; reprinted in Hamilton et al. 1977: 29)

Despite the seductive claims of this model and the allure of objectivity, there are a number of pitfalls in this approach which are deep enough to have justified looking for altogether different methods of evaluation. These have a particular relevance for TIE.

VALUES AND SUBJECTIVITY

Although the objectives model is linear, simple and apparently straightforward, the type of work it is used to evaluate may not be. Many of the actual effects of an educational programme are not planned in advance at all and may be completely unexpected. The problems and dangers of trying to evaluate a TIE programme using the objectives model become clear if we consider some of the aims and objectives of the Greenwich Young People's Theatre Company, in devising their anti-racist programme *Race Against Time* (1979):

to combat racial prejudice; to show young people of all races that there are common problems that we share, and that race is often used to divert attention from those shared problems;
to dispel some of the myths and preconceptions that often form the basis for prejudice;
to explore the background of immigration, pointing out that we live in a multiracial society and must learn to accept and value all its members.

The programme took a day in each school and consisted of a simulation piece in the morning followed by a performance by the company and group discussions in the afternoon. The company felt that schools had reacted in very different ways to both parts of the programme and that it was impossible to say in general whether it had achieved all its objectives. But as one member of the company put it:

The after-effects and side-effects of the programme have been enormous . . . . No other programme with which I have been associated has resulted in such widespread concern and co-operation among teachers . . . there have been staff meetings about it, school policies towards racism have been evolved, reports have been written . . . head teachers have debated the programme, so have ILEA officials, and the Minister for Arts saw part of it. It has also helped to raise political awareness of the company. My observations are impressionistic but obviously something important happened.

The programme did have a very wide effect on many of the schools it went to. But did it achieve its stated objectives? Does it matter? Many of these actual effects were certainly unforeseen. But then most of what goes on during any educational programme is unforeseen. In practice programmes are adapted to meet the demands of different groups. Although an educational programme needs clear initial aims, they may be modified in view of the children's actual responses, or even changed altogether. The actual effects of the programme may be more important than those intended. This process of adapting objectives and methods to the work in hand is at the very centre of how education works. The objectives model encourages us to use only the initial objectives as the reference points for evaluation. Using this model the TIE company which has adapted and responded to the challenge of different groups may conclude that they have failed altogether because they did not achieve what they set out to do.

There is another problem with this approach. How do you define the objectives in the first place? Tyler said that objectives should specify changes in student behaviour. It may well be possible to define objectives in this way for some sorts of work, particularly where specific skills are involved. Even then the outcomes are often unpredictable and this is especially true in the arts. The fact is that there are different types of educational objectives and this has important implications for evaluation.

When a TIE company sets out to consider attitudes, as Greenwich did in *Race Against Time*, there may be no immediate effects on the children's behaviour at all, especially not during the period of the programme and its evaluation. 'It was clear', said a member of the company, that some pupils have changed their views of racial issues as a result of the programme. Similarly some pupils have understood the arguments against racism but at the end of the day have reverted to irrational racist statements. Other pupils have been apparently unmoved by the whole affair. In all cases it is difficult to evaluate the long-term effects.

This is precisely the point. The effects on individuals of a programme may be imperceptible in the short term. The actual effects of *Race Against Time* for many children may have been to stir their thinking about issues they had taken for granted. It may have begun a process of thought that will continue to evolve after the experience of the programme has faded. In this context Eisner distinguishes between two types of educational objective: 'instructional' objectives, which specify skills and information to be learnt, and 'expressive' objectives:

> An expressive objective describes an educational encounter: it identifies a situation in which children are to work, a task in which they are to engage: but it does not specify what they are to learn. . . . An expressive objective provides both the teacher and the student with an invitation to explore, defer, or focus on, issues that are of peculiar interest or import to the enquirer. An expressive objective is evocative rather than prescriptive.
>
> (Eisner 1969: 17)

The point is not that TIE programmes always have expressive objectives. Companies sometimes set out to teach quite specific skills. It is that instructional objectives only specify part of the business. In any case the initial objectives should not tyrannize our perception of what is actually going on during the work.

OBJECTIVE EVALUATION

One of the hopes of the scientific approach to evaluation is that the evaluator should be 'objective' and thereby establish the 'real', 'correct' value of the programme. The trouble is that educational evaluation is inevitably tied up in values and these tend to vary between individuals and groups both in terms of the values they bring to a programme and the capacity in which they actually experience it: as teacher, children, funders, etc. A work of art 'has no single true value. A programme has no single true value. The value of an arts in education programme will be different for different people, for different purposes' (Stake 1975: 25).

A full evaluation would involve getting information on the responses of everyone involved in the programme. But a programme stimulates a huge number of personal reactions and interactions. It is not possible to gather every last scrap of potentially relevant information and even if it were the problem of what to do with it all would still remain. Information gathering involves choices and selection. By what criteria, and by whose, are these choices made? Gathering information, asking questions, performing analysis all involve acts of personal judgement. They are not neutral. The social sciences may provide some useful techniques for processing information; standardized tests may provide a way of making relevant comparisons. But when the statistics have been coded, analysed and tabulated, the need to interpret them is still there. At the heart of the most seemingly objective procedures there is a large element of personal judgement. The efforts to develop ever more sanitized processes of clinical analysis will not exorcise it. The attempt to do so is in any case inexplicable. Personal judgement is the most sensitive 'instrument' that any evaluator has.

Part of the task of evaluation is to make explicit the different values of the various participants in their view of the programme. Values pervade every step of education from the distribution of resources to the framing of objectives and the way teachers behave with children. Evaluation which is based on limited experience of a programme or on one point of view may not be useful to those with different interests in the programme.

EVALUATION AS ILLUMINATION

Methods of evaluation emerging from these considerations have been variously called 'holistic', 'illuminative' and 'responsive'. There is no set pattern to them. They are attempts to find forms of evaluation which are compatible with what is being evaluated. In general:

1 They take account of responses of all those with an interest in the programme – the team, the children, the teacher and the funders – and of their different values.

2 They are naturalistic: that is they seek to establish the actual effects of the programme rather than the intended effects.
3 They are adaptable in that the design of the evaluation may change with changes in the programme.
4 They are not restricted to test data. Although some statistical approaches may be used the results are just one element in the evaluation.
5 They are descriptive and discursive and try to report on the 'flavour' of the programme as well as on its effects.
6 They look at the process of the work rather than just at its intended outcomes or products.
7 They evaluate the objectives along with everything else.

(see Hamilton 1976: 39)

The function of 'illuminative evaluation' has been described as seeking to 'open out an educational situation to intelligent criticism and appraisal' (ibid.). Michael Scriven (1976) distinguishes between 'formative' evaluations, which help to shape the development of an educational programme, and 'summative' evaluations which reflect on its overall effects. TIE companies must do both. One of the reasons for evaluation is to improve the quality of the present programme and the next one by looking clearly at the work in hand. This calls for ways of feeding information and judgements back into the work, both during a programme's operation and from one programme to the next. 'Illuminating' the programme is part of this.

THE *ACTION* AND THE *ACT* OF EVALUATION

It is useful to distinguish between the action of evaluation and the act of evaluation. By the action of evaluation I mean the process of gathering, recording and organizing information about the working of the programme. It is a kind of trawling for information in the flow of the programme's activity. Acts of evaluation are the judgements made in the light of this information.

Problems in evaluation tend to arise when acts of evaluation are unsupported or impressionistic: that is, when the action of evaluation is narrowly focused and random. The action of evaluation must be systematic. It involves deliberately canvassing as many interpretations and responses as possible from everyone involved in or affected by the programme, and looking for areas of consensus and disagreement. The next step is to identify the key issues raised about the programme and its operation and to focus attention on them, recognizing the different personal values involved.

Acts of evaluation are difficult and unreliable where the action of evaluation is unsystematic and where relevant material is not recorded. Teachers may make quite specific comments about the programme as the team are packing up the van at the end of the day, or over lunch. These insights into how the children are responding may be invaluable for setting the impact of the programme in context. This is precisely the information that needs to be recorded as part of the action of evaluation.

It is important to see evaluation not as a post-mortem but as an integral part of a programme's life and development, and as a way of involving all those who are affected by it. This is especially important for TIE. Companies spend relatively little time with groups in schools. If they are committed to affecting children's attitudes to various issues it is essential that the programme should be followed up. The common failure of schools to do any follow-up may be rooted in misunderstandings about the functions of TIE and can seriously limit the effects of a programme. The point of integrating evaluative actions into the programme is not only to help the company adapt the work but also to encourage the school to understand the programme by looking for its effects and therefore to build upon its initiative.

Acts of evaluation by the company should blend systematic observations with personal judgements based on professional experience. Judgements will vary according to who makes them and why. No one can be relieved of the burden of sorting out their own values and criteria in education. The general problem is to sort out the action of evaluation for a TIE programme.

THE ACTION OF EVALUATION

The company should compile an evaluation file consisting of field notes, interview material and other responses of the team and participants. The purpose is to record and comment on the working of the programme for the benefit of anyone with a claim on, or use for, this information. It is also to provide a stock of evaluations from different viewpoints so as to build up an even view of the programme's overall effects. The file should be organized around the issues which the planning and operation of the programme have generated. It will therefore evolve and be modified with the programme itself. There are four main questions to address in setting about the action of evaluation: Who is evaluating? For whom? What is being evaluated? Why?

Who is evaluating and for whom?

Anyone affected by a TIE programme may have a view of it: (a) members of the company; (b) the schools – teachers and children; (c) the funders; (d) anyone else who sees it – school inspectors, advisers, parents, etc. These are also the possible audiences of the evaluation. Somebody has to collate these points of view if they are to be of general use. The responsibility for this rests with the company. Being most involved in the programme they have more opportunities to think out its implications. Schools are caught up in the problems of how to evaluate their own work; they may well need help from the company in knowing how to evaluate the programme and how to build on it. If companies cannot provide this sort of help, the failure of schools to follow up the work can be understood. The programme will be evaluated after a fashion whether or not the company step in; it is therefore not really a matter of whether it will be done but how, and it is in the company's interest to see that it is done well. No other group has the opportunity to evaluate the programme in so wide a range of circumstances. Different groups will evaluate for different purposes and it is essential that decisions made by funders, for example, are based on information from as many viewpoints as possible and not solely on their own necessarily limited personal contact with the programme. The company should be able to supply the necessary information.

What is being evaluated and why?

There are four areas for evaluative action in a TIE programme: operation, content, context and responses.

Operation

Companies need to consider carefully the effects of their own actions on children. The relatively stable features of the programme are one area for evaluation – for example, the running order of the programme, the content of the presentation piece, the music, the visual design, the organization of stimulations – as well as the more variable factors such as individual performances both during the presentation section and when in direct contact with the children in other parts of the programme.

Content

In looking at social issues TIE programmes in the 1970s and 1980s became increasingly polemical. Given the short time available, the less committed a programme is the less effect it is likely to have. The educational problem is that the issues may be presented in such a way as to block opportunities for personal judgement by the children. The children need time to weigh the issues against their own values. One of the functions of TIE is to open doors to further enquiry, not close them with arguments so closely riveted as to make personal interpretation or further questioning by the children unlikely or redundant. Both the selection and treatment of the issues need to be considered in terms of their accessibility for the children, and how many opportunities they create for further enquiry.

Context

In her enquiry into the roles of community artists, Su Braden (1978) has criticized the common distinction in the arts between form and content. Particularly for community-based and TIE groups it is essential to consider the relationship between form and context: that is, the circumstances in which the work takes place and the prevailing attitudes and values of those with whom it takes place. The value of a programme depends on how the company adapt it in practice to the different contexts in which it is used. Parlett and Hamilton talk of the 'learning milieu' in which students and teachers work together. This represents 'a network . . . of cultural, social, institutional and psychological variables. These interact . . . to produce in each class . . . a unique pattern of circumstances, pressure, customs, opinions and work styles which suffuse the teaching and learning that occur there' (Parlett and Hamilton 1977: 6). TIE teams are constantly moving into quite different learning 'milieux' and it is because of these changes in context that a TIE programme does not have a single, constant value. The action of evaluation needs to alert the company to this diversity and it needs to take account of it in offering any judgements about the programme as a whole.

Responses

Evaluation needs information and this may be lacking when contact time is short. Opinions should be gathered from the various participants together with their criteria. Although the company may have relatively constant criteria for evaluation, those of schools may vary considerably from one to the next. The company and the schools work within quite different cycles of evaluation. Teachers' evaluations of a group's responses can be fed back immediately into work with the same group. The company, being peripatetic, works within a rolling cycle of evaluation, using its judgements of one group's responses to adjust its work with the next group and so on. The company needs the teachers' judgements during and immediately after the programme before its detailed perceptions have hardened into broad generalizations about the programme like 'They really got a lot out of it.'

EVALUATION AND ENABLING

Teachers cannot be held entirely accountable for what children actually learn or fail to learn. The complexities of the learning milieu, together with many other factors affecting individual motivation and achievement, do not warrant firm guarantees about learning outcomes. Teachers are enablers: their role is to provide the best possible opportunities for learning to take place. This is what they are responsible and accountable for. There must be adequate opportunities for the children to challenge the attitudes of the company. The company spends a great deal of time in preparing and making their statement: the children must be given time to make theirs. Programmes often include role-play, discussion and 'hot-seating' – where company members in role answer the children's questions about aspects of the programme's content. In using these techniques it is important that character-roles are balanced with the teaching roles.

In the *Marches* programme for example, the fascist leader, Oswald Mosley answered the children's questions in role (Cockpit TIE 1977; see also page 5). 'Mosley' may well have to feed questions in here. The children coming new to the material may not be able to formulate the most productive questions in the heat of the moment and may need considerable help. While the children are keeping an eye on Mosley, therefore, 'Mosley' himself has to keep an eye on the point of the programme and create opportunities for learning while not cauterizing them with his responses. Similarly if the children are debating in role, as in some simulations, they may have to express views which they do not actually hold. This may be worthwhile. But if the programme sets out to challenge and affect their real views of an issue, the company have got to make time to find out just what they are – and help the children find out. Some time for out-of-role discussion may be needed for them to sort through the issues as themselves. This will also yield evaluation material within the programme.

EVALUATION AND ACCOUNTABILITY

TIE companies, along with everybody else, do not always achieve all they think they do. The reasons for this do not necessarily lie with the company. They may be to do with the circumstances of the work and lack of follow-up. TIE is still an innovatory approach to education, and innovations will not take root if the attitudes of the schools are unfavourable. Because of this the dominant pattern of short visits to schools may not be the best. Some companies have experimented with alternatives, such as visiting a school for a week to work with a wide range of pupils and with the staff. Such an approach can enormously increase the school's interest in the programme and its material value for them.

As an experiment a number of schools took the Greenwich programme for a week, bringing in children from across the whole year group and arranging special viewings for the staff. A senior teacher from one of the schools commented later:

> The staff were eager to have this particular production in school. Many teachers have been trying to raise the race issue but were unsure how to approach it . . . the school had consistently avoided making any positive moves; in this school the subject departments rarely work together. Under the stimulus of *Race Against Time* however the Social Studies, English, Geography, History and RE Departments fell to swopping ideas; even to integrating their programmes for follow-up work.

The Greenwich company did not solve the race issue in the school. It enabled the issue to be discussed and this is the key function of TIE.

When a school genuinely feels that it has benefited from the work of a company it will be reflected in the overall evaluation. Companies which can prove their value in this way are more likely to produce a body of evidence to vindicate their methods of work to funders and others and to license their own terms of accountability. Cost-effective criteria of accountability work straight against this. Bureaucracies tend to confuse the price of TIE with its value. Consequently they judge value for money in terms of the numbers of children contacted and the amount of time spent moving from school to school.

In staying in one school for a week the team are not in fact working with fewer children at all, although they would of course get round fewer schools. The gain is in the quality of the work for the schools and it is precisely the quality of TIE which may suffer in trying to answer the calls of cost-effectiveness. Working towards effective forms of evaluation which both reveal and help to improve the quality of TIE is at the centre of all this. The way in which companies respond to the two pressures to evaluate will, as in the rest of education, determine whether the movement goes forward or backward.

Acknowledgement

I am grateful for the co-operation I received from members of the Greenwich Young People's Theatre Company during observations of their 1979 programme *Race Against Time*, for the original research for this chapter. The quotations from the

Greenwich Company are taken from their individual written comments on the programme.

Bibliography

Bloom, B. S. (ed.) (1956) *Taxonomy of Educational Objectives: the Classification of Educational Goals. Handbook 1: The Cognitive Domain*, New York: McKay and Co.

Braden, S. (1978) *Artists and People*, London: Routledge & Kegan Paul.

Eisner, E. (1969) *Instructional and Expressive Objectives: Their Formulation and Use in Curriculum* AERA monograph series on curriculum evaluation, Chicago: Rand McNally.

Hamilton, D. (1976) *Curriculum Evaluation*, London: Open Books.

Hamilton, D., D. Jenkins, C. King, B. MacDonald and M. Parlett (eds) (1977) *Beyond the Numbers Game: A Reader in Educational Evaluation*, London: Macmillan Education.

House, E. R. (ed.) (1973) *School Evaluation: The Politics and the Process*, New York: McCutcheon Publishing Corp.

National Curriculum Council (1990) *The Arts 5–16: A Curriculum Framework*, London: Oliver and Boyd.

Parlett, M. and Hamilton, D. (1977) 'Evaluation as illumination: a new approach to the study of innovatory programmes', in D. Hamilton, D. Jenkins, C. King, B. MacDonald and M. Parlett (eds) (1977) *Beyond the Numbers Game*, London: Macmillan Education.

Robinson, K. (ed.) (1982) *The Arts in Schools: Principles, Practice and Provision*, London: Calouste Gulbenkian Foundation.

Scriven M. (1976) 'The methodology of evaluation', in R. Tyler, R. Gagne and M. Scriven (eds) *Perspectives on Curriculum Evaluation*, AERA monograph series on curriculum evaluation, Chicago: Rand McNally.

Stake, R. (1975) 'To evaluate an arts programme', in R. Stake (ed.) *Evaluating the Arts in Education*, New York: Merrill Publishing Corp.

Tyler, R. W. (1949) *Basic Principles of Curriculum and Instruction*, Chicago, University of Chicago Press, reprinted in D. Hamilton, D. Jenkins, C. King, B. MacDonald and M. Parlett (eds) (1977) *Beyond the Numbers Game*, London: Macmillan Education.

Chapter 15

New partnerships in new contexts

A consumer's viewpoint

Geoff Readman

In this chapter, I will suggest that the organization and provision of statutory education in the United Kingdom has
changed so radically since the Education Reform Act of 1988
that changes in the professional relationship between a school
and a TIE company are inevitable. In her article for the first
edition of this book, Kathy Joyce highlighted the significant
educational benefits that can result from a productive relationship between schools and those companies that are funded to
offer TIE within specific geographical areas. Such companies
have been able to offer schools a free service of TIE which has
been devised to meet agreed objectives.

> The company is able to build up a close relationship with
> schools and teachers, and, more generally, with the com-
> munity – a relationship which, in turn, influences the nature
> and content of the work and its extended influence within
> the school. . . . The recognition of the intrinsic nature of the
> school–company relationship is implicit in the policy of the
> area-based TIE company.
>
> (Joyce 1980: 25)

How will that relationship manifest itself in the future? It is
unlikely that local education authorities (LEAs) will be able to
continue to provide large-scale or guaranteed long-term funding, and schools are being pressurized to allocate their limited
finances to other priorities created by the National Curriculum.
Consequently, new funding relationships will need to be explored. Whilst the excellent work of the many children's theatre
companies is acknowledged, this chapter is principally concerned with the relationship between those schools, companies

and LEAs that have long recognized the contribution that TIE as an art form can make to cross-curricular learning for all students.

WHAT HAS BEEN LEARNT?

TIE companies have made significant contributions to the development of arts education in the United Kingdom over the last three decades. They have challenged, refined and developed their practice in order to extend the nature of the learning being offered to young people, and, by so doing, have played a considerable part in the development of drama teaching. The schools and colleges that have had the benefit of regular contact with permanent locally based TIE companies readily acknowledge the value of their input across the whole curriculum. The educational value of TIE has consistently received recognition from teachers and schools. Headteachers often describe the rich qualities of their students' subsequent work following participation in a programme and enthuse about aspects of the curriculum which have been given new meaning by the TIE process. These achievements were formally highlighted in a recent HMI Primary Report:

> Where TIE groups have worked in schools and with teachers, more adventurous and in-depth work has resulted. The work reveals that primary children are capable of achieving far more from the teaching of drama than is often supposed.
>
> (HMI 1990: 22)

There has been specific research which has highlighted the learning impact of TIE as evidenced by students themselves, research which indicates the lasting effect of the experience:

> The evidence from the pupils in this case study would indicate that the long-term impact of a TIE programme is considerable. There were occasions when recall of the event was limited or confused, but they were the exceptions. In the main, pupils talked animatedly and in some detail about a programme they had experienced between one and four and a half years ago.
>
> (Clark 1985: 35)

The growth of TIE has reflected a determination to develop

learning theory in relation to practice and to employ theatre forms which make social issues accessible and relevant for young people.

I will take this further and suggest that it has been within the TIE movement that genuinely innovative theatre practice in respect of writing, directing, designing and performing has taken place. Specific examples invariably reflect personal preference, but the effectiveness of David Holman's TIE writing in engaging young people in narrative has surely given main house directors new insights into what is possible in children's theatre. Similarly, the influence of the designer in utilizing shape, space and colour to facilitate participative action, has led to new understandings of the actor–audience relationship.

The teaching of drama has been enriched by the rigorous analysis of their own work by the permanent companies, which has been explicitly disseminated through the *SCYPT Journal*. TIE has helped teachers to develop a clearer grasp of the implications of such concepts as distancing, alienation, positive imagery, narrative, symbol, forum theatre, role, dramatic tension and cross-cultural forms.

In addition, companies have offered schools new and radical perspectives on contemporary themes and events, enabling students of all ages to recognize the significance of values and attitudes. The achievements in utilizing historical content to stimulate student-questioning of society have been considerable. For example, programmes such as *Raj, School on the Green* and *Brand of Freedom* have offered students opportunities to develop new perspectives on different cultural eras and social processes.

In their search for knowledge and expertise in drama teaching methodology, companies have been strongly influenced by the practice of Gavin Bolton and Dorothy Heathcote, two figures who have contributed so significantly to our understanding of the nature of the learning experience young people have in drama. However, this exploration of the interrelatedness of TIE and drama teaching has, in my view, tended to take place mostly within the TIE movement itself; any broader interaction with drama teachers has been minimal. This is in spite of the fact that HMI have felt able to claim that 'Theatre-in-Education groups are influential in stimulating and promoting developments in drama and in contributing effectively to the in-service training of teachers in some LEAs' (HMI 1990: 7).

My view is that closer working relationships over the last ten years would have yielded still more professional development for both teachers and company members. This need is now even more acute. If drama is to have any future, there must be creative collaboration and the establishment of positive networks and partnerships amongst everyone with a concern for education and drama. Schools, theatres, colleges, artists, TIE companies, even museums, health authorities and other such agencies must all be encouraged to ensure that students are offered the quality drama and theatre experiences to which they are entitled. The new educational context has created a need for the 'close relationship' between companies and schools (identified by Joyce) to be replaced by the concept of partnership.

This is not, however, to suggest that the excellence of the last thirty years will be replaced, but rather that it will be the basis from which new practice will evolve.

Within the geographical areas where permanent companies have existed, and where active school curriculum drama policies have been formulated, high expectations have developed with regard to the work. Schools have grown to expect that a professional TIE company:

will create productive dilemmas which offer learning opportunities that raise further questions for students;

will create programmes which have educational objectives as the key priority of the work, and which involve structures which are appropriate for specific age groups;

will locate any contentious issues within the security of the art form, enabling students to examine the implications of those issues;

will be fully prepared with regard to issues of equality of opportunity, in terms of the imagery in the programme, follow-up material and workshop activities;

will organize preparatory meetings to ensure the effectiveness of the company's time in school;

will offer schools detailed follow-up material;

will have the skills to interact with teachers in a supportive and adaptable way.

In addition, I suspect that those schools with long-standing relationships with companies will have recognized the greater variety of form now being employed. The long and important debates about the respective benefits of participation and performance, which began in the 1970s, do seem to be resolved. There is now far greater flexibility about structuring and a greater clarity about its relationship to learning experiences than there has been in the past. There have been previous occasions when, say, the performance of a play has not been perceived, by some, as representing 'authentic' TIE, or when participation has been identified as the uniquely distinguishing characteristic. These different approaches were important landmarks from which we have all learnt and the TIE movement should be prepared to recall and celebrate its history and development rather more readily.

I believe that schools do now recognize the value of both performance and participation, although it is often the participatory sequences which stimulate debate and discussion amongst teachers – perhaps because it is a format which relates so closely to active learning. In a recent case-study of a project called *Gulfs Apart*, by Nottinghamshire's Roundabout Company, it was interesting that, although teachers recognized that the performance work had the greater impact, it was the accompanying workshops which were more readily analysed and discussed (Readman 1992).

In schools where an understanding and respect for TIE has developed, the power of the theatre images and the vigorous challenging of social issues have been welcomed. Effective practice has often involved a whole-school approach, with companies making two or three visits to a school, or sometimes spending a week in residency. Liaison can always be improved, but the benefits of longer-term planning and teachers' meetings have enhanced the impact of the work.

In turn, where TIE has been given the appropriate support it has been able to make a significant and enriching contribution to the whole curriculum, both in terms of content and methodology. The basis of this support has been the relationship with the teacher. When this relationship is at its most effective, it fosters a climate of professional trust and respect.

WHAT HAS CHANGED IN SCHOOLS AND COLLEGES SINCE 1988?

The implementation of the Education Reform Act (ERA) has been a rapid, bludgeoning process, characterized by minimal consultation. Despite flurries of resistance and creative manoeuvring, through which schools have tried to yield something positive for arts education, the sad fact is that many are currently reeling from all the changes that have been imposed upon them.

Drama's omission as a foundation subject was initially regarded as being a 'mixed blessing' by many practitioners but, sadly, as the ERA has been implemented the implications of that decision have become clearer. Many primary schools are finding it difficult to teach anything which is outside the National Curriculum and their curriculum planning is, out of necessity, in advance of timescales operated by many TIE companies. Primary teachers, who have curriculum responsibility for drama, are aware of a lack of status and priority due to the absence of National Curriculum guidance, and secondary teachers are growing anxious about drama's future as a GCSE subject. Many specialist teachers are finding it difficult to convince their colleagues of a potential role for drama in the new context.

Local Management of Schools (LMS) is making it difficult for both schools and, indeed, companies to maintain a clear view of their educational priorities, or to resist the 'market place' ethos encouraged by successive Conservative governments. A comprehensive survey of companies by James Robinson in 1992 identified that teachers felt they had little time for any issue outside the National Curriculum, that they were under heavy scrutiny regarding their practice, and that the move to building-based management (LMS) was not leading to more flexible spending power as has been suggested by the government. Robinson also noted that some companies were reducing workshops and increasing audience numbers in response to the growing inflexibility of the curriculum organization.

What follows is an attempt to illustrate the impact of some of the new structures in a simplified format which frames the implications for TIE in critical questions.

Statutory requirements	Implications	Questions
Schools are being required to take responsibility for their own budgets.	However, since those budgets are inadequate and there is no compensatory funding for schools with particular needs, economy is often perceived as the priority.	Will schools be prepared, or able, to allocate funding to TIE? Which schools?
Governing bodies of schools have been given greater responsibility and autonomy for the running of the school and the appointment of staff.	Governors are being placed in a position of making decisions about matters of which they have little knowledge or experience.	How will Governing bodies become informed about TIE? Who will decide, or advise on, what constitutes relevant material to bring into schools?
The establishment of a National Curriculum with core and foundation subjects.	The introduction of the NC has been so ill-managed that there is minimal room for adaptation or creative curriculum planning. The implications of drama not being designated as a foundation subject grow ever more clear (see page 272 above).	Will drama survive at examination level? How will teachers respond to TIE in the light of curriculum pressure?
The establishment of national testing, with formal reporting procedures.	Teachers are anxious about test results and do not want the reputation of their school to suffer. This is resulting in heavy emphasis on testing and reporting.	Are teachers willing to give time to non-NC projects? Will teachers bring into school work which is outside NC attainment targets?
The reduction in the power and influence of LEAs and their ability to retain funding for centrally provided services.	LEAs are unlikely to have any real influence as strategic planners and will have minimal funding (if any) to invest in permanent TIE companies, locally based arts events or curriculum arts initiatives.	Where will future funding come from? Will new companies be created? How will new work emerge? Will there be any geographical or LEA based identity? Will companies have to widen their catchment areas?

There are two further dimensions which may have even more serious consequences for arts in education generally, and TIE in particular.

The first relates to teacher training. Once this current National Curriculum has become established, there is a danger that funds will no longer be available for subjects which are not part of the defined core or foundation. This will not only severely restrict the theoretical momentum which has been sustained about learning in drama, but will also reduce, if not completely remove, the number of new teachers in schools who understand and value TIE work. As TIE companies have rightly maintained, their work is relevant to all young people, but the absence of drama specialists, primary as well as secondary, would sever an important point of contact.

Plans to make training more school-based, reducing the amount of time spent at a specialist training institution, will make it unlikely that teachers of the future will have any genuine opportunity to debate or explore theories of drama and theatre. Only the pedagogical models of the host (or base) school will be offered to teachers.

The second dimension, although more serious still, will mark the end of my pessimistic pronouncements within the chapter! This dimension relates specifically to how drama and theatre practitioners have chosen to respond to the ERA legislation and is an issue which has, sadly, created yet another major divide amongst writers, teachers and TIE workers alike. One side of the divide is characterized by those who see the present context as an opportunity to promote drama as a natural member of the larger family of the arts and who would prefer drama to be represented in the National Curriculum with its own set of attainment targets and programmes of study. It is a view often shared by those who claim that concepts such as role-play and 'drama as a learning medium' have prevented drama from establishing its rightful curriculum identity. The work of Gavin Bolton and Dorothy Heathcote is bearing the brunt of the attacks being launched by this particular lobby, and, since these are the two practitioners who have contributed so significantly to TIE, then the implications within the context of this chapter should be clear.

An alternative view is based on a desire to reject the National Curriculum and the values that it represents. It is fair to say that this view has largely been attributed to many TIE teams, but it is also one which has the support of those teachers who see the ERA legislation as detrimental to the kind of learning they would wish to promote in their school.

At the time of writing, this debate is polarizing educational drama and theatre development, to such an extent that it is preventing the creation of one strong association for all drama workers in the United Kingdom. It is certainly an energy-sapping argument at a time when drama needs to be communicating effectively to policy-makers.[1]

WHAT DO SCHOOLS NEED?

As the funding and structural basis for TIE changes, so too will relationships with schools and the artistic forms of the work. The TIE movement has, rightly in my view, always insisted on maintaining certain key principles relating to autonomy which has enabled companies to present their own artistic statements about selected issues. Whether or not such freedom, with regard to the identification and prioritizing of needs, can remain is a question which cannot be avoided.

To put the question bluntly, can companies work outside the parameters of the ERA when all their clients are being compelled to implement it on a day-to-day basis?

Schools need to be confident that any external curriculum input will contribute to their agreed 'development plan', and that the educational aims of the input will complement those of the school. One of the few benefits of the National Curriculum is that it has created the necessity for schools to review their total curriculum and highlighted the need for clearer policies and strategies. The days have gone when an individual teacher might book a TIE company for the benefit of his or her children without the support or knowledge of the rest of the school. Indeed, one of the potential changes in the relationship of the future is that schools may well expect to be more influential and active in their contributions to the whole TIE process.

The nature of their response to the Education Reform Act needs to be at the centre of any development planning for all TIE companies. Schools are being shaped by two major forces. On the one hand, they are teaching to national requirements (testing, curriculum, etc.) and, on the other, they are being forced to develop a singular identity (due to the progressive dismantling of LEAs, introduction of Local Management of Schools, competitive school league tables, etc.). An inflexible response to individual school development could eventually jeopardize the contact between schools and companies, even amongst those companies who have had long-established relationships within their LEA. At least for the immediate future, I suspect that many schools will want the reassurance and support of TIE work which relates directly to the curriculum demands being placed upon them. This is not to say that TIE programmes must be geared directly to the attainment targets, as laid down by the National Curriculum Council, but that there must be a recognition of the schools' developmental concerns and of a programme's potential to complement curriculum policy.

The issue that needs to be addressed is the extent to which schools, on the one hand, can have TIE which enriches their curriculum, and companies, on the other, can devise TIE which allows them to make an independent artistic statement, without compromise.

THE WAY FORWARD

The most obvious consequence of the present situation would appear to be an increase in larger-scale theatre performances which encompass educational issues. New funding bases and changes in the curriculum will influence the ultimate shape of TIE and make it necessary for artistic roles and responsibilities to be redefined. On the positive side, this could lead to new styles and art forms in contexts which have not yet been thoroughly explored.

The need for new forms of TIE has already been anticipated and identified by several writers and practitioners during the last ten years, such as Chris Vine, Brian Woolland and Steven Lacey. Much of this writing has focused upon a re-evaluation of the 'participant–spectator' concept (the elements of which and the theory of 'imaginary spectatorship in social context' were identified by Harding in 1937). It is a focus which has also received recent attention from drama in education writers, such as Cecily O'Neill (1989) and Jonothan Neelands (1990).

The participant–spectator relationship cannot be simplistically categorized into 'taking an active part', as opposed to 'watching', for the richness of its learning potential is encapsulated within the interplay and fusion of the two states of mind. Neelands, in defining theatre as an interactive process which offers the participants opportunities as 'meaning makers', emphasizes the importance of 'interactive forms of interchange, even fusion, of the role of spectator and actor rather than those conventions associated with performance where the roles of spectator and actor tend to be more clearly defined' (Neelands 1990: 5).

In an attempt to alert TIE workers to the dilemmas of power and ownership within TIE, Chris Vine, drawing on the work of Augusto Boal, the Brazilian theatre director, points out that

> Boal's central thesis is to give the theatre back to the people, give them back the means of theatrical production. They need to stop being spectators and start being protagonists. They need to be able to change the theatrical reality to enable them to recognise the possibilities for change within the social reality. . . . I do not debase the actor at all, but there is a need to re-examine the skills in terms of the value and the intention behind them.
>
> (Vine 1985: 70)

From a different perspective, Brian Woolland and Steven Lacey advocate that drama in education should be viewed as a radical form of theatre practice, linking it to post-Brecht modernism. Their thesis highlights the fact that when students are engaged in group improvisations, 'these groups are not only authors of a series of potential narratives, but also actors within them: in practice, the process of improvisation involves a constant shift between acting and observing, doing and watching, creating and criticizing' (Lacey and Woolland 1989: 4).

These examples will suffice to highlight the fact that there have been indications that the best practices of the TIE tradition might evolve into new formats, if there can be closer collaborations with drama practitioners. The creation of productive partnerships will offer companies contexts within which new forms and styles of work can develop. This conceptual fusion of 'partnership' and 'participant–spectator' is likely to be complementary. Growth-points need not be restricted to single types of institution, such as youth clubs or museums, but could well emerge from clusters of schools being prepared to allocate funding for TIE work which addresses their specific needs. I am thinking here of a group of schools that might recognize the need to address bullying as a common issue, and consequently want to fund a major input from a TIE company, in terms of both performance and workshop. Similar projects might well relate to local history, language usage and urban development. In the future, schools will need to combine resources and become familiar with short-term project funding and planning.

Similarly, art galleries, museums, health authorities or higher education establishments, may well be establishing educational programmes in which TIE provides a significant dimension. The basis of these potential partnerships will vary, and may lead to work in alternative locations, such as hospital wards, urban dwellings, country parks, libraries and college campuses.

I would like to describe an initiative which began in Nottinghamshire in 1991; it provides evidence of a company working in partnership and is an example of TIE in which the interplay of the 'participant–spectator' concept is central. This initiative has resulted in a formal partnership between the Education Committee, Nottingham Playhouse and Clarendon College of Further Education. Through the imaginative pooling of resources, a new training course in community theatre has been established which has involved the TIE company, Roundabout, operating in a variety of ways with schools and colleges all over the county. The company has been able to make inputs into the training courses, develop residencies in individual schools, and relate its work more closely to the strategic planning of the Education Committee. In turn, the Playhouse has taken responsibility for developing the concept of a 'teaching theatre', and has offered a host of student placements, organized festivals and given a lead in community-based theatre projects. For its part, Clarendon College has facilitated the establishment of more vocationally orientated courses in the performing arts, validated by the Business and Technician Education Council (BTEC).

The organization of Roundabout has been based upon a small permanent 'core' company of four, which is extended by freelance artists for specific projects. The introduction of freelance artists enables the creation of work which reflects a cross-arts dimension; two projects influenced by this decision are a revised production of *Peacemaker*, by David Holman, which includes Asian dance, and a major programme of work based on Asian story-telling techniques. The benefits of this particular partnership have yet to be evaluated, but it is already apparent that students in Nottinghamshire schools are in receipt of a far greater quantity of TIE work than the traditional company concept might have delivered. In addition, the work has had greater breadth, in terms of the range of artistic genres, as both students and actor–teachers work with rural, urban and inner-city communities in ways which were not previously possible. The extended company concept makes genuinely multiracial casting possible and enables companies to reflect a broader range of expertise.

In addition, a recent initiative has involved the Nottinghamshire Education Committee commissioning a writer, Tony Coult, to write a TIE piece on the Civil War for their young people's theatre company. This programme, *Plague of God*, toured Edinburgh schools as part of the Festival Fringe, before being adapted by Roundabout for Nottinghamshire schools. This is an initiative which has involved professional actors, teachers, a writer and young people working in a creative collaboration to discover new and effective forms of TIE.

Roundabout's project *Gulfs Apart* arose in response to the Education Committee's decision that children in Nottinghamshire schools had an entitlement to proper debate and information relating to the war in the Gulf. The minutes of policy meetings reflected these concerns:

1 Families have relations engaged in active service in the Gulf – this will impact in schools and colleges particularly if extensive casualties result from a land war.
2 The Nottinghamshire community includes a significant number of Muslims who, along with other elements of the black community, may be identified with the Iraqi cause and become targets for abuse and harassment. Such abuse and harassment could be manifested in schools and colleges.
3 The Gulf war throws up fundamental, moral and philosophical issues which will concern pupils and students, not only in issues relating to the immediate military conflict, but

in terms of the underlying political and historical stance in the Middle East.

(Nottinghamshire Education Committee 1992)

The Education Committee gave its overwhelming support to TIE as a learning medium capable of dealing with important issues within the crisis, claiming that 'TIE has the ability to promote a lively focus for young people to explore complex issues' (ibid.).

In response to this, Roundabout then devised a comprehensive package of work, which included *Frankie's Friends* by David Holman and *Dirty Rascals* by Leeds TIE. These two performance pieces were supported by two workshops, devised by freelance workers, which were designed to connect the issues of the performance pieces with those of the war in the Gulf. These workshops represent my most recent contact with TIE that has attempted to employ a structure to maximize the 'participant–spectator' interplay, as described above.

The style of these workshops was that of an 'unfolding story', during which the students (7 to 9 year-olds or 10 to 11 year-olds), led by two actor–teachers, were engaged in decision taking, reflective action and performance. The workshop included dance, group discussion, music, poetry and sequences of prepared performance. The structures within these workshops have enormous potential for enabling young people to examine social episodes and specific contexts in a vibrant and exciting way. Students were able to engage in an interactive relationship with the actor–teachers, whose expertise was not at all diluted by this open and flexible format. In addition, the interplay and juxtapositioning of the 'participant–spectator' mode offered the students a range of perspectives on the context being explored.

For example, one workshop explored the culture and history of Flora, a fictitious refugee from Albania. The two actor-teachers used dramatic narrative and theatre forms to establish the context of the scenes, which were then reflected upon and responded to by the participating students. In one depicted scene, a photographer arrived in Flora's village offering her a 'Walkman' in exchange for the right to take photographs of her plight. This moral dilemma was then explored in various ways with the pupils being asked to make connections with incidents from their own lives.

I am not suggesting that this style of work is completely original or that it has not been attempted at various times by other companies. However, it is a form which genuinely harnesses the dual skills of the actor–teacher and one which could enable companies to respond effectively to specific requests.

There are some delicate issues involved in this way of working. It demands a high level of teacher skill, for the structuring is more flexible than many workshop formats, and new on-going learning objectives will emerge which will require teacher intervention. There are other questions too:

How can the teacher be integrally involved?
Who has the ultimate responsibility for decisions relating to structuring?
What will be the nature of the contracting (i.e. between class–company, company–museum, company–school, etc.)?
How will the combined knowledge of all the partners be utilized?
How will companies ensure that their distinctive use of the art form is preserved?

The shape of the art form in this style of work will be influenced both by the quality of the interplay of 'participant–spectator' roles and by the interaction between company members and students. The nature of the partnership and the degree of ownership experienced by the pupils will create a unique dynamic stemming from the cultural values of the context and the moment-to-moment engagement in the process:

Where the work is structured so that there is a powerful public dimension, where the participant's sense of being both actor and audience is strengthened, where their life within the drama logically includes a strong sense of being onlookers as well as performers, the drama will live.

(O'Neill 1989: 29)

The form will also be influenced by the environment within which it takes place and this is a dimension which has received minimal attention, though there have been companies who have specialized in historical, location-based theatre, such as the Young National Trust Theatre Company. The influence of the gallery, museum, or community centre has yet to be comprehensively explored.

But is this the kind of work in which companies will want to engage?

If this work is to flourish, then there will be a cost. There is likely to be a reduction in the number of independently devised programmes, since more time will be spent in workshop contexts and in planning specific projects with individual clients. The additional influence of the client and the location may well lead to other art forms being identified. The permanent-company concept will need to be re-evaluated in terms of skills and expertise, which will be evident only when requests for projects begin. But the contentious issue is the extent to which artistic autonomy can be genuinely preserved and recognized by all the partners.

Artistic autonomy is a principle which permanent companies have fervently protected, and partnership does not necessarily mean that it will be sacrificed. It will, however, be essential that roles are explicit and that the company's right to make an artistic and independent response is preserved. It will not be easy, but the work undertaken by Roundabout, through the *Gulfs Apart* project, does seem to offer one model which did not involve compromise. It was a project which meant working to a particular brief, requiring skills in negotiation and long-term planning. It demanded that the company communicated the precise kinds of learning they could address, distinguishing it from that learning which teachers facilitate in their day-to-day work. The schools, the Playhouse and the LEA all recognized the importance of Roundabout's artistic response within the overall framework.

SUMMARY

In this chapter I have tried to emphasize the nature of the contribution that TIE has made to education generally. It is a contribution which has informed the practice and theory of drama teaching. The ERA is now affecting the relationship between schools and companies and it is crucial that new patterns of work are developed quickly.

My view is that TIE can only survive by the creation of new partnerships and by a willingness to work in a range of contexts. There have been indications, in the professional literature, that new forms of TIE are in embryo and that these forms are developing out of a reappraisal of the 'participant–spectator' concept. This is not of course to discount the possibility of a future increase in large-scale educational theatre shows as well.

If my speculation is accurate, then the future will result in participative TIE which builds upon the traditions of the last thirty years, and which will be characterized by a closer relationship with drama in education practice. It will also result in TIE which is composed of or influenced by other art forms, reflecting the traits of the partnership from which it has grown. The process of devising interactive TIE within specific locations will create yet a further influence on form.

Finally, it is certain that if students in schools are to continue to experience TIE as part of their arts entitlement, then all practitioners will need to support each other. TIE has proved itself to be a medium through which students have developed their knowledge of the world, and perhaps more interactive contexts will offer them new opportunities to formulate their own artistic statements more effectively.

NOTE

1 The situation was not helped by the fact that the National Curriculum Council chose not to publish any of the papers which its own drama task group had prepared. Fortunately, the Arts Council was able to retrieve something positive from a rather bleak situation with the publication *Drama in Schools*, which reflects some of the task group's work. However, it is a publication which follows the National Curriculum style and format and does not rest easily with the views of many TIE companies.

BIBLIOGRAPHY

Arts Council of Great Britain (1991) *Drama in Schools*, London: Arts Council of Great Britain.

Clark, L. (1985) 'Theatre, memory, and learning: the long term impact of theatre', MA dissertation, University of East Anglia.

Harding, D. W. (1937) 'The role of the onlooker', *Scrutiny* 6 (3).

Heathcote, D. (1984) *Collected Writings On Education and Drama*, London: Hutchinson.

HMI (1990) *Teaching and Learning of Drama*, Aspects of Primary Education series, London: HMSO.

Joyce, K. (1980) 'TIE in schools: a consumer's viewpoint', in T. Jackson (ed.) *Learning Through Theatre*, Manchester: Manchester University Press.

Lacy, S. and Woolland, B. (1989) 'Drama in Education: a radical theatre form', *2D* 8 (2).

Neelands, J. (1990) *Structuring Drama Work*, Cambridge: Cambridge University Press.

Nottinghamshire Education Committee (1992) *The War in the Gulf: A Memo to Schools*, Nottinghamshire: Nottinghamshire Education Committee.

O'Neill, C. (1989) 'Ways of seeing', *2D* 8.

Readman, G. (1992) 'Performance and participation in TIE', MA dissertation, Loughborough University.

Robinson, J. (1993) 'The path from why to what', unpublished thesis, University of Harvard.

Vine, C. (1985) quoted in 'Theatre, memory and learning: the long term impact of theatre', MA dissertation, University of East Anglia.

Select bibliography

THEATRE IN EDUCATION AND YOUNG PEOPLE'S THEATRE: DESCRIPTIONS, DEFINITIONS, ASSESSMENTS

Arts Council of Great Britain (1966) *The Provision of Theatre for Young People in Great Britain*, London: ACGB.

Deary, T. (1977) *Teaching through Theatre*, London: Samuel French.

Dept of Education and Science (1976) *Actors in Schools*, Education Survey no. 22, London: HMSO.

Dodd, N. and Hickson, W. (eds) (1971) *Drama and Theatre in Education*, London: Heinemann.

Doolittle, J. with Barnieh, Z. and Beauchamp, H. (1979) *A Mirror of Our Dreams: Children and the Theatre in Canada*, Vancouver: Talon Books.

England, A. (1990) *Theatre for the Young*, London: Macmillan.

Jackson, T. (ed.) (1980) *Learning through Theatre: Essays and Casebooks on TIE*, 1st edn, Manchester: Manchester University Press.

Klein, J. (ed.) (1988) *Theatre for Young Audiences: Principles and Strategies for the Future*, Kansas: University of Kansas Press.

McCaslin, N. (ed.) (1978) *Theatre for Young Audiences*, New York: Longman Inc.

—— (1987) *Historical Guide to Children's Theatre in America*, Westport, CT: Greenwood Press.

McGillivray, D. (ed.) (1992) *British Alternative Theatre Directory 1992–93*, Cardiff: Rebecca Books.

O'Toole, J. (1976) *Theatre in Education: New Objectives for Theatre – New Techniques in Education*, London: Hodder & Stoughton.

Redington, C. (1983) *Can Theatre Teach?: An Historical and Evaluative Analysis of TIE*, Oxford: Pergamon Press.

Robinson, K. (ed.) (1980) *Exploring Theatre and Education*, London: Heinemann.

SCYPT Journal (1977–) 1–22 (15–18 retitled *New Voices*, 1985–90).

Siks, G. and Dunnington, H. (1961) *Children's Theater and Creative Dramatics: Principles and Practices*, Seattle: University of Washington Press.

Swortzell, L. (ed.) (1990) *International Guide to Children's Theatre and*

Educational Theatre, Westport, CT: Greenwood Press.

Way, B. (1981) *Audience Participation: Theatre for Young People*, Boston: W. H. Baker & Co.

Webster, C. (1975) *Working with Theatre in Schools*, London: Pitman.

Wright, L. (1984) *Professional Theatre for Young Audiences*, Tempe, AZ: Arizona State University Press.

TIE PROGRAMMES AND PLAYS: A SELECTION

Belgrade TIE Company, Coventry (1976) *Rare Earth: A Programme about Pollution*, ed. S. Wyatt and M. Steed, London: Methuen.

—— (1972) 'Four plays for less able pupils', *Drama in Education* 1: 197–206.

Bolton Octagon TIE team (1975) *Sweetie Pie: A Play about Women in Society*, ed. E. Murphy, London: Methuen.

Bolton, Sheffield and Leeds TIE teams (1975) 'Production casebook: three TIE entertainments (*Holland New Town, Gowky Arthur, The Visitor*)', *Theatre Quarterly* 17: 74–94.

Jackson, T. (ed.) (1980) *Learning Through Theatre*, Manchester: Manchester University Press, includes scenarios and casebooks on *It Fits* (Infants, Perspectives TIE Co.), *Poverty Knocks* (Junior/Secondary, Bolton Octagon TIE Co.) and *Marches* (Upper Secondary, Cockpit TIE team).

Leeds Playhouse TIE Company (1984) *Raj*, London: Amber Lane Press.

—— (1973) *Snap Out of it: A Programme about Mental Illness*, ed. R. Chapman and B. Wilks, London: Methuen.

McNeil, F. (1991) *Trappin'*, in R. Robinson (ed.) *Ask Me Out*, London: Hodder & Stoughton, Upstage series.

Pit Prop Theatre and Neil Duffield (1984) *Brand of Freedom*, a three-part video with accompanying notes, Manchester: Manchester University Television Productions.

Redington, C. (ed.) (1987) *Six TIE Programmes: Dirty Rascals, Peacemaker, Under Exposure, School on the Green, Questions Arising in 1985 from a Mutiny in 1789, Lives Worth Living*, London: Methuen.

Schweitzer, P. (ed.) (1980) *Theatre in Education*, 3 volumes: *Five Infant Programmes: Pow Wow, Polly the All-action Dolly, Ifan's Valley, Hospitals, Navigators*; *Four Junior Programmes: The Price of Coal, Rubbish, Travellers, Big Deal*; *Four Secondary Programmes: No Pasaran, Example: The Case of Craig and Bentley, Factory, Holland New Town*, London: Methuen.

Sheffield Crucible TIE Co. (1988) *Home Movies*, Sheffield: Sheffield Academic Press.

DRAMA IN EDUCATION AND RELATED SUBJECTS

Allen, J. (1979) *Drama in Schools: Its Theory and Practice*, London: Heinemann.

Arts Council of Great Britain (1991) *Drama in Schools*, London: ACGB.

The Arts in Schools: Principles, Practice and Provision (1982) London: Calouste Gulbenkian Foundation.

Boal, A. (1979) *The Theatre of the Oppressed*, London: Pluto Press.

Bolton, G. (1980) *Towards a Theory of Drama in Education*, London: Longman.

—— (1984) *Drama as Education: An Argument for Placing Drama at the Centre of the Curriculum*, London: Longman.

—— (1986) *Selected Writings*, ed. D. Davies and C. Lawrence, London: Longman.

—— (1992) *New Perspectives on Classroom Drama*, London: Simon & Schuster.

Bradby, D. and McCormick, J. (1978) *People's Theatre*, London: Croom Helm.

Brecht, B. (1972) *Brecht on Theatre*, ed. J. Willett, London: Eyre Methuen.

Brook, P. (1972) *The Empty Space*, London: Penguin.

Bruner, J., Jolly, A. and Sylva, K. (eds) (1976) *Play: Its Role in Development and Evolution*, London: Penguin.

Coggin, P. (1956) *Drama and Education: An Historical Survey*, London: Thames & Hudson.

Courtney, R. (1974) *Play, Drama and Thought: The Intellectual Background to Dramatic Education*, London: Cassell.

Craig, S. (ed.) (1980) *Dreams and Deconstructions: Alternative Theatre in Britain*, London: Amber Lane Press.

Dept of Education and Science (1968) *Drama*, Education Survey no. 2, London: HMSO.

—— (1989) *Drama from 5 to 16*, Curriculum Matters no. 17, London: HMSO.

Freire, P. (1972) *Pedagogy of the Oppressed*, London: Penguin.

Heathcote, D. (1984) *Selected Writings*, ed. L. Johnson and C. O'Neill, London: Hutchinson.

Hodgson, J. (ed.) (1972) *The Uses of Drama: Sources Giving a Background to Acting as a Social and Educational Force*, London: Eyre Methuen.

Hodgson, J. and Banham, M. (eds) (1972–5) *Drama in Eduction 1–3*, London: Pitman.

Holt, J. (1965) *How Children Fail*, London: Pitman.

—— (1967) *How Children Learn*, New York: Pitman.

—— (1976) *Instead of Education*, London: Penguin.

Hornbrook, D. (1989) *Education and Dramatic Art*, Oxford: Blackwell.

—— (1991) *Education in Drama: Casting the Dramatic Curriculum*, London: The Falmer Press.

Illich, I. (1970) *Deschooling Society*, New York: Penguin.

Landy, R. (1982) *Handbook of Educational Drama & Theatre*, Westport, CT: Greenwood Press.

McCaslin, N. (1985) *Children and Drama*, Lanham, MD: University Press of America.

McGregor, L., Robinson, K. and Tate, M. (eds) (1977) *Learning through Drama: Report of Schools Council Drama Teaching Project, 10–16*, London: Heinemann.

Postman, N. and Weingartner, C. (1971) *Teaching as a Subversive Activity*, London: Penguin.

Robinson, K. (ed.) (1989–90) *The Arts in Schools Project*, London: Calouste Gulbenkian Foundation.

Ross, M. (1975) *The Arts and the Adolescent*, London: Evans/Heinemann Educational.

—— (1978) *The Creative Arts*, London: Heinemann.

—— (ed.) (1980) *The Arts and Personal Growth*, Oxford: Pergamon.

Rowell, G. & Jackson, A. (1984) *The Repertory Movement: Regional Theatre in Britain*. Cambridge: Cambridge University Press.

Slade, P. (1954) *Child Drama*, London: University of London Press.

Taylor, J. & Walford, R. (1972). *Simulation in the Classroom*. London: Penguin.

Wagner, B. (1978) *Dorothy Heathcote: Drama as a Learning Medium*, Washington DC: National Education Association.

Way, B. (1967) *Development through Drama*, London: Longman.

Winnicott, D. (1971) *Playing and Reality*, London: Tavistock Publications.

Witkin, R. (1974) *The Intelligence of Feeling*, London: Heinemann.

Index

THE
HYPNOBIRTHING
BOOK